The Role of Labour Standards in Development

The Role of Labour Standards in Development

From theory to sustainable practice?

Edited by

Tonia Novitz and David Mangan

Published for THE BRITISH ACADEMY
by OXFORD UNIVERSITY PRESS

Oxford University Press, Great Clarendon Street, Oxford OX2 6DP

Oxford New York
Auckland Cape Town Dar es Salaam Hong Kong Karachi
Kuala Lumpur Madrid Melbourne Mexico City Nairobi
New Delhi Shanghai Taipei Toronto

With offices in
Argentina Austria Brazil Chile Czech Republic France Greece
Guatemala Hungary Italy Japan Poland Portugal Singapore
South Korea Switzerland Thailand Turkey Ukraine Vietnam

Published in the United States by Oxford University Press Inc., New York

British Library Cataloguing in Publication Data
Data available

Library of Congress Cataloging in Publication Data
Data available

Typeset in Palatino by Keystroke, Station Road, Codsall, Wolverhampton
Printed in Great Britain on acid-free paper by
MPG Books Ltd, Bodmin, Cornwall

ISBN 978–0–19–726491–1

Contents

Notes on contributors

Mark Bell is Professor of Law at the University of Leicester. He conducts research in the areas of national and European anti-discrimination law and labour law. He is the author of *Racism and Equality in the European Union* (Oxford University Press, 2008) and *Anti-discrimination Law and the European Union* (Oxford University Press, 2002). From 2004–2010 he was a member of the European Commission's network of legal experts in the non-discrimination field and he is an active participant in the European Working Group on Labour Law. He is a member of the Executive Committee of the Society of Legal Scholars. In 2008, he chaired an ad hoc expert group on anti-discrimination law for the European Network Against Racism. During 2008–2009 he was a partner in an EU-funded research project studying the use of positive action in Europe and beyond. His current research focuses on EU law and precarious work, such as part-time, fixed-term and agency work.

Sonia Bhalotra is Professor of Economics, Centre for Market and Public Organisation, at the University of Bristol. Her research is in applied micro-economics, with applications relating to development economics, household economics, demography, labour economics and political economy. Her work is motivated by welfare issues in low-income economies. Her recent research is concerned with health, education and gender and, in particular, child mortality, fertility and birth-spacing, child labour, intra-household resource allocation and imperfections in credit and labour markets. She was a member of the expert committee for elimination of child labour at the International Labour Organisation, advised the United Nations Development Programme on the construction of a new Human Development Index, and contributed evidence to an international project on progress towards the Millennium Development Goals.

Adelle Blackett holds a doctorate in law from Columbia University, where she taught as an Associate in Law. She is currently Associate Professor and William Dawson Scholar, Faculty of Law, McGill University, and a member of the Quebec Human Rights and Youth Rights Commission (2009–2014 appointment). Widely published in international labour law, trade law, and development, she has recently co-edited *Social Regionalism in the Global Economy* (with Christian Lévesque, Routledge, 2011), and guest-edited both a special issue of the *Comparative Labor Law and Policy Journal on Labour Law and Development* (Volume 32(2)) and a special issue of the *Canadian Journal of Women and the Law on Regulating Decent Work for Domestic Workers* (Volume 23(1)). Professor Blackett has held short visiting appointments at the African Development Bank, the Australian National University, the University of Melbourne, and the University of Sydney. A former official of the International Labour Office, she has continued to serve as an academic expert on standard setting and labour law reform. In particular, she was engaged by the ILO from 2008–2011 to write its law and practice report, to provide expert advice to the committee during the International Labour Conference, and to draft the questionnaire that provided the basic textual architecture of the recently adopted Decent Work for Domestic Workers Convention (No. 189) and Recommendation (No. 201), 2011. She is the recipient of the 2010–2011 Bora Laskin National Fellowship in Human Rights Research.

Surya Deva is Associate Professor at the School of Law, City University of Hong Kong. His research interests lie in the fields of corporate social responsibility, international human rights, globalisation and sustainable development. He has published extensively on these issues. He is the Faculty Editor of the *City University of Hong Kong Law Review* and sits on the International Board of Editors, *Journal of Law and Development*. He has also been a Visiting Research Fellow at the University of New South Wales, Sydney.

Judy Fudge is Lansdowne Chair in Law at the University of Victoria, Canada. Her research interests are employment and labour law, feminist approaches to law and the political economy of law. She has been widely published in law, history and industrial relations journals, and she has co-authored and co-edited several books. Professor Fudge has held editorial positions with a number of journals in different disciplines, including Editor-in-Chief of the *Osgoode Hall Law Journal* (2000 to 2003). After beginning her academic career at Osgoode Hall Law School in 1987, Professor Fudge joined the University of Victoria Faculty of Law in January 2007 as the Lansdowne Chair in Law. She has been a Visiting Fellow at the European University Institute, McGill University's Centre for Human

Rights and Legal Pluralism, the London School of Economics, the University of Melbourne and the University of Oxford, and she has held visiting chairs at the University of British Columbia and the University of Saskatchewan. In 2009, Professor Fudge received the Bora Laskin National Fellowship in Human Rights for her research project 'Labour Rights as Human Rights: Unions, Women and Migrants'. She is a member of the Inter-University Research Centre on Globalisation and Work. Her publications include *Labour Before the Law: The Legal Regulation of Workers' Collective Action* (with Eric Tucker, Oxford University Press, 2001), *Privatization, Law and the Challenge to Feminism* (with Brenda Cossman, University of Toronto Press, 2002), *Precarious Work, Women and the New Economy: The Challenge to Legal Norms* (with Rosemary Owens, Hart Publishing, 2006) and *Work on Trial: Canadian Labour Law Struggles* (with Eric Tucker, Irwin Law Inc., 2010).

Sir Bob Hepple QC FBA is Emeritus Professor at the University of Cambridge. He was Senior Vice-President of the UN Administrative Tribunal and a barrister at Blackstone Chambers. He was Master of Clare College from 1993–2003 and Professor of Law at the University of Cambridge from 1995–2001. He was appointed Queen's Counsel (honoris causa) and a Bencher of Gray's Inn in 1996, and was elected as a Fellow of the British Academy in 2003. He was knighted in the New Year Honours 2004 'for services to legal studies'. He has an LL.D degree from Cambridge University and has been awarded honorary doctorates by the Universities of the Witwatersrand, Cape Town, Bari and UCL. From 1975–1993 he was a chairman of industrial tribunals (England and Wales), and from 1986–1990 a Commissioner for Racial Equality. He was an Honorary Professor of Law in the University of Cape Town. His publications include *Labour Law and Global Trade* (Hart Publishing, 2005). He has acted on numerous occasions as an independent legal expert for the International Labour Organisation and for the European Commission.

Brian Langille is Professor of Law at the University of Toronto. His research and teaching interests include labour law, contract law and legal theory. His numerous publications are concerned principally with labour law and legal theory, and his recent work addresses issues of international economic integration and labour policy. Professor Langille has been a member of Canadian delegations to both the Governing Body and the International Labour Conference of the International Labour Organisation (ILO), a consultant to the Federal and various provincial governments on domestic and international labour issues, a consultant to the ILO, and a Rapporteur to the Organisation for Economic Cooperation and Development. He is an editor of the *International Labour Law Reports*, a former member of the Executive of the International Society for Labour Law and Social Security, a member of the editorial committee of the Labour Law Casebook Group (Canada), and has acted as an arbitrator in labour matters in both the private and public sectors.

David Mangan is Lecturer in the Law of Obligations at the University of Leicester. Research and teaching interests include employment, tort and contract law with an emphasis on professional services. He has been a consultant in public sector labour relations and is a barrister and solicitor in Canada. His doctorate was recently completed at the London School of Economics. Publications have dealt with employment, tort and education law.

Tonia Novitz is Professor of Labour Law at the University of Bristol. She first studied law in New Zealand and qualified there as a barrister and solicitor, specialising in employment law and civil litigation. She then studied at Balliol College, Oxford, where she was awarded the BCL and completed her doctorate. She has been a Visiting Fellow at the International Institute for Labour Studies (Geneva), a Jean Monnet Fellow and a Marie Curie Fellow at the European University Institute (Florence) and a Senior Visiting Fellow at the University of Melbourne. She has written extensively on UK labour law, including a book on *Fairness at Work: A Critical Analysis of the Employment Relations Act 1999 and its Treatment of Collective Rights* (with Paul Skidmore, Hart Publishing, 2001). She is also a member of the editorial board of the *Industrial Law Journal*, with special responsibility for the Recent Legislation section. In addition, she has written on international labour standards, EU social policy, EU external relations and mechanisms for the protection of human rights. She is author of *International and European Protection of the Right to Strike* (Oxford University Press, 2003), and has been co-editor of a number of edited collections, including *Human Rights at Work* (with Colin Fenwick, Hart Publishing, 2010).

Beate Sjåfjell is Professor in the Department of Private Law, Faculty of Law, at the University of Oslo in Norway. She is the author of *Towards a Sustainable European Company Law. A Normative Analysis of the Objectives of EU Law, with the Takeover Directive as a Test Case* (Kluwer Law International, 2009). Her field of interest includes European company and securities law, law and economics, general EU law, environmental law and labour law.

She is the project leader for the research project 'Sustainable Companies', the general objective of which is to examine how to integrate the goal of sustainable development and especially its environmental dimension as a decisive factor in the minds of decision-makers in companies. The project began in January 2010 and has financing from The Norwegian Research Council from August 2010 to the end of 2012, as part of the research programme Environment 2015. Professor Sjåfjell is the Norwegian country reporter for the legal periodical *European Company Law*, Kluwer Law International. Many of her articles and papers in English are available at http://ssrn.com/author=375947

David Tajgman is External Lecturer at Aarhus University School of Law, Aarhus, Denmark. He holds degrees in industrial relations from Cornell University (1979), in law from the University of California (1982) and in financial economics from the University of London (2003). Mr Tajgman practiced labour law in California from 1982 to 1987, was an ILO Official in Geneva and Southern Africa between 1987 and 1996, and has since been engaged full time in international labour and development consultancy. He has worked in virtually all the English-speaking countries of Africa, and many in South and South-East Asia, Eastern Europe and the Middle East. He has written extensively and developed practitioner training programmes and materials on labour standards and corporate social responsibility. Publications include *Employment-Intensive Infrastructure Programmes: Labour Policies and Practices* (with Jan de Veen, ILO, 1998), *Freedom of Association: A User's Guide* (with Karen Curtis, ILO, 1999), *Extending Labour Law to All Workers: Promoting Decent Work in the Informal Economy in Cambodia, Thailand and Mongolia* (editor, ILO, 2006) and 'Employment, Economic Activities, and Livelihoods' in *Incorporating the Guiding Principles on Internal Displacement into Domestic Law: Issues and Challenges* (ASIL, 2010).

Jacqui True is Associate Professor in Political Studies at the University of Auckland. She is a specialist in international relations, the social dimensions of globalisation and global political economy, global governance and gender mainstreaming, ethical and feminist research methodologies. Her articles on gender mainstreaming and global governance rank among the most highly cited in the field. As well as having published numerous articles in peer reviewed journals, Jacqui is the author of five books. Most recently, with Dr Brooke Ackerly, Vanderbilt University, she is the author of *Doing Feminist Research in the Political and Social Sciences* (Palgrave, 2010).

The book provides a methodological guide from research question to presentation of research for all researchers, feminist and non-feminist, seeking to address the ethical dilemmas that inhere in the research process in social and political science. She is currently completing a book, *The Political Economy of Violence Against Women*, to be published by Oxford University Press. Jacqui is an editor of *International Studies Perspectives*. In 2010–2011 she is the elected Chair of the Feminist Theory and Gender Studies Section of the International Studies Association of North America (ISA).

Rolph van der Hoeven is Professor of Employment and Development Economics at the Institute of Social Studies (ISS) in The Hague. He holds a Ph.D. in Development Economics from the Free University and a M.Sc. in Econometrics from the Municipal University, both in Amsterdam. Until June 2008, he was Director of the International Labour Organisation's (ILO) Policy Coherence Group and was previously Manager of the Technical Secretariat of the World Commission on the Social Dimension of Globalisation. Other positions include Chief of the Macroeconomic and Development Policy Group at the ILO in Geneva and Chief Economist of the United Nation's Children's Fund in New York. He has also worked in Ethiopia and Zambia. His research concentrates on issues of employment, inequality and economic reform, focusing on problems relating to basic needs, structural adjustment, poverty alleviation and decent work, on which he is widely published. He serves on the board of a number of international institutions and journals.

Charlotte Villiers is Professor of Company Law at the University of Bristol. She studied law at the University of Hull and the London School of Economics and Political Science, and is a qualified solicitor. She has taught at the Universities of Sheffield and Glasgow, and was a Visiting Lecturer at the University of Oviedo in Spain. Her publications include *European Company Law – Towards Democracy* (Ashgate, 1998) and *Corporate Reporting and Company Law* (Cambridge University Press, 2006). She has also written extensively on UK industrial relations. Her current research sponsored by the Arts and Humanities Research Council concerns female participation in company boards.

An introduction to the role of labour standards in development

From theory to sustainable practice?

TONIA NOVITZ* AND DAVID MANGAN**

There are separate academic and policy disciplines which centre on 'labour law' or 'labour relations' as distinct from 'development studies'. In this way the language of 'sustainable development' has often been thought to be a discrete area of concern, lying apart from labour markets. One reason may be that international debates over policy have traditionally also been situated in different fora, such that the United Nations Conference on Trade and Development (UNCTAD) addresses development, while it is the business of the International Labour Organisation (ILO) to consider labour standards. However, it is no longer possible to ignore the role of labour standards in economic, social and environmental development, if such development is to be sustainable.

This was the conclusion of the participants of a conference held at the British Academy Rooms in London in May 2009. They came from a variety of backgrounds, as policy makers, lawyers, economists, trade unionists, environmentalists, political scientists and specialists in international relations. They also came from a diverse range of countries. This was truly an international discussion. We cannot present in this collection of essays the full array of comment and debate at the conference, which took the form of short papers and comments from the audience. However, the contributions to this collection do at least reflect the discussion and expertise present on that date.[1]

---

* Professor of Labour Law, University of Bristol.

** Lecturer in the Law of Obligations, University of Leicester.

[1] For podcasts from contributors unable to write a chapter for this final edited book, see: http://www.bristol.ac.uk/law/research/centres-themes/labour-law-research/labconfpod casts.html

The aim of this volume of essays is to generate debate beyond the scope of previous literature relating to the justificatory basis of labour standards, so as to consider alternative ways of understanding their function. In so doing, we consider what this means for the governance of labour markets, whether at local, national, regional or international levels. We also wish to challenge mainstream assumptions relating to 'sustainable development'. We consider it necessary for those writing in the frame of economic, social and environmental development studies to consider the impact of the policies that they advocate on workers, as well as the scope for worker participation in development processes.

Labour standards have been the subject of global debate and international regulation since the late nineteenth century. Workers have organised internationally to advance trade union interests from the establishment of the International Working Men's Association (the First International) in 1864 to the present date. Currently, the International Trade Union Confederation (ITUC) represents 168 million workers in 155 countries and territories and has 311 national affiliates.[2] Perhaps even more significantly, since the first treaty containing a prohibition against slavery, the General Act of Berlin of 1885, there has followed a vast number of international instruments which seek to promote the protection of labour standards. These have been adopted, for example, under the auspices of the International Association for Labour Legislation (IALL), the League of Nations, the ILO and the United Nations (UN).[3]

Development, and indeed the notion of 'sustainable development', is a rather malleable term, which seems to have different meanings in different contexts (Robinson 2004: 369). For the contributors to this volume, it is both a goal to be achieved and a means to promote well-being (Sen 1999: 37). We contest the notion that 'sustainable development' is to be taken to refer exclusively to environmental management, but assert that this term has a broader application such that it includes various facets of social and economic planning. This contention is supported by the Johannesburg Declaration on Sustainable Development 2002, paragraph 5 of which states that 'we assume a collective responsibility to advance and strengthen the interdependent and mutually reinforcing pillars of sustainable development – economic development, social development and environmental protection – at the local, national, regional and global levels'. Notably, the

---

[2] Website: http://www.ituc-csi.org
[3] Discussed in Rodgers et al. 2009: 4.

Johannesburg Declaration drew together the rights enshrined in the UN Declaration on the Right to Development of 1986, which related primarily to 'economic, social, cultural and political development' (Article 1(1)) and the Rio Declaration on Environment and Development 1992, which introduced the language of sustainability. This is self-evidently an idealistic statement of aims, but one which generated universal approval at the 2002 World Summit on Sustainable Development convened by the United Nations in Johannesburg. The idea is to arrive at a mode of governance of the economy, society and the environment so as to ensure not only short-term satisfaction but longer-term workable (sustainable) solutions to contemporary and future problems.

What is evident from the UN Declaration of 1986, the Rio Declaration of 1992 and the Johannesburg Declaration of 2002 is that the right to development recognised therein is not just an entitlement to certain outcomes but also an entitlement to be an active participant in the process by which those outcomes are achieved. So, for example, Article 1(1) of the UN Declaration not only stressed that development is a human right, but that it is one 'by virtue of which every human person and all peoples are entitled to participate in, contribute to, and enjoy'. Principle 10 of the Rio Declaration likewise observed that 'environmental issues are best handled with participation of all concerned citizens'.

Previously, the reasons for international activity in the pursuit of labour standards have been generally regarded as oriented towards 'social justice' and the protection of human rights (Leary 1992, Gross and Compa 2009, and Supiot 2010); or alternatively towards regulation of the terms of trade (Chisholm 1925, Barnes 1926, Imber 1989, and Kaufmann 2007). Development (and its sustainability) forms a significant matrix within which to understand contemporary policy debates regarding labour law and cannot afford to be neglected; thereby necessitating consideration of the substantive and procedural aspects of development which may justify and, alternatively, in a more negative manner, impact upon labour standards. While political activity is now occurring in this field, academic literature analysing this shift in paradigms and policy orientation is still in its infancy (Langille 2006, Fudge 2007, and Novitz 2010). It is in this setting that the opportunity arises to consider how labour standards fit within the matrix of development.

It should also be noted that since May 2009, and as the contributions to this collection have been redrafted and edited, there has been a further wave of political activity led by non-governmental organisations (NGOs) and regional and international trade unions. These have included Asian civil society and trade unions, who are demanding a voice within the Association of Southeast Asian Nations (ASEAN) on matters relating to economic integration and climate change.[4] The current economic crisis has, if anything, intensified workers' concerns with such matters, as is reflected in the 'Resolution on combating Climate Change through sustainable development and Just Transition' adopted at the ITUC 2nd World Congress in Vancouver in June 2010, whereby the ITUC declared its commitment 'to promoting an integrated approach to sustainable development through a just transition where social progress, environmental protection and economic needs are brought into a framework of democratic governance, where labour and other human rights are respected and gender equality achieved'.[5]

Linking labour standards to sustainable development

This edited collection starts from the premise that labour standards can be implemented in developed and developing states in a sustainable manner. The participants articulate that the success of attempts to promote development must be assessed, at least in part, on how they affect working people, but also on the extent to which workers contribute to defining and implementing development objectives. The authors of the following essays suggest various (non-exhaustive) ways in which labour standards and sustainable development interrelate.

First, it is evident that labour standards which secure access to material well-being, such as non-discrimination in access to jobs and provision of a living wage, can assist in addressing poverty, thereby raising levels of economic development. Second, regulation of working conditions, such

[4] See report 'Asian Unions Want a Voice on Climate Change and Involvement in Forest Certification in ASEAN': http://www.bwint.org/default.asp?index=2022&Language=EN; and more recently the Bogor Statement of ASEAN Trade Unions Unity Towards ASEAN Regional Economic Integration (2009) available at: http://www.workersconnection. org/articles.php?more=112; and Advancing a Peoples' ASEAN: Continuing Dialogue: Statement of the 2nd ASEAN Peoples' Forum (APF)/5th ASEAN Civil Society Conference (ACSC) (2009) available at: http://www2.asetuc.org/media/5_0%20ASETUC%20and%20 Civil%20Society%20in%20ASEAN_5.pdf
[5] See for reportage, *Trade Unions and Climate Change* Conference News 01, July 2010.

4

as hours of work and health and safety, can enable workers not only to make economic provision for their families but to care for their dependents, thereby promoting social cohesion, well-being and stability. Third, procedural entitlements to freedom of association, worker information and consultation, collective bargaining and industrial action can enable workers to assist employers in making better managerial decisions, which may lead to sustainable income for the employer and jobs for the workers. These kinds of action may also lead to enhanced income for workers, again alleviating poverty and creating a larger consumer base. Furthermore, such procedural mechanisms may allow for worker representation of and coalition with environmental concerns felt in the local community, which can experience the effects of pollutants more directly than management.

This is a picture of the potential role of labour standards in development which even goes beyond promotion of the 'core' Conventions identified by the ILO: ILO Conventions Nos 87 and 98 on freedom of association and collective bargaining (1948 and 1949); Conventions Nos 29 and 105 on the elimination of all forms of forced and compulsory labour (1930 and 1957); ILO Convention No. 138 on the minimum age for admission to employment (1973); ILO Convention No. 182 on the worst forms of child labour (1999); and ILO Conventions Nos 100 and 111 on the elimination of discrimination in respect of employment and occupation (1957 and 1958). Nor is it centred solely on the fundamental principles identified in Article 2 of the ILO Declaration on Fundamental Principles and Rights at Work 1998. Rather, this sketch is grounded in the broader 'Decent Work Agenda' advocated by ILO Director-General Juan Somavia, which consists of essentially four limbs: the protection of fundamental rights, employment promotion, social protection and social dialogue; the latter being an objective in itself, but also instrumental to the effective achievement of the three other objectives. Attention to gender has also cut across these overlapping aspects of the ILO's project, all of which are emphatically linked to development objectives, as is evident from policy statements issued by Somavia in 2007,[6] and the International Labour Conference Declaration on Social Justice for a Fair Globalisation 2008.[7] The 2008

---

[6] 'Decent Work for Sustainable Development', Director-General's introduction to the International Labour Conference 2007 (ILC 96-2007/Report I(A)).

[7] Declaration on Social Justice for a Fair Globalization, Articles II(A) and II(B). See also Global Jobs Compact 2009, especially Articles 7 and 9.

Declaration stresses that the role of the ILO is to 'facilitate meaningful and coherent social policy and *sustainable development*' (our emphasis).[8] Indeed, in the Preface to the published Declaration, Somavia has observed that: 'It contributes to policy coherence for sustainable development in national policies, among international organisations and in development cooperation, bringing together social, economic and environmental objectives.'

One might think that the ILO would be concerned predominantly with the social and economic aspects of development, as opposed to environmental issues. However, the Decent Work agenda has been extended to a 'Green Jobs Initiative', which is a joint project carried out by the United Nations Environment Programme (UNEP), the ILO, the International Organisation of Employers (IOE) and the ITUC. They have embarked jointly on a significant research endeavour and aim to disseminate instances of best practice and other findings as they become available.[9]

Justification of labour standards in terms of sustainable development may nevertheless cause alarm in certain quarters. It might be feared that this change of perspective could render labour standards merely instrumental in the pursuit of a wider mission to promote certain development outcomes, thereby failing to recognise the element of human dignity which such standards seek to respect, protect and fulfil. Those familiar with development literature will note how workers do not often rank high on typical lists of priorities. Instead, the workforce is viewed as a malleable resource. Within a results-based framework for development, labour standards tend to be seen as subsidiary social goods which promote and sustain economic growth. It follows that they can readily be sacrificed where they would obstruct the achievement of these objectives, because they are purely instrumental, and we have witnessed this in the context of structural adjustment conditionality imposed by the World Bank and the International Monetary Fund (IMF) (Morgan-Foster 2003 and Bakvis 2009). There is also the potential to obscure, within a development framework, fundamental questions relating to the economic value of labour which have long manifested themselves in industrial conflict between workers and their employers.

However, it is also possible to see how these objections can be overcome. By asserting that labour standards have a role to play in sustainable

---

[8] Articles II(A) and (B).
[9] See: http://www.ilo.org/integration/themes/greenjobs/lang—en/index.htm

development, one need not be making the claim that this is their only role. The imposition of labour standards may be justified for more than one reason. Also, as shall become apparent in this volume, 'the impact of economic growth depends much on how the *fruits* of economic growth are used' (Sen 1999: 44); in other words, there is scope here for a more humane and human-centred conception of economic development. Human rights inherent in labour standards (as they reflect the dignity of workers) may also be regarded as intrinsic to a development agenda, on the basis that they are essential to the creation and exercise of capabilities (Sen 1999, Nussbaum 2000, and Langille 2005). While it is true that the existing literature on capabilities does not definitively answer certain key questions, such as the status to be given to socio-economic rights relative to civil and political rights (Fudge 2007), or the way in which we should aim to reconcile conflict between individual freedom and collective action, the fact that these matters are open to debate does not preclude engagement with a development framework. Moreover, there remains scope to examine carefully the issues of distribution of income in the context of a development paradigm, as is illustrated by economist Sonia Bhalotra's examination of the development implications of child labour in this collection and Jacqui True's concern at the economic foundation of violence experienced by women.

The theme that arguably transcends all the contributions to this conference and which perhaps distinguishes this book from others written on links between labour and development is its emphasis on human agency. This is not merely the individual's concern with the realisation of that person's functionings in society (which development will assist), but rather individual and collective engagement with the very process of defining what development aims should and can be. Rather than seeing economic, social and environmental development objectives as to be determined by technical experts and implemented according to their prescriptions, the contributors to this volume view development in procedural as well as substantive terms, in participatory as well as material terms. Obviously, the wages and working conditions of workers (as well as levels of social security) will impact on their ability to be active agents in the development process, as will the kinds of education they receive (Stiglitz 2006: 50). Yet, beyond an acknowledgement of these constraints, we can assert that there is a role for workers in challenging expert views and establishing objectives, and that their engagement with the implementation of any regulatory mechanisms attempting to achieve any eventual development objectives is crucial to sustainability. It may be this unique perspective that the labour movement ultimately can bring to the development discourse and which, for the sake of all workers everywhere, we hope is heeded.

Making connections, changes and challenging omissions

The participants at the British Academy event in 2009 considered connections between theories of development and their practical application to labour standards. In so doing, contributors to this volume have considered what changes might need to be made in response to a development-based policy impetus and they considered where omissions currently lie. The aim of this collection is to present each essay in a manner which makes its content accessible to those working outside each writer's own discipline, so that it is possible to communicate to a wider audience. Each chapter is also informed by the interdisciplinary and practical policy debates that took place at this event and contributions made by activists in this field. We hope that they contain the germs of ideas that will fertilise the debate surrounding the role of labour standards in sustainable development for years to come.

Connections between labour standards and sustainable development

This collection begins with two essays which examine the connections between the promotion of labour standards and sustainable development. They also address current controversy over these linkages.

Sir Bob Hepple QC reminds us that it has never been more important to reflect on the function that labour standards can play within development, not least in the midst of the current economic crisis. He considers the issue of comparative advantage in trade, questioning assumptions relating to the sources of such advantage, and proposing innovative regulatory means of addressing current shortcomings. He advocates positive interaction of local, national, regional and international measures which empower workers' voices.

Brian Langille offers a re-evaluation of the function of labour law, based on Sen's notion of capabilities. He states that we have fundamentally misconceived the role that the ILO can play and that it should focus not on its established standard-setting role, but on a promotional role which will enable each member state to realise their developmental capacities. He suggests that this requires the radical reorganisation of ILO activities. This perspective is notably at odds with later contributions, which highlight the role that ILO standard-setting has played in establishing the capacity of workers' organisations to influence employer conduct, and is indicative of continued debate in this field of study. Nevertheless, Langille does not deny the value of participatory strategies, but rather considers that debate and dialogue can be invigorated if the ILO does not act in a legalistic manner.

The remainder of the collection is devoted to an analysis of the role that the protection of labour standards can achieve in developmental terms, with reference to concrete issues such as discrimination, child labour, trade, aid and migration. The final section contains close critical analysis of the role of social dialogue in development, and ends with observations from an eminent economist, Rolph van der Hoeven.

Discrimination

It is perhaps self-evident that discrimination excludes potential workers from the labour market or from the benefits of employment to which they would otherwise be entitled, such as fair wages, promotion and jobs which reflect their talents. The loss of this human potential has profound effects on the economy as well as on the personal lives of those affected. Moreover, the process of globalisation has the potential to have particular effects on women and ethnic minorities experiencing social exclusion.

Judy Fudge addresses the relationship between women's equality, care work and sustainable development, and seeks to develop a conceptual framework that can be used to understand this complex relationship. In so doing, she further develops the 'decent work' and 'capabilities' discourse in a manner which offers a new perspective on care work. She draws upon the feminist insight that gender inequality is intimately tied up with women's disproportionate responsibility for care work and considers how this can be addressed to promote development. She resists a view of capabilities which centres on individual choice, for 'so long as men can choose not to do domestic labour women will have no choice but to do it'. Fudge therefore considers how incentives could be crafted to share unpaid labour and challenge the notion that this is women's work.

Jacqui True seeks to address the material basis of discrimination against women. True identifies the concrete manifestations of globalisation for women, in terms of the effects of free trade zones on women's working and domestic lives, the implications of deregulation of labour markets and the results of migration. She argues that failures to secure the labour standards which would make development sustainable have led to unacceptable forms of violence against women. She, like Adelle Blackett writing later in this volume, points in particular to female vulnerability amongst migrant workers.

Mark Bell takes the issue of discrimination beyond gender and turns to the issue of ethnicity, asking: how can emphasis placed on 'social inclusion' supplement anti-discrimination law in a meaningful manner? The treatment of 'Travellers' and 'Roma' under the collective complaints procedure of the European Social Charter under the auspices of the Council of Europe provides Bell with a provocative case study. He demonstrates how a new regulatory mechanism has the potential to 'provide an innovative bridge between complaints-based anti-discrimination litigation and social inclusion policy'. The collective nature of the complaint offers a benefit in that it enables the supervisory body, the European Committee of Social Rights, to go further than the detail of an individual complaint to examine the social reality of the circumstances of a group of people. Moreover, a pragmatic rather than legalistic approach makes the recommendations of that Committee more likely to be effective. However, as he observes, the battle fought for the Roma people in Ireland and Italy, the two countries considered, is far from won. Local social prejudice has thus far obstructed a change of government policy and it remains unclear as to how change will ultimately be achieved. It may be that social activism, manifested through the complaints and in the broader sphere of public debate, is more likely to have an impact than just the findings of the supervisory body which lends force to their claims.

Child labour

The failure to educate children and to place them in paid work has frequently been identified as an obstruction to development. It perpetuates reliance on unskilled labour and fails to realise the personal and economic potential of the children so affected. Moreover, the undercutting of adult labour leaves parents unable to find work themselves, while they watch their children suffer under the burden of long hours and poor rates of pay, if not harm to their health and well-being. Sonia Bhalotra, a renowned economist in this field, provides an explanation of the reasons for child labour and the strategies by which this phenomenon can be reversed. She is critical of legal methods for redress, demonstrating how carefully they need to be crafted to address the material basis of the harm caused to children.

By way of contrast, Surya Deva is more optimistic. He considers that there is scope to deploy the notion of corporate social responsibility to constrain exploitation of children. Corporate codes of conduct have the capacity to be 'responsive' to the dynamics of child labour, so that they do not merely provide a stock response, but craft regulation to the specific circumstances in which child labour arises. In this respect, he distinguishes between 'core measures' and 'complementary measures'. The former, which one would expect to be 'predefined and common to all', might include prohibition on the employment of children in hazardous industries, or the elimination of all practices designated the worst forms of child labour. The complementary measures might entail 'providing education or vocational training; offering childcare and health facilities; offering employment to parents; and ensuring alternative sources of income'. Deva suggests that existing legal regimes regarding the conduct of multinational enterprises offer this potential. His optimistic stance is challenged by more sceptical views regarding the efficacy of CSR in the final section of this collection concerning social dialogue.

Trade, aid, migration and development

It has been suggested that one means of addressing development is by promoting trade and providing targeted aid. Two commentators consider the ways in which regional and global structures set up for the promotion of trade can impact upon development objectives.

Beate Sjåfjell offers an analysis of the ways in which sustainable development, including environmental protection, has come to be embedded in the EU Treaties. She permits no arbitrary distinction between environmental protection and the promotion of labour standards in a trade context, arguing rather that they are interdependent. Like other authors, Sjåfjell makes a case for the empowerment of workers, but her focus is on the ways in which participation in corporate decision-making and collective bargaining can make environmental issues a priority for employers. She also offers a vision of the ways in which obligations can be shared in a sustainable fashion between states, companies and other international institutional actors (cf. Potter and McCauley Sine 2009).

Adelle Blackett questions another common distinction, namely that so neatly made between trade and migration. Instead, she observes that the unequal distribution of wealth reflected in trade relations (not ameliorated by aid) has significant secondary effects on the incidence of migrant labour. The attempt of so-called developed states to erect immigration barriers is a feature of the inequality of trade relations and the failure to provide sufficient aid to make domestic economies in developing countries sustainable. In this way, her work echoes the concerns expressed by Jacqui True. Blackett asserts that we need to address both the terms of trade and aid so as to ensure that they are more equitable and that this is a legitimate concern for labour lawyers, given the implications for labour associated with both. She offers us a new solution, namely a 'reverse' social clause which would require that fair terms and conditions of employment be provided to migrant workers. This involves the North accepting responsibility for the casualties of trade.

Social dialogue

The last substantive section of the book addresses social dialogue, which arguably offers the transformative potential, in terms of social commitment, essential to sustainable development. However, Charlotte Villiers is critical of the notion that corporate social responsibility can be achieved without radically reforming company law. The stress which contemporary company law places on shareholder value, when combined with an emphasis on managerial prerogative, means that where corporate aspirations for short-term profit tend to come into conflict with labour and environmental concerns the latter are unlikely to prevail. Moreover, limited liability gives a company the ability to act almost with impunity as regards the interests of workers who come last in their list of creditors. Her view is that, without structural mechanisms for meaningful worker participation (and by this she does not mean mere information and consultation procedures, but opportunities for co-decision), true corporate social responsibility capable of achieving development objectives will not emerge.

David Tajgman likewise doubts the efficacy of corporate social responsibility. He reflects on how corporate social responsibility has changed in response to the identification of 'core labour standards' identified by the

ILO in the 1998 Declaration. He identifies gaps in 'governance' and implementation, which leave corporations free to depart from established codes whenever it suits their short-term interests to do so. One might hope that the potential impact on reputation would offer sufficient incentive to corporations to comply with their own codes of conduct, but he observes that this is frequently not the case. Contending that these gaps have to be plugged by state action, or be redressed by social actors, he points to the potential significance of interpretation of the core labour standards offered by the ILO in guiding corporate conduct and setting the benchmark for acceptance of such conduct. Indeed, it is the 'criticism levelled on the basis of interpretations of these principles given by civil society organisations and labour rights campaigners' which seems likely to have the greatest effect.

Tonia Novitz considers an alternative means of promoting economic, social, political and environmental objectives, namely global-level collective bargaining through 'international framework agreements' (IFAs). These agreements, while not strictly speaking legally enforceable, have the advantage of not being a unilateral statement by a multinational enterprise (MNE) in a code of conduct, but are drafted in agreement with a global union federation (GUF) which then can promote its implementation through union members and officials in various localities in which that company or its subsidiaries or contractors operate. The substance of IFAs has been influenced substantially by core ILO standards, particularly freedom of association, but their content frequently extends beyond that core to other labour standards of significance to workers (such as working time) and to environmental protection. However, Novitz argues that the potential strength of the IFAs is dependant on securing not so much the inclusion of ILO standards (although this is important) but effective procedures which allow for the realisation of local participation. In this way, IFAs, which might seem like top-down governance by MNEs and GUFs, can offer a route for local engagement with economic, social and environmental issues. IFAs provide the opportunity for working communities to address conflicting development objectives, and to resolve these, not only at the international level, but regionally, nationally and locally.

The book concludes with an 'afterword', that is, a survey of papers by the well-known economist and former ILO official, Professor Rolph van der Hoeven. Reflecting on how theory has been and could be put into practice, he recognises that current trends towards globalisation and the recent economic crisis have forced us 'to be cognisant of growing (and unsustainable) inequality between and within countries'. He considers that we now need to envisage policies to counter this and seize the opportunity to ensure participation in the debates which could shape such policies. A better realisation of labour standards could 'play an important role in diminishing the social consequences of the crisis and in building a better socio-economic system to avoid or face future crises', so that it is ultimately sustainable.

References

Bakvis, P. (2009) 'The World Bank's *Doing Business* Report: A Last Fling for the Washington Consensus?', *Transfer* 15: 419.

Barnes, G.N. (1926) *History of the International Labour Office* (Williams and Norgate).

Chisholm, A. (1925) *Labour's Magna Carta: A Critical Study of the Labour Clauses of the Peace Treaty and of the Draft Conventions and Recommendations of the Washington International Labour Conference* (Longmans).

Fudge, J. (2007) 'The New Discourse of Labour Rights: From Social to Fundamental Rights?', *Comparative Labor Law and Policy Journal* 29: 29.

Gross, J. and Compa, L. (2009) *Human Rights in Labor and Employment Relations: International and Domestic Perspectives* (Labour and Employment Relations Association Series, University of Illinois).

Imber, M. (1989) *The USA, ILO, UNESCO and IAEA: Politicization and Withdrawal in the Specialised Agencies* (Macmillan).

International Labour Organization (2010) *Global Employment Trends* (ILO).

Kaufmann, C. (2007) *Globalisation and Labour Rights: The Conflict Between Core Labour Rights and International Economic Law* (Hart Publishing).

Langille, B. (2005) 'Core Labour Rights – The True Story (Reply to Alston)', *European Journal of International Law* 16: 409.

Langille, B. (2006) 'Globalisation and the Just Society – Core Labour Rights, the FTAA and Development', in J.D.R. Craig and S.M. Lynk (eds) *Globalization and the Future of Labour Law* (Cambridge University Press).

Leary, V.A. (1992) 'Lessons from the Experience of the ILO', in P. Alston (ed.) *The United Nations and Human Rights: A Critical Reappraisal* (Oxford University Press).

Morgan-Foster, J. (2003) 'The Relationship of IMF Structural Adjustment Programs to Economic, Social and Cultural Rights: The Argentine Case Revisited', *Michigan Journal of International Law* 24: 577–646.

Novitz, T. (2010) 'Core Labour Standards Conditionalities: A Means by which to Achieve Sustainable Development?', in J. Faundez and C. Tan (eds) *International Law, Economic Globalization and Developing Countries* (Edward Elgar).

Nussbaum, M. (2000) *Women and Human Development* (Cambridge University Press).

Potter, E. and McCauley Sine, M. (2009) 'Human Rights and Sustainability: A Corporate Perspective', in J. Gross and L. Compa (eds) *Human Rights in Labor and Employment Relations: International and Domestic Perspectives* (Labour and Employment Relations Association Series, University of Illinois).

Robinson, J. (2004) 'Squaring the Circle? Some Thoughts on the Idea of Sustainable Development', *Ecological Economics* 48: 369–384.

Rodgers, G., Lee, E., Swepston, L. and Van Daele, J. (2009) *The ILO and the Quest for Social Justice 1919–2000* (ILO).

Sen, A. (1999) *Development as Freedom* (Oxford University Press).

Supiot, A. (2010) 'A Sense of Measure', *Social and Legal Studies* 19(2): 220.

Stiglitz, J. (2006) *Making Globalization Work* (Penguin).

Part I
Theoretical connections between work and development

1
Comparative institutional advantage in the context of development

BOB HEPPLE QC*

This subject is made even more topical by the current economic crisis. This is a crisis started by bankers and we know it is leading to a dramatic increase in the ranks of the unemployed and those in vulnerable employment. In the West that might mean redundancy or repossession of homes, but as we know in places like sub-Sahara and Africa and South Asia it can mean life or death.

The International Labour Organisation (ILO) has recently said, in their *Global Employment Trends Report* (2009), that global unemployment could increase by more than 50 million, the number of working poor (that is, those earning less than the poverty line of two US dollars a day) may rise to 1.4 billion or 45% of the world's employed, and the level of vulnerable employment could reach 53%. The ILO has pointed out that, in the past, financial crises have tended to impact severely on labour markets, such that it has taken four or five years after the general financial recovery before there is a recovery in employment. The ILO says that this is because massive rises in long-term unemployment and greater labour market informalisation, exacerbated by returning migrants in large-scale reverse migration from urban to rural areas, are very difficult to reverse. If these trends take root, the negative effects of the crisis will be long lasting, thus yielding significant social hardship and depriving the economy of valuable resources. So any discussion that we have on the role of labour standards in promoting sustainable development over the next five to ten years is bound to focus on measures to protect the developing countries from the

* Emeritus Professor, University of Cambridge. This is a modified transcript of the paper delivered at the British Academy, London, May 2009.

worst effects of the crisis and to ensure that they are able to take full advantage of economic growth when it comes.

The solutions which were agreed at the G20 Summit in London in 2009 focused on fiscal stimulus and financial regulation, but little attention was paid to the development dimension. Most developing countries, of course, lack the capacity to undertake large-scale public investments and it remains to be seen whether the International Monetary Fund (IMF) packages will be adequate or will simply perpetuate the crisis. There is an irony in asking an institution which was at the heart of the Washington Consensus (see Langille, this volume) to actually now reconstruct development. But above all, nothing has been done to prevent the global economic imbalances which are at the root of the crisis. It seems unlikely that the stimulus measures will ensure that global growth is more equitable and sustainable. The deep structural causes of this crisis, such as the pressures for short-term profitability to the detriment of the incomes of working people, have not been addressed. That is what makes so important the endeavour to consider the role of labour standards in sustainable development.

My aim, here, is to say something about how the theory of comparative institutional advantage might be applied in the context of development. In so doing, I shall draw on the work of Hall and Soskice on *Varieties of Capitalism* (2001) and my own work on *Labour Laws and Global Trade* (2005). My argument there was that nations prosper in a globalised economy, not by becoming more similar in their labour laws, but by building their institutional advantages on a floor of fundamental human rights. I want to develop that argument here in the context of national responses to the economic crisis, but I am not dealing here with the Global Jobs Pact 2009 adopted by the ILO and all the other international measures that could or have been taken. I want to talk about the national dimension.

Hall and Soskice (2001) looked exclusively at developed countries and they showed that firms do not automatically move their activities when offered low labour costs abroad. They developed the argument that firms concentrate their activities where they see a particular institutional or regulatory framework which fits the type of industry or activity in which they are engaged. They distinguished between the liberal market economies, such as the US, Britain, Australia, Canada and New Zealand, and the coordinated market economies, such as Germany and the Nordic countries (ibid.: 8 and 36–44). They did not, as I say, go beyond the developed countries and I want to do this very briefly, by first of all looking at some economic models and secondly at some political models.

20

Economic models

The problem I find with some economists here is that they look at the impact of labour standards in a uni-dimensional and undifferentiated way. They think all legal intervention is the same. A recent example is the World Bank's survey called *Informality, Exit and Exclusion* (2007: 6 and 15), which says that labour regulation is an important cause of the informalisation of developing economies, but does not make any attempt to differentiate between different kinds of regulation. My argument is that, if we want to understand comparative institutional advantage, we need a typology at least of regulation of the employment relationship. The models that I am going to look at are, in part, the work of David Charny (2000).

The first model is that of so-called *static or direct benefits*. These might include working time, health and safety, protection against unfair dismissal. If these are economically efficient, they simply operate as substitutes for cash payments. They therefore confer no comparative advantage either in terms of trade or in attracting investment because, in theory at least, the employer's costs remain the same whether the benefit is in cash or is a non-wage benefit. So, if the net effect is zero, a country would not gain any advantage by diluting standards such as those. Of course, in reality we have to modify that, because some workers value the benefits at cost, some below cost, and some above cost. This means that an older, higher-paid worker would value a pension or a health benefit above cost, while a younger, lower-paid worker would value them at less than cost. This may mean that a country with a large supply of young, skilled, low-paid workers may be induced to maintain those low standards so as to attract trade or investment. A country with an older skilled workforce may find that employers are more prone to outsource and that has happened to some extent with, for example, call centres being outsourced to other countries.

A second model consists of benefits which are *dynamic* in the employment relation, such as, for example, a minimum wage law which outlaws sweatshops, and thereby gives employers an incentive to develop technology and invest in a skilled workforce that gives them a comparative advantage. Another leading example is child labour. There is, I would say, historical evidence that employers in textile factories in Britain realised not only that the competiveness of their factories was not jeopardised by statutory protection from child employment but that children who went to school were more productive in the long term. However, this happened at a particular point in the Industrial Revolution when you did not need the small nimble hands, when technology had developed, but clearly child labour could be phased out and was phased out because of those economic developments. We can also give examples in the so-called 'family-friendly' laws and also in anti-discrimination laws against harassment. So, the effects of laws like these are to raise skills and productivity to widen the labour market, for example by making it easier for women and people with children to enter and remain in the labour market, and therefore these generally have a positive impact on labour costs.

The third model is what we call *risk-spreading*, that is, where you have forms of social insurance pensions and those kinds of protection for workers, such as acquired rights when undertakings are transferred and so on. Now here jurisdictional competition really does begin to matter, because where an employer can shift to another country where the social costs are lower they would be very tempted to do so. David Charny (ibid: 291) suggested that the answer would be cross-border insurance, something that happened to some extent in the EU, where we have protection for acquired rights and so on, in an attempt in some ways to equalise costs. But there is, and we have to be aware of this, an incentive for capital to move to countries which have a low risk-spreading cost of these kinds. The cruel paradox is really that those countries with low social costs are most attractive to foreign direct investment in outsourcing, but that makes them the very countries in which recession has its harshest impact on working people and their families, because of the absence of a social safety net.

The final regulatory model is *empowerment*, for example by protecting the rights to organise and bargain, as well as information and consultation provisions. Here, although it is somewhat controversial, there is considerable evidence at least in Europe to indicate that giving workers a voice of some kind generally improves efficiency, creates trust and cooperation, and is actually good for business as well as being a more democratic form of running industry (Hepple 2005: 255). Diluting those rules can actually have adverse effects.

Political models

Now let me look at the political models in developing countries. The economic models set the parameters of institutional advantage, but it is political choices that are going to determine the outcomes. I think one of the best ways of doing this is by taking what are clearly 'ideal types', which do not exist in a pure form anywhere, and I would suggest four here: repression; informalisation or deregulation; developmental protectionism; and rights-based regulated flexibility. Just let me say a little about each of them, but prefaced by the reminder that these are only ideal types.

Labour laws do not develop in some kind of fixed evolutionary pattern. They are the outcome of political and industrial struggles and what can be conceded at any time. They are deeply imbedded in our national cultures and traditions (Kahn-Freund 1978). The other point I would make is that I am not dealing here with failed states, for example Somalia, where only radical political change can make a difference.

So, starting with *repression*, historically the repression of workers' movements (or freedom of association) either directly or more subtly featured in all industrial relations systems in all European countries. It was also a feature of colonial labour systems. Those regimes relied on penal laws to enforce one-sided servant systems. They tolerated forms of slavery, enforced bonded labour and child labour. They suppressed or marginalised trade union and workers' movements. That is the legacy when one talks about development today. One of the positive effects of globalisation has been to expose the economic inefficiency in the modern world of those colonial systems as well as the political unacceptability of repressive regimes. I do not think anyone, certainly intellectually, would justify repressive regimes as a means of comparative advantage, but it does take subtle forms. Adelle Blackett (2007), in her excellent paper for the International Institute for Labour Studies, gives a number of examples, such as the Republic of Korea, which started with a repressive cheap labour market that fuelled export-led industrialisation, but in the face of labour unrest and international pressures gave way to a more democratic approach that has led to greater social sustainability of the development process.

The second is *informalisation* or *deregulation*. We know that many developing countries have sought comparative advantage by maintaining or even extending the informal sector. There is no consensus as to how we should define informal employment. In general, I use that term to denote an absence of regulation, but the formal sector has many different types of regulation of the kind that I have been outlining. Within the informal labour market, a distinction is often drawn between so-called 'upper-tier' voluntary informal employment, that is those who prefer self-employment to avoid taxation or for family reasons, and forced informality, that is those who eke out a living below two US dollars a day and who have no choice but to be in the informal sector. It is a very controversial issue and of great importance to national policy making. It is sometimes suggested that formal regulation is a cause of both voluntary informal and forced informal employment. But would informalisation and deregulation really create more jobs? An excellent article, published in the *International Labour Review* by David Kucera and Leanne Roncolato (2008), highlights the very point that I am trying to make: the need for a differentiated approach to regulation. Of course, the ILO aims at 'decent work' and defines decent work as work covered and protected by formal labour institutions. The ILO has 'decent work indicators', that is, of employment and income opportunities, social protection, fundamental rights at work and social dialogue. These writers conclude and I quote:

> [the] evidence is clear: it points to the coherence of simultaneously endeavouring to reduce informal employment and improve the quality of formal employment through labour regulation. But the exceptions – raising minimum wages in the midst of a deep recession, requiring a large number of procedures to start a new company – are instructive too. They suggest that the debate should be not about regulation versus deregulation as such, but rather about the optimal design and implementation of labour regulations in country- and time-specific contexts. This holds for the design of social protection programmes as well.
>
> (Kucera and Roncolato 2008: 342–343)

I think one of the most intractable aspects of the 'decent work' programme is social dialogue. This will be discussed by other contributors, but I would just say, in that context, that the South African example shows that, if, despite the difficulties, you can organise the informal sector, you may have a number of effects wider than simply improving the living standards of those workers. For example, organisation of the taxi industry and of street vendors in South Africa not only has benefits for the workers, but also has enabled them to coordinate buying from wholesalers, to improve their access to services and helped to resolve disputes.

Let me then move to *developmental protectionism*. Theories of development often hang around this idea of displacement of competition, that is where you get countries at different stages of development, the more highly developed society and economy unleashes this process of displacement competition. So we find the 'tiger economies' of East Asia held up as an example, but it is to be noted again that, in the early stages, they engaged in repression (as opposed to protectionism) to ensure their competitive advantage. I once had the task of drafting a democratic trade union law for Hong Kong just before the Chinese took over, and immediately after the

24

Chinese Government took over, this law was repealed. So I have seen first hand how development and repression can be combined. Of course, companies may move out of economies where workers are organising to other less developed economies only to restart the process of repression. As regards the struggle for democratisation in those countries, I just want to make three brief comments about these struggles and how they relate to fundamental labour rights.

The first is the importance of regionalisation. There is a real fear on the part of developing countries that, if they adopt decent labour standards, they will be at a competitive disadvantage in international trade in comparison with other economies in their region. There has been a little empirical research and we need a lot more. It seems, however, that a decision to ratify core ILO conventions depends crucially on whether peer countries have done the same. There tends to be almost a domino effect here. Developing countries will look at the initiatives and what their competitors (in the region) are doing. I think, if we look at the European example, that much of the social progress in Europe in recent decades is attributable to EU-wide social and employment strategies, not now aimed at a level playing field, but aimed at establishing common minimum standards and common objectives to reduce destructive competition. I would say that, despite the many gaps and deficiencies in EU legislation, this has been the trend.

The second comment is that many developing states that purport to embrace democratisation and minimum labour standards in theory disregard them in practice. I said somewhere else that social standards are 'paper tigers', fierce in appearance but weak in tooth and claw (Hepple 2003: 238). This is the problem with the enforcement of labour laws. It is not merely a technical problem or a matter of lack of resources; it is a deep-seated political problem. It is reflected in various ways, like the preference for soft standards rather than hard law. I am not against soft standards in some contexts, but concerns arise from the weakening of trade unions, under-resourcing and privatisation of enforcement, and so on. Most important of all has been the growing use of contingent and informal labour to circumvent labour protections. The half a million Indian workers in the Gulf States who have been sent home have been the first to feel the effects of the global recession. Migrant labour is another way in which people seek to avoid labour protection.

The third comment I want to make goes back, in a way, both to regionalisation and enforcement and that is to say there is a very important interaction between national, regional and international labour standards. These can be utilised in different and dynamic ways. For example, for all its faults, the NAFTA North American Agreement on Labour Cooperation (NAALC) has created some kind of impetus for collaboration between unions in these different countries and non-governmental organisations (NGOs) to pursue more effective labour standards.

The final category is *rights-based regulatory flexibility*. This sees employment rights as necessary to economic development. For example, only regulation which says that there is to be equal pay for women and men can correct certain market failures, but central to the achievement of equal pay may be regulatory flexibility. One shoe does not fit all nor does it fit for all time. Employers and workers have to have the space in which to adapt labour standards to a particular sector or a particular workforce, and that can involve having different levels of social dialogue, using codes of practice which can be adapted, or setting certain minimum standards and also, in some cases, ceilings of rights having regard to the size and resources of undertakings. Now this model of regulated flexibility was one which was aimed at by those reforming South African labour relations law after the first democratic elections in 1994. I was on the Ministerial Working Party and we had long discussions about the appropriate regulatory model and that was the one opted for. The actual outcome was the result of intense negotiations between business and a fairly strong trade union movement, but regulated flexibility was reflected in ideas like promoting collective bargaining, choosing sectoral bargaining as a preferred but not a compulsory level of bargaining, allowing enforceability of collected agreements, having workplace forums for dealing with productivity and efficiency issues and local grievances. In the individual field, use was made of codes of practice and so on, and there was a Commission for Conciliation Mediation and Arbitration (CCMA) to resolve these individual disputes. I have to say that over the past fifteen years, this aim of regulated flexibility has not been fully met. First of all, business and labour failed to recognise the new role for sectoral bargaining as a means to balance job security and the operational needs of enterprises. What you find are very detailed, very prescriptive sectoral agreements, the antithesis of what was actually intended. The workplace forums could only be triggered by unions and the unions decided they would be competitive with unions and they did not go for them. Now that the unions are beginning to decline in South Africa, and are not as strong as they were fifteen years ago, they may change their views. The CCMA also, to some extent, frustrated the aims of regulated flexibility by over-proceduralising, over-bureaucratising dismissal procedures, treating codes of practice like a strict legal requirement and not looking particularly at the needs of small and medium enterprises. After all, the link between the formal and informal is going to be small and medium enterprises in the developing countries, and also, in a country like South Africa, a means of black economic empowerment. Therefore it is crucial in South Africa to reconsider how they could make this a more flexible form of regulation.

Conclusion

Briefly, in conclusion, there are no comparative disadvantages from efficiency-promoting standards and there are comparative advantages from dynamic standards to increase capabilities. We need to be concentrating on democratic alternatives which, as I have said, would be incompatible with repression, informalisation or deregulation. I have said that regionalisation is important and that we need to counter circumventions like the growth of contingent migrant workers. Above all, in enforcement, we need to keep in mind the interactions between the national, local and international and regional standards.

References

Blackett A. (2007) 'Trade Liberalization, Labour Law and Development: A Contextualization', International Institute for Labour Studies Discussion Paper No. 179.

Charny, D. (2000) 'Regulatory Competition and the Global Co-ordination of Labour Standards', *Journal of International Economic Law* 3: 281.

Hall, P. and Soskice, D. (eds) (2001) *Varieties of Capitalism: The Institutional Foundations of Comparative Advantage* (Oxford University Press).

Hepple, B. (2003) 'Enforcement: The Law and Politics of Cooperation and Compliance', in B. Hepple (ed.) *Social and Labour Rights in a Global Context* (Cambridge University Press).

Hepple, B. (2005) *Labour Laws and Global Trade* (Hart Publishing).

Kahn-Freund, K. (1978) 'Comparative Labour Law as an Academic Subject', in K. Kahn-Freund (ed.) *Selected Writings* (Stevens Publishing). [Reprinted from (1966) *Modern Law Review* 82: 40.]

Kucera, D. and Roncolato, L. (2008) 'Informal Employment: Two Contested Policy Issues', *International Labour Review* 147(4): 321.

2
Human freedom and human capital

Re-imagining labour law for development

BRIAN LANGILLE*

This book examines the role of labour standards in sustainable development and that is what I wish to address at a fairly abstract level. The essence of what I have to say is the following: if we could have clear thinking about labour standards and clear thinking about sustainable development, then we would say that there is an intimate connection and profound overlap between labour standards and development.

This is because, first, there is an intimate and profound connection between human freedom (in Sen's way of talking) on the one hand, and human capital on the other (Sen 1997). Second, development is the process of the removal of obstacles to real human freedom conceived of, according to Sen, as the real capacity to lead lives which we have reason to value. Indeed, human freedom is both the goal and the way there. Third, labour law is that part of our law which structures and mobilises the deployment of human capital, that is, which structures and mobilises the 'exploitation' (in the best sense of the word) of human capital, which is at the core of human freedom.

So, if development is about human freedom and labour law is about human capital, then my conclusion is that labour law is a key to development. Now, a lot depends on the condition I mentioned. I began by saying that if we had clear thinking, then we would see that this is the case.

*Professor of Law, University of Toronto. This is a modified transcript of the paper delivered at the British Academy Rooms, London, May 2009. A fuller article is now published as Langille, Brian A. (2010) 'Imagining Post-"Geneva Consensus" Labor Law for Post-"Washington Consensus" Development', *Comparative Labor Law & Policy Journal* 31(3). Available at SSRN: http://ssrn.com/abstract=1607939

What I want to focus on here are the obstacles to clear thinking about labour standards and their relationship to development.

Why is this such a controversial and difficult topic? I wish to approach that question by suggesting that development theorists and development economists have made some progress in their thinking, in particular about the 'Washington Consensus' and the need to move beyond it, but that labour lawyers lag behind in their thinking about labour standards, particularly international labour standards and particularly International Labour Organisation (ILO) standards. What I am going to suggest is that just as there was a 'Washington Consensus', so too has there been a 'Geneva Consensus' and it is still profoundly influential in our thinking about labour law. It needs to be addressed and, in fact, it needs to be discarded as it is well past its 'sell-by date'.

At the core of the problem is the idea of a 'Washington Consensus' and a 'Geneva Consensus'. The 'Washington Consensus' is, or was, about how development should and does work, and the 'Geneva Consensus' is about how labour standards should and do work. But the shared idea is the very idea of a 'consensus'. In other words, the problem is not the word 'Washington' in the term 'Washington Consensus', the problem is the word 'consensus'. So too in the 'Geneva Consensus', the problem is not any particular set of ideas or package of ideas, it is the very idea of a set or package of ideas in the first place. My conclusion is that we need a post-'Geneva Consensus' about labour standards for post-'Washington Consensus' development. Now let me expand upon that argument. The core claim is that we need to get rid of the commitment to the idea of a consensus.

Someone might claim, in relation to the 'Washington Consensus', that the golden age of deregulatory capture (from roughly 1978–2008) is over. That person would at least get a hearing today, a hearing that they may not have received five years ago, or perhaps even a year ago. That is because many people along with Alan Greenspan have discovered flaws in what he has called 'the critical functioning structure that defines how the world works'. Now as John Lanchester recently pointed out, the critical functioning structure that defines how the world works is one hell of a thing to find a flaw in (see Greenspan cited in Lanchester 2009). It is my view that Lanchester is precisely right, it is a hell of a thing to find a flaw in, but that is where the important flaws are located and where we should direct our efforts.

It is difficult to think about these defining critical structures precisely because they give us a way of understanding, framing and picturing our world. And as Wittgenstein famously said, these pictures hold us captive (Wittgenstein 1973: para. 115). But, as difficult as it is, I think this is where development theorists (or certain among them) have been directing their efforts and where labour law theorists should be as well.

Development economists and development theorists have made headlines recently by being rather hard on themselves and upon their discipline. Dani Rodrik began a review in the *Journal of Economic Literature* with the following sentence: 'Life used to be relatively simple for the peddlers of policy advice in the tropics' (Rodrik 2006). This way of putting things is provocatively similar to Willliam Easterly's formulation as revealed in his title, *The Elusive Quest for Growth: Economists' Adventures and Misadventures in the Tropics* (Easterly 2002). Even more provocative is Easterly's more recent title, *The White Man's Burden: Why the West's Efforts to Aid the Rest Have Done So Much Ill and So Little Good* (Easterly 2006; cf. the more thoughtful review in Sen 2006).

This is unsettling language. It is loaded with much political and historical freight, but I suggest that we should observe that there are actually two metaphors in Easterly's two titles. One is that of the 'elusive search'. The other is the idea of 'spreading the gospel'. These are related but different ideas. The former is: there is an answer and we shall keep looking until we find it. The latter idea is: we have the answer in hand and we are here to tell you what it is. Within this latter view it has been common for some time to identify the 'Washington Consensus' as the gospel in question and it is now also a commonplace view that the 'Washington Consensus' is dead. But there has also emerged recently an even more radical idea that suggests that the common denominator in Easterly's two metaphors is the idea of 'the answer', that is, of a 'consensus'. The real and fundamental problem with the 'Washington Consensus' may be not just that the recipe for development contained in the 'Washington Consensus' was wrong, but that the very idea of a recipe is a bad one, no matter whether it is cooked up in Washington or anywhere else.

It is this question which Dani Rodrik has asked most pointedly, particularly in his book, *One Economics, Many Recipes* (Rodrik 2007). But it also is one which the World Bank itself has come to ask and to answer in the affirmative. In its document, *Economic Growth in the 1990s: Learning from a Decade of Reform* (World Bank 2005), the Bank makes this fundamental point as follows (p. xiii):

> The central message of this volume is then that there is no unique universal set
> of rules. Sustained growth depends on key functions that need to be fulfilled

over time: accumulation of physical and human capital, efficiency in the allocation of resources, adoption of technology, and the sharing of the benefits of growth. Which of these functions is the most critical at any given point in time, and hence which policies will need to introduced [sic], which institutions will need to be created for these functions to be fulfilled, and in which sequence, varies depending on initial conditions and the legacy of history. Thus we need to get away from formulae and the search for elusive 'best practices', and rely on deeper economic analysis to identify the binding constraints on growth. The choice of specific policy and institutional reforms should flow from these growth diagnostics. This much more targeted approach requires recognizing country specificities, and calls for more economic, institutional, and social analysis and rigor rather than a formulaic approach to policy making.

The report is almost moving when it talks about this insight and 'the ending of a conviction'. It notes that such endings of a conviction cause 'discomfort' for those who have held them. It also notes that the central changes of attitude which flow from this ending of a belief that one's task is to deliver the truth to others are from arrogance and ignorance to 'humility' and 'understanding'.

This report is, as Rodrik notes,

> a rather extraordinary document in that it shows how far we have come from the original Washington Consensus. There are no confident assertions here of what works and what doesn't – no blueprint for policymakers to adopt. The emphasis is on the need for humility, for policy diversity, for selective and modest reforms, and for experimentation . . . Occasionally the reader has to remind himself that the book he is holding in his hands is not some radical manifesto but a report by the seat of orthodoxy in the universe of development theory.
>
> (Rodrik 2006: 974–975)

A common way of summarising what Rodrik says in his book, and what the Bank says in its report, is that we are now witnessing a shift from detailed recipes to general principles; a shift from the universal to the local, contextual and embedded; a shift from 'all at once' to 'a few things at a time'; and a shift from creating grand solutions to the idea of removing concrete and identifiable road blocks. Now these are important lessons but they beg the question: Why are these shifts necessary?

This is a difficult question which leads, in my view, to quite a radical answer. It is an answer which one of Rodrik's heroes, Albert O. Hirschman, articulated over fifty years ago (Hirschman 1958). I will return to this radical response shortly, but before I do that I want to consider this idea of the 'Geneva Consensus'.

This is in some ways a new method of putting across a point that I have been trying to make for a while. I think that there is a commonly accepted theory of labour standards, and a particular theory of international standards, that is best understood as analogous to the 'Washington Consensus' that I now call a 'Geneva Consensus'. This is not because it has the same content, but because it follows the same methodology. That is, the methodological cornerstone is, again, the very idea of a consensus.

This consensus seems to have come into being, and reflected a natural set of assumptions in place, at the time of the ILO's creation in 1919 (Standing 2008). It is not the result of anything contained in the ILO's constitution; rather, it is a result of a set of beliefs – to use Greenspan's (2008) words, a 'critical defining structure about how the world works'– and how best to interpret and use ILO constitutional machinery in light thereof. The problem is that this consensus remains basically unreconstructed and carries on as it has for the last 80 years and more. Furthermore, labour lawyers have made very little progress in reconsidering, let alone dislodging, this consensus, and far less progress than have their development theory colleagues. International labour lawyers need a parallel revolution – they still await their Greenspanian moment of insight.

Here is the parallel between the two packages of ideas, the 'Washington Consensus' and the 'Geneva Consensus'. The informing idea of both is that all states need to be disciplined by a set of universal and comprehensive policies. These comprehensive package deals are aimed at constraining the self-interest of member states who otherwise would be tempted to depart from the true path. They are to be externally imposed upon members by international institution. In the case of international labour law this consensus on what is at stake has direct and dramatic implications for ideas about the scope and kind of law required to deal with the problem. It also dictates the kinds of processes needed to administer and apply that law. Very briefly these are to be very serious legal proceedings leading eventually, it is usually hoped, to sanctions.

Once we have adopted or bought into the very idea of a consensus and all that it entails, discussions of shortcomings of the system will centre on how it is not comprehensive enough and on the need for a continual production and ratification process making the consensus even more comprehensive. Discussions of reform of the system will be dominated by allegations that the system is not 'hard' enough, that it is equipped with insufficiently strong sanctions to coerce the required behaviour across the comprehensive agenda of the consensus, and that the ILO needs to obtain some real 'teeth' in the form of, for example, economic clout (conditionality of some sort – usually trade) which those economic agencies advancing the 'Washington Consensus' can bring to bear, and so on. (In this sense the 'Geneva Consensus' is a 'wannabe' 'Washington Consensus'.)

The ideas inherent in the very idea of consensus are evident and dominant in this way of thinking. The standard entrenched views see labour standards as detailed, universal, comprehensive, top-down, one-size fits all, all at once, a-contextual, imposed, centrally enforced, and backed up with some sort of clout. Labour standards are not viewed as general principles which are actually in the rational self-interest of ILO member states. The process is exactly not seen as one in which obstacles to their realisation need to be identified and prioritised locally and contextually, informed by local feedback, and then helpfully worked on in light of local circumstances and resources, and with called-upon outside assistance, and so on.

There has been a growing internal resistance to the 'Geneva Consensus' for some time but it has had a limited success and it is not hard to see why. These attempts to rethink dominant modes of thinking have to be 'inside jobs', as it were, and this sort of inside job is fraught with difficulty. First, such thinking is hard to do because these paradigms are so powerful and these pictures are so hard to escape. Second, even if it were possible, any suggestion to move away from the Consensus and its hard law system, in order to find alternative strategies, will be seen as threats which undermine the very fabric of the system and as totally inconsistent with the Consensus. Third, as a result of this resistance to change, initial efforts and any initial success in developing new approaches 'packaged' and 'sold' as non-threatening to, outside and parallel to the processes mandated by the Consensus must never be seen to threaten to replace it. Then they will rightly, in one sense, be attacked as an alien transplant granted on a system unlikely to insidiously damage it. This is, in my view, the best way to understand the purpose, method of creation and history of the 1998 Declaration on Fundamental Rights, as well as the vigorous and negative response to it in certain quarters, within and without the ILO (Alston 2004, for example).

Here is a prediction. It will in time come to be seen as, again, the underlying logic and method of the less well understood 2008 Declaration on Social Justice – which, in essence, seeks to extend the logic of the 1998 Declaration beyond the fundamental rights to the other pillars of the Decent Work Agenda.

Meanwhile we can also predict much else that will happen. First, if it is the case that the very idea of a 'consensus', which underlies all else, is unhelpful in the real world, then member states will seek to avoid it. The consensus, and the machinery used to enforce it, will begin to be less comprehensive in theory and less used in practice (Langille 2005: 425–426). If the consensus is inappropriate, ILO member states will use it less and less, and this is precisely what is happening.

Second, there will be an increasing isolation of the labour standards system within the world of the ILO as a whole. Those in the ILO but outside the legal system will come to view it as wedded to an increasingly irrelevant set of processes unconnected to any concern about progress in the real world. Labour standards will increasingly be seen as purely formal in a legalistic sense and the whole methodology one which increasingly looks like Easterly's missionaries spreading the gospel in the tropics.

And within the ILO the legal system will be viewed as an end in itself, a separate world in which lawyers talk to lawyers on an island of their own. As a result, labour standards and the real-world development work of the ILO constitute 'two cultures' talking past each other.

Third, this in turn has operational and financial consequences. That is, we have the old system up and running while these new efforts of reform come on stream in 1998 and 2008. This makes it difficult to get the support even of prosperous nations like Canada who see the 2008 ILO Declaration as merely another reporting system on top of the already existing reporting systems. This results in the undermining of support from nations who should be supporting these reform initiatives.

It does not have to be this way. It should not be this way. The consensus is not written in stone but of course, as is the case with any 'critical functioning structure that defines how the world works', what is interesting is that most people think it is written in stone. Whilst most people think that the supervisory machinery under the ILO system is constitutionally mandated, it is not. Everything about it is a matter of administrative invention out of some pretty thinly worded and obscure articles in the constitution. And the whole Committee of Experts supervisory system, which could have been a very interesting soft law feedback from the field, became, inevitably in light of the Consensus, merely a small claims court version of the official and constitutionally explicit hard law (International Court of Justice / Article 33 / complaint driven) system. There is a large opportunity here, still being missed.

How did this happen? It is a long complicated story and one which is the product of a long institutional struggle. For example, some institutional administrative decisions which are seemingly innocuous turn out to be vitally important; to give one example, having the Committee of Experts divide up its work according to legal topic and not according to country has substantial consequences. It is both a product of, and a way of, reinforcing the consensus.

My own view is that ILO standards are kind of a public good. You cannot exclude people from using them and there are a lot of people out there trying to use these standards in various ways. If you are inside the mindset of 'consensus', this is a threat to ILO law, not an opportunity. Why? Because you now have non-experts trying to figure out what ILO standards mean, thereby circumventing the official process of the consensus. Rather than, for example, taking some of these interesting things that have happened in the real world, the ILO legal system actually resists them. For example, the 'Better Work' programme is a very interesting initiative, coming out of the Better Factories Cambodia idea. But it is carried out in almost a clandestine way completely divorced from the 'normal' supervisory mechanisms within the ILO.

Here is an interesting question: Why are both the 'Washington Consensus' and the 'Geneva Consensus' under stress? (Albeit to different degrees, but at the same time.) This is a difficult question because the usual ILO account for 'troubles at t' mill' is that the forces of neo-liberalism are at work. But this cannot be the explanation for the almost simultaneous strains upon the 'Washington Consensus' and the 'Geneva Consensus'. What can explain the need perceived, to different degrees within different institutions, for a new understanding and a new insight into the problems with the very idea of a consensus? This takes us back to the radical thought which I mentioned before, which goes back to Hirschman and which others, such as Stiglitz (2002), have also articulated.

Hirschman wrote fifty years ago: 'As long as one thinks of development in terms of a missing component be it capital, entrepreneurship, technical knowledge, one is likely to believe that the problem can be solved by injecting that component' (Hirschman 1958: 7). His view was that this was not how development occurred, nor was made possible. Expressing what I take to be a remarkable and profound philosophical insight, Hirschman suggested that we resist the impulse which this picture of development inevitably visits upon us to continue the search for the illusive missing component to be injected, as he put it. Rather, he saw that development occurs 'provided economic development itself first raises its head' (ibid.: 5). He believed that an attitude, which he called a 'growth perspective', was necessary for development. Hirschman then pointed out, in typically direct form, the seemingly tautological nature of this claim. He asked, 'are we not simply saying that development depends upon the ability and determination of a nation and its citizens to organize themselves for development?' (ibid.: 8) and noting that 'if a growth perspective is needed for growth . . . this perspective can only be acquired in the course of growth. So it would seem that all we have achieved is to saddle ourselves with . . . a vicious circle' (ibid.). Hirschman responds to his own questions as follows, making the conceptual point: '. . . the circle to which our analysis has led may perhaps lay claim to a privileged place in the hierarchy of these circles inasmuch as it alone places the difficulties of development back where all the difficulties of human action begin and belong: in the mind' (ibid.: 10–11). (Or, to paraphrase Wittgenstein, the 'injected component' itself 'is dead'.) That is a deep remark.

Stiglitz, picking up on this idea almost 50 years later, said that development is essentially a change in mindset: 'a change in mindset is at the centre of development' (Stiglitz 2002: 165). Now this is ultimately a change in self-conception from one of passivity to one of human agency and this is the idea which lies at the core of Sen's approach to human development. In Sen's view, human freedom (conceived of as the real capacity to lead a life we have reason to value) is the most important means to that end. Development consists of removing obstacles, but human freedom is not only the goal but the way there. Only this type of account can explain why, limited as they are, the conclusions that Rodrik and the World Bank have come to are true.

Without free agency, we do not know what will work or why it should work. On the view taken here, this forces us to re-imagine labour law as being about the mobilisation, deployment and exploitation of human capital. Human capital is primarily a matter of education (Nussbaum 2006: 322), but human capital not only has to be created, it has to be mobilised and be deployed.

This is what labour law is and this involves throwing away a whole history of the way that people think about labour law, and international labour law. It is not about employers and employees negotiating contracts of employment and feeling sorry for workers because they lack bargaining power and so on. This is a very thin and negative foundation for labour law. Within a Senian view there is a thicker and more positive claim available and it lays claim to a lot more territory than that to which tradi-tional labour law could lay claim.

It is clear that a lot of the subject matter of the 'Geneva Consensus' remains relevant to smart and valuable human capital policy – from non-discrimination, hiring, to health and safety at work, to pensions. But we now see limits to the Consensus. It is limited to a rationale of protecting employees who are parties to contracts under which they are exploited. But labour law is not limited to 'employees' – labour law is much bigger than that. Many things that have been outside the old purview of labour law – child care and other vital public policy issues – bear upon the deployment of human capital and therefore should be labour law's concern.

As I said in my introduction, the key is to see that human capital and human freedom are two ideas that overlap extensively. In fact, human capital, properly understood, is key to the idea of human freedom. And if that is true, then we have a really serious agenda for imagining a post-'Geneva Consensus' labour law for post-'Washington Consensus' devel-opment.

References

Alston, P. (2004) 'Core Labour Standards and the Transformation of the International Labour Rights Regime', *European Journal of International Law* 15: 457.

Easterly, W. (2002) *The Elusive Quest for Growth: Economists' Adventures and Misadventures in the Tropics* (MIT).

Easterly, W. (2006) *The White Man's Burden: Why The West's Efforts To Aid The Rest Have Done So Much Ill And So Little Good* (Penguin).

Greenspan, A. (2008) 'A Widely Reported Testimony Before a Congressional Committee on October 23 2008', available at http://oversight.house.gov/images/stories/documents/20081024163819.pdf

Hirschman, A. (1958) *The Strategy of Economic Development* (Yale).

Lanchester, J. (2009) 'Heroes and Zeroes', *The New Yorker*, 2 February: 73.

Langille, B. (2005) 'Core Labour Standards – The True Story', *European Journal of International Law* 16: 409.

Nussbaum, M. (2006) *Frontiers of Justice* (Harvard).

Rodrik, D. (2006) 'Goodbye Washington Consensus, Hello Washington Confusion? A Review of the World Bank's *Economic Growth in the 1990s: Learning from a Decade of Reform*', *Journal of Economic Literature* 44: 973.

Rodrik, D. (2007) *One Economics, Many Recipes* (Princeton).

Sen, A. (1997) 'Human Capital and Human Capability', *World Development* 25: 1959.
Sen, A. (2006) 'The Man without a Plan', *Foreign Affairs*, March/April, 85: 171.
Standing, G. (2008) 'The ILO: An Agency for Globalization?', *Development and Change* 39: 355.
Stiglitz, J.E. (2002) 'Participation and Development: Perspectives from the Comprehensive Development Paradigm', *Review of Development Economics* 6: 163.
Wittgenstein, L. (1973) *Philosophical Investigations*, 3rd edition (Prentice Hall).

Part II
Addressing social exclusion and discrimination

3
Gender, equality and capabilities

Care work and sustainable development

JUDY FUDGE*

The issue of gender inequality is one of disproportionate freedoms.

(Sen 1992: 125)

Introduction

The goal of this chapter is to consider the relationship between women's equality, care work and sustainable development, and to develop a conceptual framework that can be used to understand this complex relationship. In doing so, I define a handful of concepts – sustainable development, decent work, capabilities, and care work – that comprise the key components of the framework. The chapter builds upon the feminist insight that gender inequality is intimately tied up with women's disproportionate responsibility for care work.

I begin the construction of my conceptual framework by briefly reviewing the relationship between sustainable development, which includes the International Labour Organisation's (ILO) 'Decent Work' Agenda,[1] and women's equality. The next section answers the question on what basis or dimension women's equality should be measured. Instead of assessing a range of potential answers, I focus on Amartya Sen's notion of substantive freedom and his capabilities approach. In addition to

*Lansdowne Chair in Law, University of Victoria, Canada.

[1] Decent Work for All, ILO, http://www.ilo.org/global/About_the_ILO/Mainpillars/WhatisDecentWork/lang-en/index.htmILO definition (accessed 1 November 2009).

identifying what I (and others) consider to be the important advances that Sen's approach makes to understanding freedom and equality, I also want to indicate some of its limitations. However, these limitations are not fatal; I am using the capabilities approach as a framework of thought or a normative tool, rather than as a specified theory that gives a complete answer to all of our normative questions (Robeyns 2005: 66). In the third section, I argue that women's equality, and especially the relationship between women's equality and responsibility for care work, illustrates both the promise of, and the limitations to, Sen's capabilities approach. Some of the salient differences between paid and unpaid care work in the North and the South are sketched in the following section, which also considers the capacity of the ILO 2009 report, 'Decent Work for Domestic Workers', to respond to these differences. Drawing upon feminist scholars (mainly from the fields of economics and social policy) in the fifth section, I argue that, supplemented by a theory of choice, deliberative mechanisms, and a social theory of power, the capabilities approach can be a useful tool for conceptualising women's equality and for recognising the significance of socially necessary care work. I conclude by suggesting that a robust capabilities approach designed to address gender inequality and to incorporate care work illuminates the limitations in the current approaches of anti-discrimination law for addressing women's inequality. However, at the same time it also suggests a different role, one that is transformative, for anti-discrimination law.

Sustainable development, gender and 'Decent Work'

> *The changing agency of women is one of the major mediators of economic and social change, and its determination as well as consequences closely relate to many of the central features of the development process.*

> (Sen 1999: 202)

Amartya Sen claims that development is more than a matter of positive economic indicators, such as gross domestic production, it is also about human development. In *Development as Freedom* (Sen 1999), his basic proposition is that we should evaluate development in terms of 'the expansion of the "capabilities" of people to live the kinds of lives that they value – and have reason to value' (ibid.: 18). This is Sen's definition of freedom (Evans 2002: 54–55). For Sen, freedom includes not only well-being, an individual's own advantage in terms of valuable states of being, but also agency, the different ways that individuals act and exercise their choice to achieve valuable states.

This approach is regarded as particularly important for women since conventional measures of development are not appropriate for measuring women's well-being (Sen 1999: 189–203). Moreover, Sen demonstrates how women's equality is crucial for development, decreasing infant and child mortality and morbidity, and leads to a declining and sustainable fertility rate in developing countries. Women's equality also results in a more cohesive and productive society and, finally, is good in and of itself (Antonopoulos 2008: 4).

Sen's conception of development is compatible with the definition of sustainable development offered in the influential 1987 Brundtland Report, which is: 'development that meets the needs of the present without comprising the ability of future generations to meet their own needs' (Sen 2009: 248). At the Johannesburg World Summit on Sustainable Development in September 2002, which was organised by the United Nations, a commitment was made by the attending heads of states, national delegates and leaders from non-governmental organisations (NGOs), businesses and other civil society groups to 'promote the integration of the three components of sustainable development – economic development, social development and environmental protection – as interdependent and mutually reinforcing pillars' (ILO 2007: 3). Moreover, as part of the commitment to this multifaceted approach to development, the United Nations and the international system have endorsed the ILO's goal of 'Decent Work for All' as a vital part of the international development agenda and an essential element in shaping a fair globalisation.[2]

According to the ILO, Decent Work is central to efforts to reduce poverty, and is a means for achieving equitable, inclusive and sustainable development. Decent Work is captured in four strategic objectives: fundamental principles and rights at work and international labour standards; employment and income opportunities; social protection and social security; and social dialogue and tripartism.[3] The significance of the Decent

---

[2] The Decent Work Agenda was endorsed at the United Nation's 2005 World Summit, and in greater detail at the July 2006 United Nations Economic and Social Council (ECOSOC) High-level Segment (ILO 2007, 3).

[3] Decent Work for All, ILO, http://www.ilo.org/global/About_the_ILO/Mainpillars/Whatis DecentWork/lang-en/index.htmILO definition (accessed 1 November 2009).

Work Agenda is that these objectives hold for all workers, women and men, in both formal and informal economies; in wage employment or working on their own account; in the fields, factories and offices; and in their home or in the community. Moreover, as Juan Somavia, the Director-General of the ILO remarked, 'a gender perspective is . . . needed to quantify evidence more systematically that there are more women at the bottom of the income and wealth scale and fewer at the top' (ibid.: 9).

All over the world, women are disproportionately over-represented in unpaid, informal and precarious work (Fudge and Owens 2006). Women in the developed and developing world perform more unpaid work than do men, and men perform more paid work than do women. Time-use data show that when paid and unpaid work is combined women work longer hours than do men in the North and the South (Antonopoulos 2008).

In 2008, the ILO issued its Declaration on Social Justice for a Fair Globalisation, which institutionalises the Decent Work concept, placing it at the 'core of the Organisation's policies to reach its constitutional objectives' (ILO 2008: 1). The Declaration reaffirms that labour is not a commodity (ibid.: 6). Although the ILO has embraced this position since 1944, it has had very little to say about unpaid care work, which is the 'ghost in the ILO closet' (Vosko 2006). Women's domestic and caring responsibilities shape women's labour force participation and influence the types of employment arrangements, which are disproportionately non-standard and precarious, to which they have been relegated. It is an open question, one I shall probe in the fourth section of this chapter: What is the extent to which the Decent Work Agenda can begin to make headway in confronting women's dual – paid employee and unpaid caregiver – roles?

Equality of what? The capabilities approach

> *To eliminate discrimination and achieve equality at work, it is important to understand what it is that needs to be eliminated and how it can be done.*
> (Tomei 2003: 401)

Sen argues that the best metric or space for determining equality, which for him is the substantive freedom to be or do what one has reason to value, is the concept of capability. A capability is a type of freedom to achieve a number of different things a person may value being or doing, and the actual beings or doings are human functionings.[4] Capabilities are the powers people have as human beings and the opportunities that people have to nurture and exercise their capacities.[5]

The expansion of people's capabilities, unlike utility, income or resources, demands both the elimination of oppression, as well as the provision of the social and environmental infrastructure that people need in order to exercise their capabilities (Anderson 1999, Evans 2002). Central to this conception of capability is the idea of conversion factors, which include personal characteristics, such as an individual's metabolism or her or his biological sex, societal characteristics that could include social norms, legal rules and public policies (such as norms that result in social discrimination or gender stereotyping, or legal interventions to offset these phenomena), and environmental characteristics that could refer to climate, physical surroundings, technological infrastructure and legal-political institutions (Brown, Deakin and Wilkinson 2004: 209).

The benefit of the capabilities approach is that it rests upon a positive conception of freedom, it is committed to ethical individualism, it is pluralistic, it is context specific and it emphasises agency. However, it has a number of limitations. Sen emphasises individual responsibility, and he employs a choice-centred view of responsibility (Alexander 2008: 112). He also concentrates too much on adaptive preferences and does not devote enough attention to social relations of exploitation (Anderson 1999: 336, Robeyns 2008: 190). Moreover, justice cannot be defined simply by the satisfaction of individual preferences; it is also a matter of obligation, as the example of care work makes so clear (Fredman 2008: 16).

However, the problem is not so much with Sen's concept of capability, but rather in assuming that the concept of capability provides a complete theory of social justice. Sen is very clear in acknowledging that although the idea of capability has considerable merit in the assessment of the opportunity aspect of freedom, it cannot possibly deal adequately with the process aspect of freedom, since capabilities are characteristics of individual advantages, and they fall short of telling us about fairness or equity in the processes involved, or about the freedom of citizens to invoke and utilise procedures that are equitable (Sen 2009). A normative theory of

---

[4] Capabilities are to functionings what opportunities are to achievements (Robeyns 2005).
[5] Capabilities are broader than human capital, and in *Development as Freedom*, Sen is careful to point out the limitations of a human capability approach (1999: 292–297).

social choice is needed to supplement Sen's theory of capabilities. As Ingrid Robeyns (2005: 69) points out, we also get 'quite divergent normative results, depending upon which social theories we add to the capabilities framework'. Different social theories provide different accounts of the individual, social and environmental conversion factors that transform individual endowments into substantive opportunities that people enjoy (see, for example, Nussbaum 2005).

Gender equality and capabilities

> *What [would] a critical use of the capability approach . . . recommend us to do to make the gender division of labour more just.*
>
> (Robeyns 2008: 188)

Traditional accounts of work and labour law have ignored all of the unpaid domestic work that is involved in maintaining living spaces, buying and transforming the commodities used in the family, supplementing the services provided to family members by the public and private sectors, caring for people and managing social and personal relationships (Picchio 2003).[6] This unpaid work is a systematic transfer of hidden subsidies to the rest of the economy, and because it is women who disproportionately perform this work it functions as a time tax on women throughout their life cycle (Antonopoulos 2008). Time spent caring is a major factor limiting people's, particularly women's, participation in the formal economy (Himmelweit 2002: 231).

Elizabeth Anderson claims that the proper aim of egalitarian justice, which she calls democratic equality, is to end oppression, and she adopts a capability approach. However, unlike Sen, Anderson specifies capa-

---

[6] At the theoretical and empirical level it is possible to distinguish between domestic work, which includes all the impersonal activities in the management of the household, such as cleaning and meal preparation, that can be purchased in the market, and care work for children, elderly, or ill people that, because of its interpersonal and emotional nature, is more difficult to transfer to others and to purchase on the market (Chiappero Martinetti 2007: 2). However, domestic and care work is deeply interconnected – to feed a child one must prepare food (Antonopoulos 2008: 10). The term social reproduction activities captures domestic and care work, and I will use care and domestic work interchangeably. I am also using social reproduction as the lens to understand care work because I want to explore the gender, racial and class dimensions of care work (Duffy 2005).

46

bilities, and she focuses on capabilities to overcome oppression and exploitation. She also emphasises the need for an expansive conception of the social conditions of freedom, which includes private relations of domination, even those entered into by consent or contract, as violations of individual freedom (Anderson 1999: 315). According to Anderson (ibid.: 325), democratic equality entails that no one should be reduced to an inferior status because they fulfil obligations to care for others.

Similarly, Robeyns claims that the capabilities approach is not limited to market behaviour, and that it can encompass people's beings and doings in market and non-market contexts. In elaborating on their list of capabilities, both Anderson and Robeyns emphasise care work. Long periods of dependency on others' caregiving are a normal and inevitable part of everyone's life cycle. It is therefore an indispensable condition of the continuation of human society that many adults devote a great deal of their time to such caretaking however poorly such work may be remunerated in the market (Anderson 1999).

Robeyns' (2005: 73) list of capabilities is specifically designed for conceptualising gender inequality in post-industrialised Western societies.[7] What is distinctive about her list of capabilities is that it addresses inequalities in time allocation, leisure time and time-related stress (Benería 2008: 13). Thus, in addition to what are generally recognised as important capabilities, such as paid work and other projects (being able to work in the labour market or undertake projects), mobility (being able to be mobile) and leisure activities (being able to engage in leisure activities), her list includes domestic work and non-market care (being able to raise children and to take care of others) and time-autonomy (being able to exercise autonomy in allocating one's time) (Robeyns 2005: 74).

Concerned about how neo-liberal policies have a different impact on the reconciliation of family and labour market work in the North and the South, Lourdes Benería uses Robeyns' methodology (which included brainstorming sessions, testing the draft list by comparing it with other lists and the relevant literature, and debating the lists with academics, policy-makers, activists and workers) to determine if her list of capabilities can be adapted to conceptualise gender inequality in the South. Since Robeyns' methodology incorporates the expressed needs and views of people specific to Western societies, Benería discussed Robeyns' list of capabilities

---

[7] Her list of capabilities and her methodology for determining the list are set out at Robeyns 2005: 73–74.

with women in the South, specifically women in Bolivia. Benería notes that while some capabilities are universally relevant, such as being able to raise children and care for others as well as being able to engage in paid work, mobility, for instance, applies to different societies in different degrees. Moreover, she includes a sixth capability – being able to articulate and organise around collective needs (Benería 2008: 15). Benería explains that expanding upon the six capabilities that she has identified would help to ease the problems of balancing different types of work for women in the global South.

Care work in the North and South: 'Decent Work'

Female migration to take up domestic employment abroad creates 'transnational' households, a form of global care chain between workers with family responsibilities in the North, who require household service, and temporary migrants from the South, who can provide for them – albeit at the cost of leaving their own families behind.
(ILO 2009: 9)

Women's labour force participation has increased substantially and a growing proportion of care work has been marketised, 'even though much is still performed within the household, either as unpaid work by family members or as paid activities performed by hired domestic help' (Benería 2008: 2). Moreover, neo-liberal policies have subjected women across the globe to similar pressures. Privatisation in the North has weakened the welfare state, and in the South social protection has contracted. Although care is provided in the paid and unpaid economy, it is provided very differently in the South and the North. In the North, policies designed to reconcile the competing pressures of paid work and care work emphasise paid maternity, parental – and (very occasionally) paternal – leave, flexible hours of work and childcare services (Fudge 2005, 2011, Benería 2008). The goal of these policies is to increase women's labour force participation. Benería identifies three key differences between the North and the South – the availability of inexpensive domestic service in the South, the large informal economy in the South, and the feminisation of migration as a form of survival strategy in the South – that suggest that the policies needed in the South for balancing different types of work may differ from those in the North (Benería 2008: 6).

Shahra Razavi (2007: 2) notes that historically across a diverse range of countries, both developed and developing, women from disadvantaged racial and ethnic groups have tended to provide care services to meet the needs of more powerful social groups, while their own care needs have been downplayed and neglected. Nowhere is this process of racialisation and subordination more evident than when it comes to the globalisation of care and social reproduction. Many of the women who leave the South to work in the North are temporary migrant workers who do not enjoy either the right to become permanent residents in their host country or the right to circulate freely in the labour market. Moreover, given the basic gender division of labour in destination countries, women migrants are often restricted to traditionally 'female' occupations – such as domestic work, care work, nursing, work in the domestic services and sex work – that are frequently unstable jobs marked by low wages, the absence of social services and poor working conditions (Antonopoulos 2008: 38).

On the demand side, the feminisation of migration is fuelled by the increase in women's labour force participation, falling fertility rates, increasing life expectancy and the increasing marketisation of care in the North (Yeates 2009). On the supply side, economic trends such as growing inequalities between high- and low-income countries, and insecurity, vulnerability and instability due to economic crises combine with gender-related factors such as abuse, family conflict and discrimination to increase the numbers of women who migrate in order to obtain paid work (Benería 2008). The feminisation of migration has contradictory impacts. While women's decisions to migrate can increase their financial autonomy and increase their financial contribution to their household through remittances, their absorption into the care markets of the North reinforces the gendered nature of care. Moreover, Rhacel Salazar Parreñas (2005: 15) has demonstrated, in the case of the Philippines, how the export of women's labour results in a 'depletion of care resources' that detrimentally affects their ability to provide care for the families that they have left behind.

Benería argues that female migration can have implications for policies designed to reconcile paid employment and care responsibilities in both host and home countries.

The employment of migrant women to perform care work in the receiving countries of the North is an individual and privatised solution to the broader problem of combining paid work with unpaid care work. Since this solution is only an option for families who can afford it, lower-income families are left in the lurch. In fact, as Benería (2008: 11) points out 'the employment of migrant women from the South might contribute to a vicious circle in the host country, in which private solutions delay collective efforts to search for appropriate public policies'. Moreover, 'in home countries, the need to balance family and [labour] market work shifts from the women who migrate to the individuals who assume their roles in the family' (ibid.). Since it is mostly women who assume the family roles of migrant women, there is a growing need for reconciliation policies in the South.

Not only is there a need for public policies that provide for collective, and not individual, solutions for reconciling the competing demands of paid and unpaid work in the North and South, there is also a need for policies that provide decent work for domestic workers around the globe. In the North, well-paid women are increasingly resorting to migrant domestic workers as an individual solution to reconcile competing demands on their time. At the same time, upper- and middle-class women in the South deal with the competing pressures of balancing paid work with unpaid work by hiring women to perform domestic labour (Benería 2008: 6).

The ILO's Decent Work Agenda has begun to make some inroads in breaking down the conceptual and regulatory barriers between the workplace and the household through the issuance of the report, 'Decent Work For Domestic Workers', which was discussed at the 2010 International Labour Conference. As a result, the Conference Committee recommended the adoption at the 2011 Conference of an international instrument that would regulate domestic work (International Labour Conference 2010).[8] The specific regulation of domestic work as work is very significant for the ILO's Decent Work Agenda because it takes the 'ILO beyond the identification of non-compliance and towards the provision of specific, constructive guidance on how to regulate effectively a category of worker that is singularly in need of support' (ILO 2009: 2).

With 'Decent Work for Domestic Workers', the ILO has taken the ghost out of the closet; it recognises:

> Care work in the household – whether performed by paid employees or by unpaid household members as a part of their household responsibilities and as a 'labour of love' – is quite simply indispensable for the economy outside the household to function.
>
> (ibid.: 5, footnotes omitted)

The report also explains that domestic work is undervalued and poorly regulated because it is considered to be unskilled work performed by

---

[8] The ILO's first inroad in considering the household as a place of work was the 1996 Homeworkers Convention C177.

women. It is also attentive to the transnational dimension of domestic work, in which women from the South migrate to the North in order to provide domestic work, thus creating a type of global care chain in which the labour of one group of women in the home empowers another group of women to enter paid employment outside of the home (ibid.: 9).

Significant recognition of the value of domestic work was achieved at the June 2011 International Labour Conference, when the majority of members adopted a convention and a supplementary recommendation (International Labour Conference 2011). Although the proposed convention is an important step towards decent work for domestic workers, there is some distance to go before it provides equal protection regarding working time, health and safety and labour inspection.

Care and the question of choice

> *The politics of choice are inter-leavened with those of gender equality.*
> (Lewis and Guillari 2005: 96)

In the general discussion at the 2009 International Labour Conference on the report entitled 'Gender Equality at the Heart of Decent Work', the Employers' Group objected to the global campaign by the Workers' Group that opposed part-time work, contract work and other work arrangements that they considered to represent precarious work.[9] The Employers' Group insisted that these non-standard forms of work arrangements should not be defined as precarious, as several are part of the formal economy and in many instances involve a matter of personal choice, especially in the case of women, to enter the labour market under these new arrangements.[10] Research has demonstrated that women are disproportionately over-represented in these forms of employment, and these forms of work arrangements tend, in general, to be poorly paid, lack benefits and result in income and employment insecurity (Fudge and Owens 2006). Women choose to enter these forms of work because they allow them to balance the competing demands of paid employment and unpaid domestic and care

---

[9] Report on the 2009 International Labour Conference, Gender Equality at the Heart of Decent Work, *(General Discussion)* 18 July 2009, http://fke-kenya.org/download/International%20 Labour%20Conference%20Report.pdf (accessed 1 November 2009).
[10] *Ibid.*

work. Thus, the choices of individual women to work and to care are used to justify work arrangements that cannot provide women with a livelihood that would enable them to lead lives autonomous of male breadwinners and still support children. For this reason, it is necessary to probe the notion of 'individual choice' that is used to justify women's inequality.

Feminist economists claim that models of free individual choice are not adequate to analyse issues of dependence/independence, traditions and power (Benería 2008). Susan Himmelweit (2002: 231) argues that the rational choice model separates the influences internal to an individual at the moment of choice (preference) and those that are external (opportunities/ constraints). She proposes an alternative to rational choice that recognises the fulfilment of responsibilities that individuals feel to be theirs because of their identification as members of a group subject to particular social norms. 'It is as parents, wives, husbands, workers, employers, teachers, school-children, and friends that people hold certain specific responsibilities to certain specified others and particular expectations are made of their behaviour' (ibid.: 243).[11]

Other feminist economists, for example, Paula England and Nancy Folbre (2003), demonstrate how care has distinctive characteristics that help explain the economic vulnerabilities of those who provide it. High-quality care requires long-term commitment or contracts characterised by emotional connection, moral obligation and intrinsic motivation. It is difficult to specify and to enforce the care bargain, in part because it is very important for the well-being of dependents – children, the sick and the elderly – who are seldom in a position to negotiate. Moreover, care work limits the choices of those who perform it. However, although existing patterns in the division of labour between men and women manifest inherited differences and deeply rooted inequality, feminists argue that they are not immutable. For example, although Robeyns (2005: 88) acknowledges that there is no social consensus over whether gendered choices in care work are due to nature or to social upbringing, she argues that the burden of proof falls on those who claim that women are essentially different from men.

---

[11] Robeyns (2005) argues that the capability approach is able to recognise that the process of decision-making is itself subject to social forces, and, thus, is not committed to ontological individualism.

It is crucial to recognise the extent to which 'the politics of choice are inter-leavened with those of gender equality' (Lewis and Guillari 2005: 96). Policies that enhance individual choice need to attend to the broader structures of employment and social provisioning. Women should be free to choose the balance between employment and domestic life that is good for them. But policy discourse has barely begun to register ideas about men's greater involvement in domestic life. The problem is that so long as men can choose not to do domestic labour women will have no choice but to do it. The choices of individual women are shaped by the opportunities open to them and the cultural norms that prevail. It is important to increase the incentives for men to take on a greater share of unpaid labour and to challenge cultural norms that associate women with certain kinds of domestic labour if women are to be given a real choice about how they spend their time. Men and women must be encouraged 'to identify with each other across gender boundaries by pursuing greater equality of experience, through developing norms that require both men and women to contribute financially to their children and to care for them' (Himmelweit 2002: 247). Moreover, as Himmelweit goes on to elaborate, the benefit of widening the numbers of people who contribute time to caring is that it would not only reduce the individual costs of those who care, by extending the experience of caring throughout the members of a society, it may be that society would be more willing to contribute institutionally and financially to the costs of care (ibid.).

The role of anti-discrimination law

Developments in gender norms and relations, and in the division of labour between the sexes, might be a major source of a Polanyian 'countermovement' in the twenty-first century.

(Crompton 2002: 541)

Most gender equality indicators that are widely accepted by international organisations miss unpaid care work and put too much focus on women's increased employment rate.[12] Moreover, as the ILO noted in its 2003 Time

[12] See, for example, the United Nations Human Development Report (UNHDR) Gender-related Development Index (GDI) and Gender Empowerment Measure (GEM), neither of which measures the division of unpaid care work in a society.

for Equality report, work-family policies are so often aimed at women they may end up reinforcing the image of women as secondary earners and accruing the double burden to women (ILO 2003: 73). Thus, Nancy Fraser's distinction between affirmation and transformation is particularly appropriate when it comes to remedying gender inequality. By affirmative remedies Fraser (1997: 28) means 'remedies aimed at correcting inequitable outcomes of social arrangements without disturbing the underlying framework that generates them'. In contrast, she identifies transformative remedies as those remedies 'aimed at correcting inequitable outcomes precisely by restructuring the underlying generative framework' (ibid.).

When contemplating transformative remedies, the question is how to promote policies that foster responsibility for sharing care between men and women that enhance women's agency freedom by making men more accountable for their responsibility to care for others (Lewis and Guillari 2005: 94). This question is not only pertinent for women in the North; referring to the South, Benería (2008: 16) claims, 'the new agenda of gender equity needs to emphasize men's equal share in the reproductive activities taking place within households'. A more equitable allocation of time devoted to care by men and women is crucial for the quality of life and the development of human capabilities. As Elizabeth Anderson (1999: 324) suggests, redistribution, although crucially important, is not sufficient for eradicating gender inequality, and that gender inequality may require a change in social norms, by which men and women would be expected to share in caretaking responsibilities. Robeyns also argues that social and environmental conversion factors allow for societal factors, such as social norms and discrimination practices, to be taken into account in a capabilities approach. Thus, the role of anti-discrimination law should be to transform gender norms rather than simply reconciling women to existing work norms and a double day of labour.

However, changing men's roles and providing incentives for them to take on the socially necessary domestic labour that is crucial for a sustainable society is a necessary, but not a sufficient, condition for achieving a true balance between paid work and family life in dual-earner societies (Crompton 2002: 217). What is also required is a comprehensive rebalancing of care work between the market and the state. Moreover, it is crucial to provide Decent Work for domestic workers so that some women's choices are not expanded at the expense of other women. Whose freedom is enhanced is a crucial question for public policy. But the concern with enhancing women's freedoms must not obscure the fact that the ability to care is not only a valuable functioning, it is also an essential conversion factor that is necessary for all of us – the young, the old, the sick and the disabled – to live (Chiappero Martinetti 2007: 5–9). Thus, we must recognise, as Joan Tronto has so eloquently put it,

> care is not a parochial concern of women, a type of secondary moral question, or the work of the least well off in society. Care is a central concern of human life. It is time we began to change our political and social institutions to reflect this truth.
>
> (Tronto 1993: 180)

References

Alexander, J.M. (2008) *Capabilities and Social Justice: The Political Philosophy of Amartya Sen and Martha Nussbaum* (Ashgate).

Anderson, E. (1999) 'What is the Point of Equality?', *Ethics* 109: 287.

Antonopoulos, R. (2008) 'The Unpaid Care Work–Paid Work Connection', Working Paper No. 541, The Levy Economics Institute of Bard College.

Benería, L. (2008) 'The Crisis of Care, International Migration, and Public Policy', *Feminist Economics* 14(3): 1.

Brown, J., Deakin, S. and Wilkinson, B. (2004) 'Capabilities, Social Rights and European Market Integration', in R. Salais and R. Villeneuve (eds) *Europe and the Politics of Capabilities* (Cambridge University Press).

Chiappero Martinetti, E. (2007) 'Time and Income: Empirical Evidence on Gender Poverty and Inequalities from a Capability Perspective', Paper prepared for K. Basu and R. Kanbur (eds) *Sen Festschrift – 'Welfare, Development, Philosophy & Social Science: Essay for Amartya Sen's 75th Birthday (Volume 2: Development Economics and Policy)* (Oxford University Press), available from http://www-1.unipv.it/webdept/p_8_p07.pdf (accessed 1 November 2009).

Crompton, R. (2002) 'Employment, Flexible Working and the Family', *British Journal of Sociology* 53(6): 537.

Duffy, Mignon. (2005) 'Reproducing Labor Inequalities: Challenges for Feminists Conceptualizing Care at the Intersection of Gender, Race, and Class', *Gender & Society* 19(1): 66.

England, P. and Folbre, N. (2003) 'Contracting for Care', in M.A. Ferber and J.A. Nelson (eds) *Feminist Economics Today: Beyond Economic Man* (University of Chicago Press).

Evans, P. (2002) 'Collective Capabilities, Culture, and Amartya Sen's Development as Freedom', *Comparative International Development* 37(2): 54.

Fraser, N. (1997) *Justice Interruptus: Critical Reflections on the 'Postsocialist' Condition* (Routledge).

Fredman, S. (2008) *Human Rights Transformed: Positive Rights and Positive Duties* (Oxford University Press).

Fudge, J. (2005) 'The New Duel-Earner Gender Contract: Work-life Balance or Working-time Flexibility?', in J. Conaghan and K. Rittich (eds) *Labour Law, Work and Family: Critical and Comparative Perspectives* (Oxford University Press).

Fudge, J. (2011) 'Working-time Regimes, Flexibility, and Work-Life Balance: Gender Equality and Families', in C. Krull and J. Sempruch (eds) *Demystifying the Family/Work Conflict: Challenges and Possibilities* (University of British Columbia Press).

Fudge, J. and Owens, R. (2006) 'Introduction', in J. Fudge and R. Owens (eds) *Precarious Work, Women, and the New Economy: The Challenge to Legal Norms* (Hart Publishing).

Himmelweit, S. (2002) 'Economic Theory, Norms and the Care Gap, or Why Do Economists Become Parents?', in A. Carling, S. Duncan and R. Edwards (eds) *Analysing Families: Morality and Rationality in Policy and Practice* (Routledge).

ILO (2003) *Time for Equality at Work*. International Labour Conference, 91st Session, Report I (B), http://www.lex.unict.it/eurolabor/documentazione/oil/rapporti/report2003.pdf (accessed 1 November 2009).

ILO (2007) Director-General's Introduction to the International Labour Conference, *Decent Work for Sustainable Development*, ILC 96-2007/Report I (A), http://www.ilo.org/wcmsp5/groups/public/-dgreports/-cabinet/documents/meeting document/wcms_085092.pdf (accessed 1 November 2009).

ILO (2008) Declaration for Social Justice for a Fair Globalization, http://www.ilocarib.org.tt/projects/cariblex/conventions_24.shtml (accessed 1 November 2009).

ILO (2009) *Decent Work for Domestic Workers*, Report IV(1) International Labour Conference, 99th Session, 2010, Fourth Item on the Agenda, http://www.ilo.org/wcmsp5/groups/public/-ed_norm/-relconf/documents/meeting document/wcms_104700.pdf (accessed 1 November 2009).

International Labour Conference (2011) *Text of the Convention Concerning Decent Work for Domestic Workers*, 100th Session, Provisional Record.

Lewis, J. and Guillari, S. (2005) 'The Adult Worker Model Family, Gender Equality and Care: The Search for New Policy Principles and Problems of a Capabilities Approach', *Economy and Society* 34(1): 76.

Nussbaum, M.C. (2005) 'Capabilities as Fundamental Entitlements; Sen and Social Justice', in B. Aggarwal, J. Humphries and I. Robeyns (eds) *Amartya Sen's Work and Ideas: A Gender Perspective* (Routledge).

Parreñas, R.S. (2005) *Children of Global Migration: Transnational Families and Gendered Woes* (Stanford University Press).

Picchio, A. (ed.) (2003) *Unpaid Work and the Economy: A Gender Analysis of the Standards of Living* (Routledge).

Razavi, S. (2007) 'The Political and Social Economy of Care in A Development Context: Conceptual Issues, Research Questions and Policy Options', United Nations Research Institute for Social Development, Gender and Development Program, Paper Number 3.

Robeyns, I. (2005) 'Sen's Capability Approach and Gender Inequality: Selecting

Relevant Capabilities', in B. Aggarwal, J. Humphries and I. Robeyns (eds) *Amartya Sen's Work and Ideas: A Gender Perspective* (Routledge).

Robeyns, I. (2008) 'Is Nancy Fraser's Critique of Theories of Distributive Justice Justified?', in K. Olsen (ed.) *Adding Insult to Injury: Nancy Fraser Debates her Critics* (Verso).

Sen, A. (1992) *Inequality Reexamined* (Oxford University Press).

Sen, A. (1999) *Development as Freedom* (Anchor).

Sen, A. (2009) *The Idea of Justice* (Harvard University Press).

Tomei, M. (2003) 'Discrimination and Equality at Work: A Review of the Concepts', *International Labour Review* 143: 402.

Tronto, J. (1993) *Moral Boundaries: A Political Argument for an Ethic of Care* (Routledge).

Vosko, L. (2006) 'Gender, Precarious Work, and the International Labour Code: The Ghost in the ILO Closet', in J. Fudge and R. Owens (eds) *Precarious Work, Women, and the New Economy: The Challenge to Legal Norms* (Hart Publishing).

Yeates, N. (2009) *Globalizing Care Economies: Exploration in Global Care Chains* (Palgrave Macmillan).

4
The political economy of women's human rights

Problems of gender, violence, development and labour

JACQUI TRUE*

Introduction

What has poverty or wealth for that matter got to do with persistent and egregious violence against women globally? Violence against women includes rape and sexual abuse, forced trafficking, intimate partner violence, female genital mutilation, maternal death, femicide, dowry deaths, honour killings, female infanticide, sexual harassment and forced and early marriage. It includes violence at home, at work and in the public or transnational realms. As one women's international non-governmental organisation (NGO) has stated 'when one thinks of women's human rights issues, one usually thinks about violence against women and not about poverty, housing, unemployment, education, water, food security, trade and other related economic and social rights issues'.[1] But is there a relationship between women's poor access to productive resources such as land, property, income, employment, technology, credit, and education, and their likelihood of experiencing gender-based violence and abuse?[2] This chapter examines this important question.

* Associate Professor in Political Studies, University of Auckland.

[1] Programme on Women's Economic, Social and Cultural Rights (PWSCR) concept paper, see www.pwescr.org (accessed on 4 March 2010).

[2] The CEDAW Committee states that violence against women or gender-based violence is that 'directed against a woman because she is a woman or that affects women disproportionately'

58

Nowhere in the world do women share equal social and economic rights with men or the same access as men to these productive resources (Apodaca 1998). Economic globalisation and development, including the impact of the global recession, are creating new challenges for women's rights as well as some new opportunities for advancing women's economic independence and gender equality. Globalisation has brought about a significant movement in the geographical location, occupation and social position of women. It has expanded women's formal economic participation, while leaving unchanged the underlying patriarchal structures that perpetuate women's inequality with men, and their susceptibility to violence. Women's labour has become part of the competitive dynamic of globalisation, yet a large number of women workers in the informal economy, care sector and in unpaid work often fall outside of recognised labour standards and the human rights system. These women are highly vulnerable to new forms of gender-based violence associated with the displacement of populations, sex trafficking, home-based production, restrictive immigration and exploitation of local and migrant workers especially around special economic zones and large developments. Structural adjustment policies imposed by international institutions have disproportionately affected women and 'have led to increased impoverishment, displacement and internal strife resulting from the political instabilities caused by devaluing national currencies, increasing debt and dependence on foreign investment' (Commaraswamy 2000). The proliferation of armed conflicts, often caused by struggles to control power and productive resources, has also set back efforts to increase gender equality and prevent violence against women. Furthermore, post-conflict and post-humanitarian crisis and natural disaster processes have tended to deepen gender inequalities in economic and political participation, affecting women's vulnerability to violence.

Yet despite these glaring realities the current global political economic order is often neglected in analyses of violence against women, while violence against women is also overlooked in analyses of sustainable development, international labour practices and decent work. Official United Nations (UN) and International Labour Organisation (ILO) approaches

(CEDAW General Recommendation No. 19, 11th session, 1992). Women are often subject to violence as a result of their gender subordination, that is the construction of women as inferior to men within and across societies and multiple intersecting vulnerabilities between gender and their membership in ethnic, nationality, class, and other marginalised groups.

make no linkages between the effects of financial crises, macroeconomic policies and trade liberalisation for example, and the prevalence of violence against women in particularly affected regions. They do not contextualise pervasive violence against women within the gendered structures of economic impoverishment and lack of opportunity.

Feminist international political economy (IPE) has made it possible for us to reconsider informal economic activity, feminised economies such as the sex and domestic workers' trade, and unpaid work in the home as comprising major parts of the globalisation story (see Prugl 1999, Marchand and Runyan 2000, Peterson 2003). This chapter seeks to rectify the neglect of these contemporary global political-economic processes and their effect on the prevalence of various forms of violence against women. Given the short length, however, it cannot fully substantiate the argument that women's physical security and freedom from violence are inextricably linked to the material basis of relationships that govern the distribution and use of resources, entitlements and authority within the home, the community and the transnational realm. This is, rather, the project of my forthcoming book. Here I can only set out the key elements of a feminist political economy *method* for analysing violence against women and then sketch out how this method might be employed to analyse how global processes affect violence against women. I argue that employing such a feminist political economy method could significantly improve the way we treat violence against women and respond to its global scale and its brutality.

The chapter explores four strategic sites where structural political-economic forces can be seen to be heightening the conditions for and increasing the extent of violence against women. These sites could each be the subject of sustained political economy analysis in their own right. They consist of neo-liberal economic restructuring and men's reaction to the loss of secure employment, economic destabilisation and transition, the growth of a sex trade around the creation of free trade zones and the transnational migration of women workers. (For reasons of length I exclude my analysis of three further strategic sites: sexual violence in armed conflict; the gendered impact of natural disasters; and post-conflict/crisis reconstruction efforts, see True 2010.)

From domestic violence to decent work: outline of a feminist political economy method

A feminist political economy method seeks to comprehend broader, global political-economic structures that underpin gender inequality and women's vulnerability to violence. In general, political economy as a method analyses political and economic power as part of the same authority structure. All forms of power – including the use of violence – are understood as having a material basis, and are often founded on material relations of inequality. The method directs us to investigate the interconnections between the economic, social and political realms. Such investigations reveal that power operates not only through direct coercion but also through the structured relations of production and reproduction that govern the distribution and use of resources, benefits, privileges and authority within the home and transnational society at large (e.g., Whyte 2009). Political-economic processes interact with and reconfigure the institutional and ideological formations of society where gender identities and relations are shaped. As Bina Agarwal (1994: 1459) states: 'those who own and/or control wealth-generating property can directly or indirectly control the principal institutions that shape ideology, such as educational and religious establishments and the media . . . These can shape views in either gender-progressive or gender-retrogressive directions.'

Feminist political economy highlights the masculine nature of the integrated political-economic authority structure. The three elements of a feminist political economy method summarised below can be employed to analyse the material situation of women and men particularly with respect to their unequal access to productive resources, toward a more comprehensive explanation of the prevalence of different forms of violence against women in wide-ranging global contexts.

The first element is the gendered public-private sphere division of labour, which is supported by gender ideologies that hold women primarily responsible for unremunerated and often invisible unpaid work in the family or 'private' sphere, thus creating inequalities in household bargaining power between men and women (Mackinnon 1988). Caring professions in the 'public' labour market akin to the unpaid care work women traditionally do in the home are devalued as a result of this prior gender structure (Okin 1989). The internationalisation of reproductive work has extended this division of labour to the transnational realm as women from poorer, developing countries migrate to provide care services for families in wealthier countries. In a mutually-constitutive way, the strict division of roles in the domestic sphere constrains women's public participation and their access to economic opportunities in the market, in turn creating hierarchical structures that entrap many women into potentially violent environments at home and at work. Some women, especially those in developed countries, avoid patriarchal, and potentially violent, situations in the family / private sphere by contracting out care work to poor women, including migrant women from the global South.

The second element highlighted by a feminist political economy method is the contemporary global, macroeconomic environment. Capitalist competition encourages firms to seek cheap sources of labour and deregulated investment conditions that maximise profits locally and transnationally. In this context, the relocation of industries has disrupted local economies and dramatically changed labour markets, increasing a poorly regulated economy of low pay and insecure jobs, and attracting women from developed and developing societies into wage employment on a scale unseen before.

While the neo-liberal policy environment has led to the expansion of women's employment, it has also led to the intensification of their workload in the market and at home, and to the 'feminisation of poverty' especially among unskilled and marginalised poor women in developing countries who lack access to productive resources or public services. Such poverty, marginalisation and lack of protective mechanisms make women easy targets for abuse and undermine the prospects for their empowerment (Elson 2002: 78). These conditions also disempower many men who may react to the loss of employment and economic opportunities by reasserting their power over women through violence.

The third element of a feminist political economy method relates to the gendered dimensions of war and peace, which are intimately connected to both private patriarchy and the differential gender impacts of economic globalisation. Violent conflict, which often results from struggles to control power and productive resources, normalises violence and spreads it throughout the societies involved. State- and group-sanctioned violence frequently celebrate masculine aggression and perpetuate impunity with regard to men's violence against women, viewing this violence, *inter alia*, as the 'spoils of war'.

A feminist political economy approach implies that stability without justice is not possible. The prioritisation of national security and electoral machinery by governments over the social and economic security of citizens in many post-conflict situations is usually destabilising in the long run. Insofar as women are unable to gain access to physical security, social services, justice and economic opportunities, their particular vulnerability to violence continues in peace time.

The remainder of this chapter illustrates with specific examples rather than comprehensive analysis how such a feminist political economy method, especially the first two elements, might be used to analyse violence against women in four strategic sites, also increasingly examined by international and labour law scholars.

Roots of gender violence and unsustainable development

Competitive globalisation

Due to the impact of global economic restructuring in some regions some men have experienced long-term unemployment and the loss of their previous breadwinner status. These men admit to feelings of powerlessness and to using violence against their women partners to regain a sense of control. One of the ways we see globalisation processes perpetuating violence against women is through men's reactions to these processes and the loss of male entitlement they often bring about. As mentioned above, firms in competitive, global markets may prefer to hire women over men where their labour is deemed 'cheaper' due to prevailing gender structures and ideologies. Thus, where neo-liberal reforms open economies to global competition there may be increased opportunities for women to enter the labour market and gain economic independence. The obverse of women's economic empowerment is men's economic disempowerment. Thus, violence against women may actually rise as women assume non-traditional roles and gain greater access to these economic opportunities and resources; contradicting the association between women's employment and empowerment in indicators like the gender development index (Heise and Garcia-Morean 2002: 99, Jewkes 2002). Male violence against intimate women partners may increase especially when the male partner is unemployed, and/or feels his power is undermined in the household (UNICEF 2000).

To the extent that men have been socially constructed to be breadwinners, assuming control over income and resources as well as women, these masculine breadwinner identities are threatened by women's newly valued economic roles. In the context of neo-liberal restructuring and economic crises, men may be unable to find alternative employment which fulfils their visions of themselves as dominant breadwinners. This may lead them to act out violently against women and children in the home and in public spaces compensating for the loss of economic control. Research evidence also shows that a reduction in male incomes challenges norms of masculinity and exacerbates tensions between men and women (Schuler, Hashemi and Badal 1998, Chant 2001). In Latin America and the Caribbean, the severely inequitable distribution of wealth is considered to be one of the chief factors fuelling a rise in the rates of domestic violence, which are also two of the highest rates in the world (Larrain 1999). Yet, because conventional economic and legal analyses do not consider power dynamics in the household, unlike feminist political economy, the relationship between high returns to business and poverty and violence against women at the household level remains invisible (Sweetman 2008).

In South Africa where there is a history of state-sponsored violence and the contemporary context is marked by poverty, unemployment, crime and deprivation, several forms of violence against women are prevalent. Rape, in particular, has been found to be extremely pervasive. In one epidemiological study, it has been argued that rape plays a crucial role in male peer group positioning and that it must be understood within the context of the limited number of other recreational opportunities available to poor township and rural youth. 'Competition over women has achieved overwhelming importance because it is one of the few available and affordable opportunities for entertainment and arenas where success may be achieved and self-esteem gained' (Jewkes and Abrahams 2002: 1231). Given the context of poverty, relationships and the input of resources they require may not be realistic options, whereas rape and violence may be more readily deployed to achieve the same goals.

Another South African study of 15 men and their female partners, recruited via two agencies that provide programmes for victims and perpetrators of intimate violence, connected men's economic disempowerment to domestic violence against women (Boonzaier 2005: 99). The study found that men react to the greater economic opportunities for women and rising male unemployment by attempting to maintain their hold on dominant forms of masculinity through the perpetration of violence. Interviews with men revealed that their ideas of 'successful masculinity' were linked to their ability to become or remain economic providers for the family. Men facing chronic unemployment described feeling powerless and employed this feeling as a justification for violence against women (ibid.: 100).

In a different context, Kuwait, Muslim men reacted against economic restructuring by acting out violently against women. These men draw on traditional patriarchal discourses and objectify women as symbols of liberalisation. Tétreault argued that 'women are implicated . . . not only because they are themselves objects of value and symbols of communal identity, but also because their emancipation introduces a new class of competitors for political and economic positions' (Tétreault 2003: 236). In the struggle between tradition and economic liberalisation women are subject to men's violence in their quest to maintain their dominant masculine identity and place.

Free trade zones of gender violence

> *In the Mexican border town, Ciudad Juarez, 377 women have been murdered in just over a decade, many of them young women who migrated to work in the Maquila factories. The murders, one third of which involved sexual violence, are said to have different motives from domestic violence to drug trafficking but several analysts see femicides as the outcome of men's reactions to globalization and the feminization of employment in the border region.*
>
> (Camacho 2005: 259)

Trade liberalisation has facilitated the globalisation of export-oriented, labour-intensive industries. The creation of free trade zones exacerbates gendered inequalities and creates deregulated environments in which violence against women thrives. These industries, set up in 'free trade' or special economic zones exempt from many government regulations, have largely employed women's labour; often young, migrant women from rural areas hired on temporary contracts at lower wages than men and with minimal benefits. Violence against women workers, including the abuse of reproductive rights (e.g., through mandatory pregnancy screening), sexual harassment, rape and femicide, has been highly prevalent in many of these free trade zones in developing countries (Erturk 2005).

The epigraph concerning the femicides in Ciudad Juarez on the US-Mexico border, where 'Maquiladora' factories are located, illustrates the destabilising effects of neo-liberal globalisation (Albuquerque and Vemala 2008). Thousands of young rural women came to Mexico's tax-free border cities when the 1992 North American Free Trade Agreement (NAFTA) liberalised trade with the United States and the Mexican government created these zones to attract foreign investment. They were treated as dispensable workers and constructed as 'cheap labour' (relative to men), leading to high male unemployment in the border cities and towns (Livingstone 2004: 60). Studies show that their influx resulted in lower wages for all, which, combined with male unemployment, created resentment toward young women workers. Both the multinational firms and the states concerned failed to protect these women from targeted, violent abuse. Alicia Camacho (2005: 267) argued that just as women emerged as new political and economic agents they lost their claim to the fundamental rights of personal security.

The femicides in Ciudad Juarez were the subject of the first inquiry under the optional protocol of the Convention on the Elimination of All Forms of Discrimination against Women (CEDAW) undertaken by the CEDAW Committee (2005). The report of the Committee revealed the multiple vulnerabilities of women to violence in the border city: 'they were young, come from other parts of Mexico [*sic*], living in poverty, working in *maquilas* where protection for their personal security was poor, subject to deception and force' (para. 63–64). The Committee observed that the women did not enjoy basic social and economic rights including the right to decent work, education, health care, housing, sanitation infrastructure and lighting (para. 289). The panel recommended ensuring compliance with the human rights provisions of CEDAW (para. 290) (Chinkin 2008).

Some multinational export industries located in impoverished regions need to import foreign male workers. Their presence may encourage the development of prostitution and sex trafficking as well as gender-based violence. For example, it is argued that liberalisation of the fisheries industry in the Pacific has encouraged the development of prostitution and sex trafficking on shore, and gender-based violence, which has been shown to rise during an economic recession or crisis such as the loss of markets (Pacific Islands Forum Secretariat 2008). A case study of Padang province in Papua New Guinea (PNG) has linked the development of canneries by multinational firms and the import of foreign male workers to an increase in the sex trade, child prostitution and HIV/AIDS. Moreover, many women working in fisheries' processing plants in PNG and Fiji are unmarried and face problems of security and harassment, especially when they either live at cannery hostels or travel to and from their shifts in darkness (PANG 2008). In another example of an extractive, multinational industry, in the Solomon Islands local government officials have accused foreign logging companies of exploiting not only their natural forestry resources but their teenage girls as well. Loggers from Asian countries working for multinational companies are said to employ these girls to work as domestic live-in servants, subjecting them to sexual abuse and leaving them pregnant when they return home (Radio Australia 2008).

Liberation from what? Transitions to a market economy

The destabilisation of economic patterns in society by macroeconomic policies that facilitate a state's global integration is associated with growing inequalities and increasing levels of violence against women in several regions, including Latin America, Africa and Asia (UNICEF 1989, Agnihotri and Mazumdar 1995). The market transitions in Eastern Europe and the former Soviet Union led to widespread increases in poverty, unemployment, hardship, income inequality, stress and violence against women. These factors also indirectly raised women's vulnerability by encouraging more risk-taking behaviour, more alcohol and drug abuse, the breakdown of social support networks and the economic dependence of women on their partners (UNICEF 1999: 7, True 2003).

Some have viewed Eastern Europe and Central Asia as 'test regions' for judging the impact of neo-liberal policies. Rather than revealing positive impacts of market reform, almost all the countries in these regions have exhibited regressions in women's economic and social status (Erturk 2006). The biggest regression has been in Eastern Europe according to Social Watch's 2008 Gender Equity Index. As well as increases in rape and domestic violence, this region has seen hundreds of thousands of young women trafficked for prostitution and other indentured labour each year due to the loss of economic opportunities emanating from liberalisation.

Women are often the hardest hit by economic transition, financial crises and rising unemployment. 'Economic and political insecurity provoke private and public backlash against women's rights that may be expressed through violence and articulated in the form of defending cultures and traditions' (Montréal Principles 2004). Widespread discrimination against girls and women in education, employment and business, and the lack of a state social safety net can mean they are not protected from violence when economies rapidly expand and contract. Export-oriented development in East Asia has had detrimental impacts on women and girls due to patriarchal family-firm structures and the lesser value attributed to women's paid and unpaid labour. There is considerable evidence that economic growth in East Asian countries such as Korea, Taiwan, China and Hong Kong was accelerated by increasing women's employment, while at the same time widening gender wage gaps in the labour market (Gupta 2002, Berik 2004).

When the Asian Financial Crisis hit in 1997–1998, the impact on women and girls in the region was disproportionate as early indications of the impact of the 2008 financial crisis also suggest. Girls were removed from school to help at home or they were forced to seek work in the sex sector to support household incomes as a result of cutbacks in public service jobs and salaries (Truong 2001, Young 2004). In some East Asian countries women's paid labour intensified while in others, notably South Korea, their labour participation shrank. The resulting increased financial burdens strained intra-household relationships, boosted suicides, family violence and abandonment (Floro and Dymski 2000).

Since the 2007–2008 global financial crisis, girls in poor and low-income countries with pre-existing low female schooling have also been highly vulnerable to being pulled out of school and may be led into sex work or trafficking as households cope with declining household income (Buvinic 2009). This response to the crisis has seriously jeopardised the achievement of the Millennium Development Goals which aim to slash poverty, hunger, infant and maternal mortality, and illiteracy by 2015, as well as jeopardised the realisation of gender equality and efforts to protect, prevent and, ultimately, to eliminate violence against women.

Crossing borders: exploitation of migrant women workers

> *All over the world, but especially in labour receiving countries, women domestic workers are abused and exploited. They work in the home where violence among family members is still acceptable or at least beyond the purview of national and international law.*
>
> (Piper 2003: 724)

The expansion of women's labour market participation in developed countries and the reduction of state welfare provisions have fuelled a growing demand for workers in the growing service sector. The employment of foreign-born women has partially met this demand extending across an increasingly broad range of economic sectors, from prostitution and sex work to domestic service, child- and aged-care, and including highly regulated occupations such as nursing. Neo-liberal structural reforms have created debt and unemployment, reduced social services and increased poverty especially in developing countries, requiring more women from those countries to become income earners for their families.

Migration has been one option for women to receive an income, providing economic security for their families. Women are often chosen by their families to migrate based on the expectation that they will sacrifice themselves to a greater degree than men for the welfare of their families – i.e., work harder, remit a higher proportion of their earnings, spend less on themselves and endure worse living conditions (Kofman and Raghuram 2008, UN INSTRAW 2008). In 2005, women made up nearly half of all economic migrants (95 out of 191 million) and they dominate in migration streams to developed countries. Remittances from international migration in 2005 totalled US$251 billion and have had a significant impact on diminishing poverty in developing countries, although these remittances have been falling since the onset of the financial crisis with households cutting back on services (UNFPA 2006: 62). Migrant women and domestic workers have been among the first to be laid off due to prevailing gender ideologies that consider their labour dispensable as well as their part-time, flexible and vulnerable work conditions (Seguino 2009).

Vulnerability to violence is frequently part of the employment relationship for migrant women workers due to the highly unequal power relations at work based on the combined oppressions of gender, class, nationality and ethnicity (Piper 2003: 724). Migrant women usually work in poor conditions with low social status, live in degrading housing situations and lack basic legal protections and opportunities for redress. Domestic workers, for instance, are typically excluded from standard labour practices such as the minimum wage, regular payment of wages, a weekly day off and paid leave. Employers evade domestic labour laws and governments rarely monitor their observance in the domestic sphere (Varia 2007: 1). Labour-sending countries for their part have an economic incentive to ignore their breach as they benefit from the high levels of remittances and may not wish to jeopardise their relations with relevant host countries.

Structural inequalities in global trade regimes allow freedom of movement for firms, investors and professional workers typically from developed countries, but limit the movement of low-skilled workers usually from developing countries. Very few countries have ratified the international conventions that extend citizenship and labour rights to migrant workers. Just 23 per cent of states have ratified the 1949 ILO Convention on Migration for Employment, only ten per cent have ratified the 1975 ILO Convention Concerning Migration in Abusive Conditions and the Promotion of Equality of Opportunity and the Treatment of Migrant Workers, and a mere 17 per cent of states have signed the 1990 International

Convention on the Protection of the Rights of All Migrant Workers and Members of Their Families (United Nations 2006). There are clear linkages between violence against migrant women workers and the failure of states to protect these women workers by monitoring minimum labour standards and ensuring access to adequate housing, education and alternative employment opportunities.[3]

Migrant women working in the sex sector as well as those trafficked for prostitution face extreme vulnerabilities. Trafficking is the underside of migration and inseparable from processes of globalisation and trade liberalisation (Truong 2003). Yet it is more often addressed as a state security and immigration issue or even as a problem of violence against women (in the 1995 Beijing Platform for Action) but not as an economic issue, relating to the loss of economic opportunities brought about by state and global restructuring. The trade in human beings is part of the globalisation of trade in goods, investment, production and services, and needs to be part of trade policy discussions at the World Trade Organisation (ibid.: 53). This recognition would make it clear that all trade occurs in an institutional and moral context and that trade policy as a result must be held accountable for its social as well as its economic impacts.

Increasing rates of trafficking are linked with women's low socio-economic status, gender discrimination in education, employment and business and their relative lack of economic opportunities in specific contexts of neo-liberal globalisation. The majority of trafficked women have made a decision to migrate in search of better economic opportunities, not to be abducted, kidnapped, or to work in indentured labour conditions. State policies that treat trafficked women as criminals or mere victims in need of rescue and rehabilitation fail to take account of their economic agency and their basic human rights in the prevention, protection and prosecution of trafficking. States often seek to control women and police their bodies rather than empower them (Sullivan 2003). Indeed, some argue that it is not migration for sex work that should be abolished, but rather the power relations between trafficked women and traffickers that involve physical, psychological and economic violence against women. When slavery was abolished, for instance, it was the power relationship that was abolished, not working in the cotton fields or in domestic work (Lasink 2006).

[3] For the recommendations and best practice measures undertaken by states to address violence against migrant women workers see United Nations (2007).

Globalisation introduces new vulnerabilities to violence, as well as offering potential for empowerment through labour migration. But neo-liberal government policies that fail to attend to the basic social and economic entitlements of individuals and families make violence against women a more likely outcome than empowerment (Commaraswamy 2000). Restrictive immigration policies focused on national security and a narrow construal of economic interests lead to greater economic exploitation, physical abuse and violence against migrant women workers. Research evidence shows that where countries have male-biased immigration laws, women migrants are more vulnerable to violence. Prostitutes and domestic workers require not just cultural 'recognition' to redress their experiences of violence but material 'redistribution' (Varia 2007). Rather than restricting women's and girls' right to migrate and seek work, 'the real challenge lies in creating the guarantees for them to do so safely and with dignity' (Ramírez, Mar and Morais 2005, Varia 2007: 10).

Conclusion

Patterns of violence against women from the home to the transnational realm are structurally linked to patterns of global transformation instigated by economic, political, military and natural environmental forces. This chapter has sought to highlight rather than comprehensively analyse some strategic sites where we can see global processes implicated in reinforcing existing gender inequalities and creating new forms of marginalisation and violence against women.

For scholars, advocates and policy makers who seek to end violence against women, the lack of analysis of the political economic processes that shape and perpetuate gender-based violence worldwide is deeply troubling. Employing a feminist political economy method, the outlines of which I have suggested here, reveals the destabilisation brought about by economic globalisation and neo-liberal policies promulgated by states and international institutions, and how they exacerbate violence against women. Women's experiences of violence and abuse are shown to be intertwined with the feminisation of poverty, transnational labour exploitation, trade liberalisation, limitations on their sexual and reproductive rights and ongoing control of their mobility.

Feminist political economy analysis, although undertaken only at a general level here, should make us sceptical that current global initiatives, such as the United Nations 'UNITE' Campaign to end violence against women by 2015, will have a significant impact on eradicating violence against women. While these international initiatives remain disconnected from the larger transnational struggle for social and economic equality they will most likely fail to achieve this goal.

Nancy Fraser (2009: 115) has argued that the emancipatory promise of feminism depends on our 'reconnecting struggles against personalized subjection to the critique of a capitalist system'. She entices feminists to 'think big' by bringing back and integrating feminist political economy with cultural critique (ibid.: 117). This chapter and the larger book project of which it is a part aim to contribute to that rejoining of critical, feminist interdisciplinary analysis to address the deep-rooted structural causes and consequences of violence against women. If ending violence against women globally is one of the key struggles and wishes of our age, then it matters greatly that we marshal the best feminist-informed analysis to interpret and to transform the causes of this violence.

References

Agarwal, B. (1994) 'Gender and Command Over Property', *World Development* 22(10): 1459.

Agnihotri, I. and Mazumdar, V. (1995) 'Changing Terms of Political Discourse', *Economic and Political Weekly* 30(29): 1869.

Albuquerque, P.H. and Vemala, P.R. (2008) 'A Statistical Evaluation of Femicide Rates in Mexican Cities along the US-Mexico Border', *Canadian Law and Economics Association (CLEA) 2008 Meetings*, October.

Apodaca, C. (1998) 'Measuring Women's Economic and Social Rights Achievement', *Human Rights Quarterly* 20(1): 151.

Berik, G. (2004) 'Mature Export-Led Growth and Gender Wage Inequality in Taiwan', *Feminist Economics* 6(3): 1.

Boonzaier, F. (2005) 'Woman Abuse in South Africa: A Brief Contextual Analysis', *Feminism and Psychology* 15: 89.

Buvinic, M. (2009) 'The Global Financial Crisis: Assessing Vulnerability for Women and Children, Identifying Policy Responses', written statement to the Interactive Expert Panel on Emerging Issues: The Gender Perspectives on the Financial Crisis, held at the Commission on the Status of Women, 53rd Session, 2–13 March.

Camacho, A.S. (2005) 'Ciudadana X, Gender Violence and the Denationalization of Women's Rights in Ciudad Juarez, Mexico', *The New Centennial Review* 5: 255–292.

Chant, S. (2001) 'Men In Crisis? Reflections on Masculinities, Work and Family in Northwest Costa Rica', in C. Jackson (ed.) *Men at Work* (Frank Cass).

Chinkin, C. (2008) 'The Protection of Economic, Social and Cultural Rights Post-Conflict', OHCHR Women's Human Rights and Gender Unit 3 at http://www2.ohchr.org/english/issues/women/

Commaraswamy, R. (2000) 'Report of SRVAW, on Trafficking in Women, Migration and Violence Against Women', UN Doc. E/CN.4/2000/68, 2 February 2000.

Committee on the Elimination of Discrimination against Women (2005) *Report on Mexico*, CEDAW/C/2005/OP.8/MEXICO.

Elson, D. (2002) 'Gender Justice, Human Rights, and Neo-liberal Economic Policies', in M. Molyneux and S. Razavi (eds) *Gender, Justice, Development and Rights* (Oxford University Press).

Erturk, Y. (2005) 'Report of UN Special Rapporteur on Violence against Women in El Salvador' E/CN.4/2005/72/Add.2; Report on Guatemala E/CN.4/2005/72/Add.3; and Report on Mexico E/CN.4/2006/61/Add.4.

Erturk, Y. (2006) 'Report of UN Special Rapporteur on Violence against Women in the Russian Federation' E/CN.4/2006/61/Add.2; Report on Moldova, A/HRC/11/6/Add.4; and Report on Tajikstan A/HRC/11/6/Add.2.

Floro, M. and Dymski, G. (2000) 'Financial Crisis, Gender, and Power', *World Development* 28(7): 1369.

Fraser, N. (2009) 'Feminism, Capitalism and the Cunning of History', *New Left Review* 56: 109.

Gupta, N.D. (2002) 'Gender, Pay and Development', *Labour and Management in Development Journal* 3(2): 1.

Heise, L. and Garcia-Moreno, C. (2002) 'Violence by Intimate Partners', in E. Keug et al. (eds) *World Report on Violence and Health* (World Health Organization).

Jewkes, R. (2002) 'Intimate Partner Violence: Causes and Prevention', *The Lancet* 359: 1411.

Jewkes, R. and Abrahams, N. (2002) 'The Epidemiology of Rape and Sexual Coercion in South Africa: An Overview', *Social Science & Medicine* 55: 1221.

Kofman, E. and Raghuram, P. (2008) *The Implications of Migration for Gender and Care Regimes in the South* (UNRISD).

Lansink A. (2006) 'Human Rights Focus on Trafficked Women: An International Law and Feminist Perspective', *Agenda* 70 (see http://www.agenda.org.za/content/blogcategory/2/88889070/ accessed 4 March 2010).

Larrain, S. (1999) 'Curbing Domestic Violence: Two Decades of Action', in A. Morrison and M. Loreto Biehl (eds) *Too Close to Home: Domestic Violence in the Americas* (Inter American Development Bank).

Livingstone, J. (2004) 'Murder in Juarez: Gender, Sexual Violence and the Global Assembly Line', *Frontiers* 25(1): 55.

Mackinnon, C. (1988) *Feminism Unmodified: Discourses on Life and Law* (Harvard University Press).

Marchand, M. and Runyan, A.S. (2000) *Gender and Global Restructuring* (Routledge).

Montreal Principles on Women's Economic, Social and Cultural Rights (2004) *Human Rights Quarterly* 26(3): 758.

Okin, S.M. (1989) *Justice, Gender and the Family* (Basic Books).

Pacific Islands Forum Secretariat (2008) *Gender Issues in Tuna Fisheries: Case Studies in Papua New Guinea, Fiji, and Kiribati* (Fishtech Consultants).
PANG (Pacific Network on Globalization) (2008) 'Social Impact Assessment of the Economic Partnership Agreement (EPA) being negotiated between the European Community and Pacific ACP States', available online at http://www.pang.org.fj/45.html
Peterson, V.S. (2003) *A Critical Rewriting of Global Political Economy* (Routledge).
Piper, N. (2003) 'Feminization of Labor Migration as Violence against Women', *Violence against Women* 9(6): 718.
Prugl, E. (1999) *The Global Construction of Gender* (Columbia University Press).
Radio Australia (2008) 'Solomon Official Accuses Foreign Logging Companies of Exploitation', 19 September.
Ramírez, C.D., Mar, G. and Morais, J.M. (2005) *Crossing Borders: Gender, Remittances and Development* (UN INSTRAW Santo Domingo).
Schuler, S.R., Hashemi, S.M. and Badal, S.H. (1998) 'Men's Violence against Women in Bangladesh: Undermined or Exacerbated by Microcredit Programmes?', *Development in Practice* 8(2): 141.
Seguino, S. (2009) 'The Global Economic Crisis and its Gender Implications', written statement to the Interactive Expert Panel on Emerging Issues: The Gender Perspectives on the Financial Crisis, held at the Commission on the Status of Women, 53rd Session, 2–13 March.
Sullivan, B. (2003) 'Trafficking in Women: Feminism and New International Law', *International Feminist Journal of Politics* 5(1): 67.
Sweetman, C. (2008) 'Feminist Economics: From Power to Poverty', background paper contributing to the development of D. Green *From Poverty to Power* (Oxfam International).
Tétrault, M.-A. (2003) 'Kuwait: Sex, Violence and the Politics of Economic Restructuring', in E.A. Doumato and M.P. Posusney (eds) *Women and Globalization in the Arab Middle East* (Lynne Rienner Publishers).
True, J. (2003) *Gender, Globalization and Post Socialism* (Columbia University Press).
True, J. (2010) 'The Political Economy of Violence Against Women', *The Australian Feminist Law Journal* 32: 39–59.
True, J. (forthcoming) *The Political Economy of Violence Against Women* (Oxford University Press).
Truong, T.-D. (2001) 'A Feminist Perspective on the Asian Miracle and Crisis', *Journal of Human Development* 1(1): 140.
Truong, T.-D. (2003) 'Organized Crime and Human Trafficking', in E. Veriano, J. Magallenes and L. Bridel (eds) *Transnational Organized Crime* (Carolina Academic Press).
UNICEF (1989) *The Invisible Adjustment: Poor Women and Economic Crisis*, UNICEF Americas and the Caribbean Regional Office.
UNICEF (1999) *Women in Transition*, Regional Monitoring Report No 6.
UNICEF (2000) 'Domestic Violence against Women and Girls', *Innocenti Digest* 6, June, Innocenti Research Centre.

UN INSTRAW (2008) *Gender, Remittances and Development: The Feminization of Migration: Working Paper*.

United Nations (2006) *International Migration and Development: Report of the Secretary-General* A/60/871.

United Nations (2007) *Violence Against Women Migrant Workers: Report of the Secretary-General, Sixty-Second Session* A/62/177.

Varia, N. (2007) 'Globalization Comes Home: Protecting Migrant Domestic Workers' Rights', *Human Rights Watch World Report 2007* (Human Rights Watch).

Whyte, D. (2009) 'Naked Labour: Putting Agamben to Work', *Australian Feminist Law Journal* 31: 57.

Young, B. (2004) 'Financial Crises and Social Reproduction', in I. Bakker and S. Gill (eds) *Power, Production and Social Reproduction: Human In/Security in the Global Political Economy* (Palgrave).

5
Promoting equality through social inclusion

Case studies from the European social charter

MARK BELL*

There can be little doubt that equality is one of the pivotal labour standards enjoying global recognition. A natural point of reference is the ILO 1998 Declaration on Fundamental Principles and Rights at Work, which included the elimination of discrimination in employment as one of its four strands. In addition, there are a range of UN Conventions which seek to promote equality in the labour market.[1] Although these instruments do not necessarily link equality to sustainable development, it is not difficult to uncover the connections. Societies in which substantial inequalities are permitted to arise and fester are vulnerable to the social tensions which they can produce. At one end of the scale, there is the waste of valuable human resources if certain groups are excluded from the labour market and trapped in poverty and/or dependence on state-provided social welfare. More dramatically, examples abound of situations where these fissures in society eventually erupt with violence and unrest.[2]

This chapter explores how equality is pursued, comparing two approaches. In Europe, legal responses to inequality have tended to focus on anti-discrimination legislation. This approach attempts to bring about

---

* Professor of Law, Centre for European Law and Integration, University of Leicester.

[1] E.g., Article 5 of the Convention on the Elimination of All Forms of Racial Discrimination 1965 obliges states to prohibit racial discrimination in areas such as the free choice of employment and just and favourable conditions of work.

[2] E.g., in the past decade both the UK and France have experienced urban rioting in socially disadvantaged neighbourhoods with significant ethnic minority populations.

76

equality by giving individuals a right to challenge discrimination through litigation before courts or other adjudicatory bodies. In contrast, the promotion of social inclusion has been more typically linked with policy-based mechanisms, not amenable to judicial enforcement (Fredman 2008: 177). A dichotomy thus arises between two pathways for advancing equality: anti-discrimination and social inclusion. The chapter begins by reviewing in more detail the characteristics, strengths and pitfalls of each of these two approaches. It then seeks to explore whether these approaches might be brought together and, to this end, it examines the European Social Charter. This appears to marry some of the qualities of both approaches; it is an instrument of international law, yet it has a holistic outlook on social rights and their implementation in practice. In order to make a more concrete assessment of the Charter's potential to promote equality, two discrete case studies are considered, focusing on the social situation of Travellers in Ireland and Roma in Italy.

Approaches to the pursuit of equality

Anti-discrimination

Within Europe, anti-discrimination legislation varies greatly in its contents. This section does not intend to pronounce any 'universal truth' about what is, or is not, anti-discrimination legislation, but simply to identify some of its main hallmarks. Probably the most defining characteristic of an approach to equality founded on anti-discrimination is conferring the right on individuals to bring legal challenges to acts of discrimination. This is certainly not the sole dimension of such laws, but it seems to be an irreducible minimum. This reflects a rights-based approach to equality; individuals have a right to be free from discrimination and hence there should be a legal procedure through which they can challenge its occurrence and, ultimately, receive effective redress (such as annulment of the original act of discrimination, or compensation from the discriminator). The anti-discrimination approach endeavours to empower individuals and implicitly seeks broader social change through the spillover effects of individual cases. This can arise because of the educative function of litigation; cases elucidate how legal concepts materialise in everyday workplace practice, bringing to life abstract notions such as direct or indirect discrimination. Case law, and its media reporting, can also exercise a deterrent effect, raising awareness amongst employers and the general public about the legal prohibition of discrimination.

Notwithstanding these salutary qualities, experience with the anti-discrimination approach has exposed some of its shortcomings. Individuals encounter a range of legal and practical obstacles which can deter them from bringing cases. Accusations of discrimination are highly sensitive in today's workplace and they are likely to be met with considerable resistance.[3] As Fredman has observed, litigation becomes embroiled in retrospective fault-finding and the attribution of responsibility to specific individuals (Fredman 2002: 177), rather than seeking to prevent inequalities or to identify those actors in a position to advance equality. Litigation-based approaches have also tended to become focused on an individualised analysis of discrimination, dissected from the socio-economic context within which inequalities breed. Considering the situation of Roma in Europe, there is abundant evidence of disadvantage in multiple sectors of life: housing, healthcare, education and the labour market (European Commission 2004a). Anti-discrimination litigation can be a valuable tool in tackling a specific instance of discrimination against Roma people, for example, where Roma job applicants are turned away because of their ethnic origin. Yet such litigation tends to scrape the surface of inequality, dealing with the symptoms but struggling to find a remedy for the underlying causes. Disadvantage in the education system means that many Roma possess fewer formal educational qualifications than their non-Roma counterparts. Even if there was no direct discrimination in the recruitment process, the legacy of educational disadvantage implies that employers will often prefer non-Roma candidates on the basis of 'merit', that is, better qualifications.

The anti-discrimination approach has evolved over time and it increasingly engages with the need to tackle structural forms of disadvantage. The concept of indirect discrimination can be used to unpick disadvantage that flows from organisational culture and practices which, on the face of it, appear to apply equally to all persons. A notable example is *DH* v. *The Czech Republic*.[4] In this case, children were allocated to special schools for

---

[3] Research by the former Department of Trade and Industry showed that employers were more likely to attend Employment Tribunal (ET) proceedings under the Race Relations Act 1976 than under any other type of discrimination or employment litigation. In a sample of around 500 cases, the employers attended ET hearings in 96% of RRA cases: Peters, Seeds and Harding (2006).

[4] *DH and others* v. *The Czech Republic* [GC] (2008) 47 EHRR 3.

those with learning disabilities on the basis of supposedly neutral psychological tests. In practice, Roma children in the town of Ostrava were 27 times more likely to be allocated to such schools than a similarly situated non-Roma child. Crucially, the European Court of Human Rights held (at para. 209) that it was not necessary to show that any individual Roma child had been subject to prejudicial treatment in the conduct of the tests. The 'disproportionately prejudicial effect on the Roma community' was sufficient evidence to support a finding of unlawful discrimination. Whilst such litigation illustrates the potential of anti-discrimination law to expose those practices which perpetuate inequality, it simultaneously imposes significant constraints on the tools available to remedy past and ongoing disadvantage. Compensatory measures, labelled 'positive action', are foreseen in EU anti-discrimination legislation, as well as in the national legislation in most EU member states. (See de Schutter 2007: 757.) These, though, have traditionally halted at the point of selection for employment. In its case law on gender equality, the Court of Justice has repeatedly rejected the notion that overcoming historic under-representation of women in the labour market might entail preferential treatment in selection for employment (ibid.: 801). Even if there seems little appetite in Europe to pursue strong forms of positive action, such as job quotas, perhaps the deeper impact of anti-discrimination legislation is to create a legal climate which is suspicious of group-specific measures. The symmetrical nature of most anti-discrimination legislation implies that providing specific advantages for Roma persons runs the risk of legal challenge from the non-Roma who are excluded.

Social inclusion

The parameters of 'social inclusion' as an approach to pursuing equality are less defined than the anti-discrimination approach. Within Europe, social inclusion has emerged as a successor to what might previously have been described as 'anti-poverty' policy (Schoukens and Carmichael 2001: 76). The term was popularised within EU discourse after the creation in 2000 of a policy coordination process on 'social inclusion' (Ferrera, Matsaganis and Sacchi 2002). As a concept, the following definition of social *exclusion* provides an insight into what social *inclusion* seeks to overcome:

> Social exclusion is a process whereby certain individuals are pushed to the edge of society and prevented from participating fully by virtue of their poverty, or lack of basic competencies and lifelong learning opportunities, or

as a result of discrimination. This distances them from job, income and education opportunities as well as social and community networks and activities. They have little access to power and decision-making bodies and thus
often feeling [*sic*] powerless and unable to take control over the decisions that
affect their day to day lives.

(European Commission 2004b: 10)

A number of characteristics emerge from this definition. First, social
inclusion adopts an open and holistic perspective on inequality. The interaction of disadvantage in spheres such as housing, education and employment is recognised from the outset. As mentioned above, this contrasts with
the blinkered vision imposed within litigation processes, where the
emphasis is normally on a sole dimension of inequality, such as denial of
employment. Indeed, anti-discrimination legislation often carefully circum-
scribes its material scope meaning that only those inequalities falling within
the remit of the law can be effectively addressed.

A second characteristic of social inclusion is its blended approach to
socio-economic inequality (poverty) and discrimination. Social inclusion
differs from anti-poverty policy insofar as it broadens its horizons beyond
relative income levels. It acknowledges that socio-economic disadvantage
is not solely located in low income; rather, it is interlinked with other factors
leading to marginalisation. Even those enjoying stable work and adequate incomes can encounter social exclusion within the labour market if
they are segregated into certain occupational sectors or driven into self-
employment. One of the shortcomings of the anti-discrimination approach
is its tendency to render socio-economic inequalities invisible. Neither the
European Union nor the Council of Europe have expressly recognised
socio-economic status as a protected ground of discrimination within their
legal frameworks. Instead, the emphasis has been on sources of collective
identity, such as gender and ethnicity. This downplays the correlation often
found between socio-economic status and such characteristics. In relation
to Roma communities, there is a particularly acute relationship between
poverty and ethnicity.[5]

---

[5] The overlaps between socio-economic disadvantage and membership of the Roma
community are highlighted in *European Roma Rights Centre* v. *Bulgaria*, Complaint no. 48/2008,
18 February 2009. In this case, the European Committee of Social Rights was divided on
whether restrictions on unemployment benefits should be characterised as direct discrimination based on socio-economic status or indirect discrimination against Roma.

A third distinction between social inclusion and anti-discrimination lies in the instruments used within each approach. Social inclusion generally falls under the category of 'policy', implying a relative absence of legally-enforceable norms. Although anti-discrimination is not exclusively pursued through law, legislation and litigation have tended to occupy centre stage. It would be a mistake, however, to equate the policy/law dichotomy with weak/strong interventions. Social inclusion policy has much less reticence about redistribution of resources from the advantaged to the disadvantaged, and it does not endeavour to be even-handed in its approach (Collins 2003: 22). Measures such as subsidies for employing the long-term unemployed, state-sponsored apprenticeships or even preferential access to employment in the public service are not vulnerable to litigation claiming that they discriminate against those who are socio-economically advantaged.

Although the policy terrain seems more focused on achieving certain outcomes (for instance, reduced long-term unemployment) than the anti-discrimination approach, a corollary of this may be this disempowerment of individuals. By eschewing legal remedies, the social inclusion approach implicitly rejects complaints mechanisms with the consequent sidelining of courts. The policy prescription seems reliant on initiatives taken from above, whereas one virtue of the anti-discrimination approach is the potential for individuals to provoke change by mounting a legal challenge to the specific discrimination which they have encountered. In the *DH* case (discussed above), a wide range of initiatives by the Czech Republic to reduce the segregation of Roma children in schools were mentioned by the state in its defence (see paras 65–79), but the factual circumstances confronted by the children in that case provided a graphic illustration that these measures were not sufficient. Cases such as *DH* more generally expose the difficulty in measuring progress and effectiveness within the social inclusion approach. The absence of courts renders it difficult for individuals or civil society to compel states to take action. They must therefore fall back on political campaigning and persuasion; yet the political leverage of socially excluded groups is inherently likely to be limited. This is especially true in relation to Roma communities, where high levels of public antipathy can be encountered, as well as anti-Roma populism within politics and the media.

The European Social Charter

The discussion above has identified some of the main differences between approaches to equality based on anti-discrimination or social inclusion. Both offer potential, whilst each contains its own internal weaknesses. Nevertheless, the two approaches often remain rather isolated from each other. Within European Union law and policy, for example, there is both an elaborate framework of anti-discrimination legislation and a policy coordination process focusing on social inclusion. There is, though, relatively little evidence of crossover or interaction between the two.[6] Against this backdrop, the European Social Charter warrants further scrutiny because it has attempted to integrate both approaches.

The Charter is an instrument of the Council of Europe and it guarantees a broad swathe of social rights in fields such as employment, education, healthcare and housing. The original 1961 Charter was more heavily focused on labour market rights, but a revised Charter agreed in 1996 expanded its horizons to embrace a wider range of social rights. The Charter has two mechanisms to oversee its implementation within the contracting states. First, there is a duty on states to report on their implementation of the Charter. Reports are submitted on an annual basis, but there is a four-year thematic cycle of reporting, so that different parts of the Charter are monitored at intervals. A *legal* assessment of whether the state has complied with the Charter is then made by the European Committee of Social Rights (ECSR). The following-up of these assessments (called 'Conclusions') is the responsibility of *political* bodies. Initially, the Conclusions of the ECSR are considered by the Governmental Committee, composed of one representative from each of the states who are party to the Charter. The final step is for the Governmental Committee to ask the Committee of Ministers to make a recommendation to the state concerned. The Committee of Minsters is comprised of the Foreign Affairs Ministers of all the member states, or their permanent diplomatic representatives in Strasbourg, so it represents high-level political engagement.

The second mechanism for monitoring enforcement of the Charter is a collective complaints procedure. This allows a limited range of organisa-

---

[6] E.g., in the first EU joint report on social inclusion in 2002, the section on 'access to rights' discussed combating discrimination without mentioning the EU anti-discrimination Directives adopted in 2000: European Commission 2002: 53.

tions, such as trade unions and listed international non-governmental organisations (NGOs), to bring a complaint that the state is in breach of the Charter. The complaints are adjudicated by the ECSR. This dual enforcement structure means that the Charter combines programmatic oversight with the possibility for complaint-based litigation. Although 43 states have ratified either the 1961 or 1996 Charter, only 14 have accepted the collective complaints procedure. Both of the case studies selected involve countries which adhere to the 1996 Charter and the collective complaints procedure.

In principle, the Charter holds considerable potential for an effective joining of the anti-discrimination and social inclusion approaches. Reflecting the social inclusion approach, the ECSR has regularly emphasised that it looks to see that rights are guaranteed not only in law, but also in practice.[7] For example, it routinely collects data from states on topics such as the labour market situation or the utilisation of government programmes. Such analysis illustrates that the outlook of the Committee is broad and often more wide-ranging than the typical purview of courts. There are, though, elements of the Charter which are consistent with the anti-discrimination approach. Notably, the Revised Charter includes a horizontal non-discrimination clause (Article E) and the case law under the collective complaints procedure frequently concerns claims of discrimination in national law and policy. Although the Committee's assessment is devoted to an analysis of the general situation, evidence of individual cases is sometimes advanced within the collective complaints procedure as a means of establishing the overall picture.[8]

Given the diversity of states and social rights covered by the Charter, it is beyond the confines of this chapter to make a generalised assessment of its effectiveness. In order to shed some light on how it functions in practice, two discrete case studies have been chosen, focusing on the social situation of Travellers in Ireland and Roma in Italy. This seemed an apt topic for investigation. 'Roma' is an umbrella term that stretches across a multiplicity of diverse social groups, each with its own cultural and historical background. As a label, it may be understood differently when used in the

---

[7] E.g., *Mental Disability Advocacy Centre* v. *Bulgaria*, Complaint no. 41/2007, 3 June 2008, para. 38; *International Movement ATD Fourth World* v. *France*, Complaint no. 33/2006, 5 December 2007, paras 59–61.
[8] *International Movement ATD Fourth World* v. *France*, Complaint no. 33/2006, 5 December 2007, paras 52–53.

national or European context. From a European perspective, the Travelling community in Ireland fall under the 'Roma' umbrella due to their history of a nomadic lifestyle. In everyday discourse in Ireland, the label Roma is typically reserved for ethnic Roma migrants from other parts of Europe, who are distinguished from the Travelling community. In contrast, in Italy, Roma is used as a catch-all label to cover groups that have a long history in Italy, as well as more recent migrants. Notwithstanding the differences between the various groups, there is a clear pattern of socio-economic disadvantage that makes these cases suitable for comparison. In 1993, the Parliamentary Assembly of the Council of Europe adopted a Recommendation identifying Gypsies as 'a true European minority', whilst recognising that they lived in a 'deplorable situation'.[9] Ten years later, a study published by the European Commission concluded that 'many Romani communities are uniquely exposed to the forces of social exclusion' (European Commission 2004a: 6). It would, therefore, be reasonable to expect that this topic is germane to the implementation of the European Social Charter.

Ireland

The Travelling community is an indigenous ethnic minority group in Ireland. There are estimated to be around 20–27,000 Travellers in Ireland (European Commission 2006: 101–102). The 2006 census revealed that, of those in the labour force, the unemployment rate for Traveller men was 76%, and 73% for Traveller women.[10] The social situation of Travellers in Ireland has been on the radar of the ECSR for some time. In 2003, the Committee asked Ireland to report on the extent of accommodation available for Traveller families, in its remarks under Article 16 on the right of the family to social, legal and economic protection.[11] The following year, the Committee noted that this information was still missing and reiterated its request.[12] In 2005, no conclusions on any topic could be reached by the Committee as Ireland failed to submit its annual report.

[9] Recommendation 1203 (1993) on Gypsies in Europe, 44th Ordinary Session.

[10] Central Statistics Office Ireland, 'Irish Travellers aged 15 years and over classified by principal economic status, age group and sex, 2006', available at: http://beyond2020. cso.ie/Census/TableViewer/tableView.aspx?ReportId=75507 (accessed 6 August 2009).

[11] Conclusions XVI-1, Volume 1 (2003).

[12] Conclusions 2004 (Ireland), Article 16.

In 2006, the issue of the rights of Roma under Article 16 assumed a higher profile across the entire reporting exercise. This was stimulated by the Committee's first decision in a collective complaint concerning Roma. In *European Roma Rights Centre (ERRC) v. Greece,*[13] the Committee held that Greece had violated Article 16 in relation to the shortage of permanent housing for Roma, the lack of temporary stopping facilities and the manner in which forced evictions were conducted. In the course of the decision, the Committee indicated (at para. 19) that it viewed the goals of social inclusion and equality as inextricably linked:

> States must respect difference and ensure that social arrangements are not such as would effectively lead to or reinforce social exclusion. This require-ment is exemplified in the proscription against discrimination . . .

The Committee chose to highlight this decision in its 'General Introduction' to its 2006 conclusions, indicating that comprehensive information would be sought from all states on 'nomads' as a particularly vulnerable group.[14] In relation to Ireland, the Committee had received data which indicated that housing provided by local authorities for Travellers had increased in the past three years and it concluded that the situation was 'satisfactory'. The degree of scrutiny applied to these figures is, though, open to question. The data reported that 6,991 Travellers were in housing of all types during the relevant period. Whilst this may have represented an increase, it remains well below the total estimated Traveller population.[15] Indeed, the issues raised in *ERRC v. Greece,* such as insufficient temporary halting sites, have familiar echoes of the controversies that often surround the Travelling community in Ireland.

The 2006 report is the first occasion on which the Committee starts to consider Travellers beyond the sphere of housing rights. It requested that Ireland submit a more detailed analysis of unemployment rates for ethnic minorities.[16] Whilst noting that domestic legislation prohibits discrim-ination in employment on grounds of, *inter alia,* membership of the Travelling community, the Committee held that the legislation was not in conformity with the Charter because it includes a predefined upper limit on the amount of compensation that can be awarded. The Committee views

---

[13] Complaint no. 15/2003, 8 December 2004.
[14] Conclusions 2006, Volume 1, para. 34.
[15] Conclusions 2006 (Ireland), Article 16.
[16] Conclusions 2006 (Ireland), Article 1, para. 1.

such limits as inconsistent with the need for damages to be commensurate with the loss suffered.[17] This finding of non-compliance with the Charter was referred to the Governmental Committee and, in 2007, it formally requested Ireland to bring its legislation into conformity with the Charter.[18] Nevertheless, 2008 witnessed another failure by Ireland to submit any report to the ECSR, so no conclusions could be issued.[19]

The relative paucity of information in relation to this case study tells its own story. During the five years of monitoring from 2003–2008, the Committee has gently probed into the situation regarding the social and labour market situation of Travellers. Ireland's response could be characterised either as neglect or disdain. By repeatedly failing to submit information, the monitoring function of the Committee was effectively frustrated. In the one instance where a clear finding of non-compliance was issued, Ireland demonstrated a casual disregard for the subsequent procedure. When asked to respond to the finding before the Governmental Committee, the written submission was simply a reproduction of a guide on the Internet to making a complaint under the Employment Equality Acts.[20] This document did not even attempt to engage with the substantive issue, which was the adequacy of the remedies for discrimination in employment. At the time of writing, Ireland had yet to make any amendment to the legislation in order to address the finding of the ECSR or the request from the Governmental Committee.

Italy

Estimates vary, but in 2006 it was reported that there are around 85–120,000 Roma living in Italy (European Commission 2006). This is an internally diverse population split between those who are Italian citizens and historically resident in Italy, and those who have migrated to Italy in recent years, from the Balkans and Romania in particular. Unlike the tentative

---

[17] Conclusions 2006 (Ireland), Article 1, para. 2.

[18] Governmental Committee of the European Social Charter, 'Report concerning Conclusions 2006', T-SG (2007) 11, 19 July 2007, para. 34.

[19] Conclusions 2008 (Ireland).

[20] The document submitted by Ireland (Governmental Committee 2007) matches a guide produced by the Equality Tribunal, available at: http://www.equalitytribunal.ie/uploaded files/AboutUs/EE1_Making%20Complaint.pdf (accessed 3 August 2009).

engagement described in the Irish case study, the issue of Roma rights in Italy has been the subject of extensive discussion within the Charter mechanisms. A key milestone was the collective complaint brought against Italy by the ERRC. This focused on the right to housing under Article 31 of the Charter, as well as Article E on the right to non-discrimination.[21] In brief, the ERRC presented evidence that Italy had a policy of housing Roma in camps with very poor living conditions. The camps often lacked basic amenities, such as water or sewage facilities. Where Roma resorted to unauthorised settlements, these were subject to forced eviction with inadequate procedural safeguards, accompanied by destruction of personal property and violence by law enforcement officers.

In approaching the right to housing, the Committee explained its starting point (at para. 18): 'the right to housing secures social inclusion and integration of individuals into society and contributes to the abolishment of socio-economic inequalities'. This philosophy tends to ground the interpretation of the Charter in the social inclusion approach. Although the complaint relates to a specific 'identity group' (Roma), the Committee identified the link with poverty. It does not pursue a traditional discrimination analysis; there is no search to discover how an appropriate comparator group would have been treated. Indeed, the Committee (at para. 21) rejected any assumption that the approach to the housing of Roma needs to be measured by equivalent treatment of the non-Roma population: 'equal treatment implies that Italy should take measures appropriate to Roma's particular circumstances to safeguard their right to housing and prevent them, as a vulnerable group, from becoming homeless'. Such an approach focuses on achieving a particular socio-economic outcome, in this case avoiding homelessness. On the facts, the Committee considered a range of empirical evidence from the ERRC concerning the social picture for Roma in Italy overall, as well as some identified instances of forced evictions. Ultimately, it held (at para. 36) that there was a 'practice of placing Roma in camps' and breaches of the rights to housing and non-discrimination.

The approach that has evolved for following up collective complaints is a subsequent Resolution by the Committee of Ministers, accompanied by a statement from the respondent state on the measures it will take to address the decision. In this case, Italy promised to take a range of steps,

---

[21] *ERRC* v. *Italy*, Complaint no. 27/2004, 7 December 2005.

including: adopting a framework law setting out a national strategy on Roma; the addition of Roma to the legally-recognised list of historic minority groups (with associated rights); and the promotion of Roma rights via the National Office against Racial Discrimination.[22] On the face of it, this seems to provide an ideal example of how the Charter mechanisms can utilise a complaints-based enforcement model to provoke a ripple of changes that deliver collective benefits. Subsequent events, however, have illustrated the limited capacity of the Charter process to compel states to honour their undertakings.

The state reporting procedure is the primary mechanism through which the Committee controls whether its decisions on collective complaints have actually been respected. In 2007, the Committee noted that the framework law had still not been adopted and that the measures taken by regional authorities were patchy.[23] In relation to evictions, the Committee sounded its concern at the intention of certain local authorities to close down camps under the auspices of 'Security Pacts'. Concretely, it pointed out that closing down the camps in Rome was intended to reduce accommodation by 10,000 places, yet there were only 4,000 places in the planned alternative villages. In this period, the Committee can also be seen to widen its scope of inquiry, asking for data on the unemployment rate of ethnic minorities in Italy,[24] as well as finding non-conformity with Article 17 on the rights of children because of the low number of Roma children in education.[25]

The situation changed dramatically after April 2008. National elections resulted in the governing centre-left coalition being replaced by a right-wing coalition which included various parties, such as Lega Nord, notorious for strong anti-immigrant and anti-Roma rhetoric. In May 2008, the government declared a 'state of emergency with regard to nomad community settlements', invoking powers under legislation designed to respond to natural disasters.[26] Under the state of emergency, a range of new measures were taken including the compulsory fingerprinting of camp residents. This was accompanied by a new wave of camp clearances. Once

---

[22] Resolution ResChS (2006) 4 of the Committee of Ministers on Collective Complaint no. 27/2004, 3 May 2006.

[23] Conclusions 2007 (Italy), Article 31.

[24] Conclusions 2006, Volume 1 (Italy), Article 1, para. 1.

[25] Conclusions 2007, Volume 2 (Italy), Article 17, para. 1.

[26] For full details, see European Roma Rights Centre and others, 'Security a la Italiana: fingerprinting, extreme violence and harassment of Roma in Italy', at 17, available at: http://www.errc.org/db/03/4C/m0000034C.pdf (accessed 6 August 2009).

again, there were reports of forced evictions during the night, destruction of personal possessions and violence by police officers.[27] Parallel to the actions by the state, Roma camps were burnt down in attacks in Rome, Naples and Catania.[28]

Unsurprisingly, this turn of events sparked a response by various international organisations. A fact-finding mission was launched by the High Commissioner on National Minorities and the Office for Democratic Institutions and Human Rights of the Organisation for Security and Cooperation in Europe (OSCE).[29] This concluded that the measures taken were 'disproportionate' and 'fuelled anti-Roma bias'.[30] The Council of Europe's Commissioner for Human Rights has since made two official visits to Italy, finding that 'the vast majority of Roma and Sinti are in urgent need of effective protection of their human rights, especially their social rights, such as the right to adequate housing and to education, by national, regional and local authorities'.[31] The Council of Europe's specialist anti-racism body, the European Commission on Racism and Intolerance (ECRI), took the unusual step of issuing a statement criticising 'persistent racist and xenophobic discourse by some Italian politicians, even at the highest levels'.[32] Within Italy, however, the national institution for combating racism (UNAR) apparently made no official comment on the developments.[33]

Against this backdrop, it is particularly salient to examine how these events were handled within the Social Charter mechanisms. Clearly, the practices occurring in 2008 were precisely the types of conduct which led to the Committee's 2005 decision that Italy was in breach of the right to housing. Moreover, the Committee's warnings in its 2007 report about the

---

[27] Ibid., 24.

[28] Ibid., 29.

[29] OSCE, 'Assessment of the human rights situation of Roma and Sinti in Italy: report of a fact-finding mission to Milan, Naples and Roma on 20–26 July 2008': http://www.osce.org/documents/odihr/2009/03/36620_en.pdf (accessed 6 August 2009).

[30] Ibid., 8.

[31] Commissioner for Human Rights, 'Memorandum following his visit to Italy on 19–20 June 2008', CommDH(2008)18, para. 44.

[32] Statement of ECRI on recent events affecting Roma and immigrants in Italy, 20 June 2008, 46th plenary meeting.

[33] A search of the website of UNAR on 6 August 2009 did not reveal any press release or statement from the body about the measures taken in 2008. In fact, the most recent annual report from UNAR dated back to 2007. See further: http://www.virtualcommunityunar.it/ and http://www.pariopportunita.gov.it/ (under 'Uffizi and servizi').

direction in which Italian policy was going proved remarkably prescient. In February 2009 it fell to the Governmental Committee to decide what stance to adopt on the Committee's 2007 report. Italy argued that the compulsory fingerprinting and incursions into the camps were designed to improve data collection on the situation of Roma and that they were in fact an appropriate response to calls from the ECSR to improve data on the living conditions of Roma.[34] With regard to the earlier commitment to include Roma within the law on historic national minorities, it was stated that this was no longer one of the government's priorities.[35] The Governmental Committee accepted Italy's explanations, stating that 'the Committee welcomed the developments occurred [*sic*] after the reference period' and referred the issue back to the ECSR for the next round of state reporting.[36]

The handling of the Italian case by the Governmental Committee exposes the risk that the legal standard-setting by the ECSR is undermined by subsequent politicisation. There can be little doubt that Italy has not complied with the 2005 decision in *ERRC v. Italy*. Few of the commitments given to the Committee of Ministers have been fulfilled and the situation on the ground has actually deteriorated. It seems doubtful to characterise the compulsory fingerprinting as a legitimate means of equality data collection. The OSCE pointed out that singling out one ethnic group for data collection, in a particularly intrusive manner, could be discriminatory and stigmatising.[37] The practice of forced evictions continues: in July 2009, a camp housing around 140 persons, which had existed for 20 years, was cleared of its residents and destroyed.[38]

In the minutes recording the discussions of the Governmental Committee, it is notable that other states with large Roma populations intervened to support the Italian position. For these states, there may be a political self-interest in avoiding any criticism of Italian policies. Bulgaria, for example, suggested that Italy should be afforded more time to deal with

[34] Governmental Committee, 'Report concerning Conclusions 2007', T-SG (2009) 4, 24 February 2009, para. 304.

[35] Ibid., para. 302.

[36] Ibid., para. 306.

[37] OSCE, 'Assessment of the human rights situation of Roma and Sinti in Italy: report of a fact-finding mission to Milan, Naples and Roma on 20–26 July 2008', 7.

[38] *Il Messaggero*, 'La Rustica, sgomberato campo nomadi dopo 20 anni, allontanate 140 persone' ['La Rustica, nomad camp cleared out after 20 years, 140 people moved on'] (27 July 2009).

90

the situation;[39] it can hardly be overlooked that in two collective complaints Bulgaria has been found by the Committee to be in violation of the Charter in relation to Roma rights.[40] Nevertheless, the issue will not disappear from the Charter mechanism. In May 2009, the Centre on Housing Rights and Evictions lodged a new collective complaint alleging violation by Italy of various rights in relation to Roma, including the right to non-discrimination. The complaint covers both the failure to comply with the 2005 decision and especially the government measures taken since 2008.[41]

Conclusions

In principle, the European Social Charter offers a positive example of how an approach based on social inclusion can enrich the concept of equality with a view to sustainable development. In its interpretation of equality in the context of Roma rights, the Committee starts from the goal of social inclusion and explicitly links this to combating socio-economic inequality. From this standpoint, the Committee does not hesitate to recognise that group-targeted measures are required, and that this may entail treating some groups differently in order to overcome social disadvantage. Indeed, in a decision on housing rights for Roma in Bulgaria, *ERRC* v. *Bulgaria*,[42] the Committee was willing to impose a duty to take positive action (at para. 42):

> the Committee finds that in the case of Roma families, the simple guarantee of equal treatment as the means of protection against discrimination does not suffice . . . this means that for the integration of an ethnic minority as Roma into mainstream society measures of positive action are needed.

This approach moves away from the asymmetrical outlook which often typifies anti-discrimination legislation. Another illustration of this tendency

[39] Governmental Committee, 'Report concerning Conclusions 2007', T-SG (2009) 4, 24 February 2009, para. 301.

[40] *ERRC* v. *Bulgaria*, Complaint no. 31/2005, 18 October 2006; *ERRC* v. *Bulgaria*, Complaint no. 46/2007, 3 December 2008.

[41] Complaint no. 58/2009, 29 May 2009. On 25 June 2010, the European Committee of Social Rights held that there had been further breaches of the Charter by Italy in its treatment of Roma communities. Notably, it found that there had been 'an aggravated violation' due to the contribution of public authorities to the violation of the human rights of a vulnerable group and that this went 'beyond ordinary breaches of the Charter' (para. 78). The Committee also held that the Italian authorities had issued 'racist misleading propaganda' (para. 139).

[42] Complaint no. 31/2005, 18 October 2006.

can be found in the Committee's approach to eviction from unlawful housing settlements. Whilst not giving an unlimited right to Roma to settle anywhere irrespective of planning laws, the extent to which evictions are viewed as permissible by the Committee is balanced against an analysis of whether adequate alternative housing actually exists (*ERRC* v. *Bulgaria*, para. 54).

The Committee's processes provide an innovative bridge between complaints-based anti-discrimination litigation and social inclusion policy. The collective complaints mechanism allows interested organisations to shine a spotlight on specific equality concerns. These avoid becoming bogged down in the analysis of the factual circumstances of any isolated individual case, but explicitly seek to establish a global picture of the real situation. The Committee's approach reveals that it is not merely concerned with what law in the books states (i.e., legislation), but it actively engages with the social reality. Moreover, it does not bind itself with formal rules of evidence and it is willing to accept diverse types of information collected by NGOs. The combination of a complaints forum with the ongoing periodic review should allow for the specific equality issues flagged up via complaints to be then reviewed more systematically through the regular reporting process.

Despite the considerable potential that the Social Charter mechanism holds, the analysis of the two case studies illustrated that it can fail to deliver on this promise. The most obvious conclusion is that the Charter can be rendered ineffective by recalcitrance on the part of the contracting states. The Irish case study showed how a state can, to a large extent, simply ignore the Charter's supervisory bodies and frustrate their work through non-communication. Eventually, political pressure would doubtless build if a recommendation from the Committee of Ministers went without any response, but reaching this point is a slow process. The Italian case study began with optimism; it appeared that the collective complaint would stimulate a revision of national policy. The anticipated measures never came to pass, however, and it was a concrete illustration of the weaknesses within the Charter mechanisms where a government pursues a course of action in evident contrast to the Committee's requirements.

The difficulty in enforcing the Charter is relatively well known, although it is worthy of note that the case studies confirm a long-held impression. From the perspective of this chapter, it is also significant that labour standards remained in the background in each case study. Given that Travellers and Roma are undoubtedly marginalised within the labour market, it is surprising that there was little evidence of the Committee exploring this dimension to their social situation. On a few occasions, the Committee requested evidence from Ireland or Italy on the labour market situation of ethnic minorities, but these inquiries generated little information and the issue was not pursued further. In this area, the Committee's periodic monitoring has focused on other social rights, notably housing and education. This coincides with, and perhaps reflects, the litigation strategy of the NGOs active in this field. None of the collective complaints relating to Roma rights has dealt with labour market issues, and similarly the Roma cases pursued at the European Court of Human Rights have so far focused on access to education,[43] as well as violence against Roma.[44] The low profile of labour market issues suggests that the rounded outlook of the Charter on social rights can be difficult to implement in practice.

The theoretical discussion at the beginning of this chapter illustrated that equality can be pursued with different approaches. Neither the anti-discrimination approach nor the social inclusion approach offered a complete recipe for bringing about equality and it seems logical to explore how both can be combined. The Social Charter provides an example of a legal framework which has travelled some distance down this path. Its application in practice suggests that putting this kind of combined equality strategy into effect encounters its own difficulties and requires further elaboration.

References

Collins, H. (2003) 'Discrimination, Equality and Social Inclusion', *Modern Law Review* 66: 16.

de Schutter, O. (2007) 'Positive Action', in D. Schiek, L. Waddington and M. Bell (eds) *Cases, Materials and Text on National, Supranational and International Non-Discrimination Law* (Hart Publishing).

European Commission (2002) *Joint Report on Social Inclusion* (Office for Official Publications of the European Communities (OOPEC)).

European Commission (2004a) *The Situation of Roma in an Enlarged European Union* (OOPEC).

---

[43] *DH and others* v. *The Czech Republic* [GC] (2008) 47 EHRR 3; Application no. 32526/05 *Sampanis and Others* v. *Greece*, 5 June 2008.
[44] E.g., *Nachova and others* v. *Bulgaria* [GC] (2006) 42 EHRR 43; *Moldovan and others* v. *Romania* (2007) 44 EHRR 16.

European Commission (2004b) *Joint Report on Social Inclusion 2004* (OOPEC).
European Commission (2006) *Gender Inequalities in the Risks of Poverty and Social Exclusion for Disadvantaged Groups in Thirty European Countries* (OOPEC).
Ferrera, M., Matsaganis, M. and Sacchi, S. (2002) 'Open Coordination Against Poverty: The New EU Social Inclusion Process', *Journal of European Social Policy* 12: 227.
Fredman, S. (2002) *Discrimination Law* (Oxford University Press).
Fredman, S. (2008) *Human Rights Transformed – Positive Rights And Positive Duties* (Oxford University Press).
Peters, M., Seeds, K. and Harding, C. (2006) 'Findings from the Survey of Claimants in Race Discrimination Employment Tribunal Cases', *Employment Relations Research Series* No 54 (Department of Trade and Industry).
Schoukens, P. and Carmichael, L. (2001) 'Social Exclusion in Europe: Testing the Limits of European Integration', in D. Mayes, J. Berghman and R. Salais (eds) *Social Exclusion and European Policy* (Edward Elgar).

Part III
Child poverty and child labour as an obstruction to development

6
Some remarks on the economics of child labour

SONIA BHALOTRA*

The responsibility for child labour is often cast as resting with (exploitative) employers. This creates a demand for legislation that bars employers from employing children. However, a careful look at household survey data suggests that the majority of employers are parents and, when not, parents have volunteered the child for work. There are important exceptions involving forced removal of children for war, prostitution and bonded labour. In such cases, there is a clearer case for legal action, although action in practice is limited by the problems of detection in these activities, many of which are conducted underground. The 'worst forms of child labour', even if less prevalent, generate most concern and motivate the 1999 ILO Convention no. 182. My focus is on the majority case of children working to help the family survive. I will briefly discuss the role of legislation in curbing child labour, while arguing that it is not a substitute for efforts directed at creating income-generating opportunities amongst the poor and improving their access to education. Even when legislation is effective in lowering the incidence of child labour, it remains relevant to consider where children removed from the labour market go, which is why so much of the emphasis in the contemporary development literature is on education.

There is considerable evidence to show that educating children is a way of breaking the inter-generational cycle of poverty, allowing children to move on to different trajectories than their parents. Education promotes

* Professor of Economics, Centre for Market and Public Organisation, University of Bristol. This is a modified transcript of a lecture delivered at the British Academy, London, May 2009.

voice, democracy and the demand for human rights. But there are well-documented market failures that result in socially sub-optimal investments by families in education. State-led intervention is needed to raise the incentive to send children to school by raising the quality and relevance of schooling (benefits), while at the same time lowering its direct and opportunity costs. Poor access raises costs of attendance so policies that improve the geographic spread and density of schools are helpful too. Education aside, child workers are more likely than adult workers to suffer human rights violations, basically because they are little and they have limited voice.

Amongst legislative interventions relevant to the problem of child labour are international labour standards, trade sanctions, bans on child labour, compulsory schooling and adult minimum wages. The effectiveness of each depends upon understanding the structure and causes of child labour, upon the state of development of the legal infrastructure and upon the wider socio-economic, legal and political environment. The rest of this chapter sketches some of the elements of this background, presenting an informal discussion of selected legislative measures.

Defining child labour – and its relation to schooling

Obviously, how much child labour there is in the world depends on how you define it and the definitions will be sensitive to definitions of the 'child' and definitions of 'labour'. The ILO Conventions define children as individuals under the age of fifteen and 'labour' as work that produces a marketable output. So, if you work on a farm owned by your parents, as long as the rice grown on the farm is sold for a price the work counts, but if the rice is eaten at home the work does not count. Obviously this is not ideal, since much domestic work, which is predominantly performed by girls, does not count as child labour. However, this is the statistical basis for the ILO estimate that nearly 211 million children (or about a third of all children below the age of fifteen) were economically active in year 2000.

It is useful to observe that school is not the exact opposite of work. First, children often combine work and school. Second, there are many children who are neither in school nor in work and this 'idleness' has been subject to very little analysis. It is probably a worse thing than child labour if child labour produces valuable work experience, although not so if child labour is hazardous or if there is home education.

The family context

Understanding solutions to the child labour problem naturally involves understanding its structure and causes. In this section we describe relevant features of the family context in which child labour arises. Many of the families that supply child labour are poor. Where public provision of schooling is limited, it falls upon the family to find resources for schooling. Schooling is an investment with delayed rewards, so families need to fork out cash today or at least give up income from children today and they only get a pecuniary reward much later when the child has grown up. Access to credit is weak in general, but weaker for long-term investments with an uncertain return. For these reasons poorer families that anticipate zero bequests may be constrained to send their children to work (Baland and Robinson 2000).

A further relevant feature of poor countries is that self-employment is widespread. Family capital is typically inherited and labour regulation does not apply to small informal (unregistered) farms or enterprises. Parents have an incentive to deploy their children on the family farm or enterprise for these reasons. First, to the extent that the child stands to inherit the family capital (typically first-born sons), there is a specific return to work experience. Second, it can be difficult to hire adult labour because of seasonality in demand. Third, while it is hard to monitor hired labour (moral hazard), one's own children may be relied upon to act upon their parent's instruction (Bhalotra and Heady 2003). While child labour was at least as prevalent in pre-industrial Europe and America as it is in today's developing countries it was concentrated in factories (Horrell and Humphries 1995), a contrast to the current situation where it is concentrated on farms.

Preferences, incentives and constraints

In situations of no coercion, parents face a choice between sending their children to work or school or neither ('leisure'). This choice depends, like any labour supply choice, on preferences, incentives and constraints. The *preferences* of parents may not coincide with the preferences of children. Yet parents are the 'agents' that typically make the child labour decision for children, the 'principals'. Thus the degree of parental altruism is a factor in the decision (Bhalotra 2001a). The *incentive* is the return to education.

Parents in poor countries often see the education provided by state schools as producing no return, whether because teachers are poorly qualified and frequently absent or because material resources are limited (PROBE 1999). *Constraints* relate to either the non-availability of schools or to the family being dependent upon the income generated by child labour to meet its subsistence requirements. Very different policy solutions emerge depending on which of incentives or constraints dominates. For example, if a survival constraint forces children into work, then no matter how attractive the schooling option is families cannot afford to send children to school. In this case, targeting employers with fines or trade sanctions could make children worse off. The appropriate policy is to relax the binding income constraint, for example by offering cash transfers or micro-credit. In the absence of binding constraints, relative returns come into play. The appropriate policy is then to improve the quality of education provided so as to incentivise parents to send their children to school.

Analysis of representative household survey data on children in wage work in rural Pakistan suggests that boys work where necessary for survival while girls work even when their income contribution is not necessary (Bhalotra 2007). This difference could arise because parents favour boys, perhaps because boys provide old-age security, or because girls' schooling brings lower returns, or because there are cultural preferences in favour of keeping girls at home. In this context, policies that improve income-augmenting opportunities for poor households would successfully discourage boys' work but discouraging girls' work would probably involve alternatives such as improving access to and the quality of girls' schools.

Economic growth

A common if sometimes unfair perception of the approach taken by economists is that they will tend to argue, whether with regard to child poverty, child labour or child death, that pursuing policies that promote growth will (eventually) resolve the problem. Child labour has largely disappeared in rich countries, so, if we wait, it should disappear in poorer countries. Of course we may wait for a long time. Also, while growth raises average incomes in society, it has a variable record in delivering what is needed, which is (a) higher average incomes *amongst the poor*, (b) less volatile incomes, and (c) higher net returns to schooling.

Redistribution, micro-credit, supply of education

There is therefore a role for governments to engage in redistribution and directly reduce poverty and income volatility. As child labour is concentrated amongst poorer households in poor countries, raising their incomes will relax the subsistence constraints that would otherwise compel poor parents to send children into work. One alternative is to invest in pro-poor and inclusive growth. Another is to offer cash transfers. The evidence suggests that cash transfers conditional upon school attendance work well (Fiszbein, Schady and Ferreira 2009). Following the success of Mexico's Progresa, a number of other developing countries have instituted cash transfer schemes. Schemes like Progresa illustrate the importance of a concert of interventions. For example, if supplementing income with cash transfers raises the demand for schooling then the programme must simultaneously build schools to accommodate the demand and avoid creating overcrowding in schools. It is also important to consider 'unintended consequences' such as that cash transfers offered per child may stimulate fertility.

Poor households in developing countries suffer income volatility as a result of their dependence upon rain-fed agriculture and the fallout of wars and financial crises. They typically enjoy no state-financed insurance. When income is volatile and its average is low, it is easy for a shock to result in the removal of a child from school. In principle, the child goes back to school once income recovers, but often it is difficult to go back and catch up. So even when child labour is used to insure household income, it can cause permanent deficits in education. Micro-finance helps households smooth consumption across income fluctuations.

Pensions policy does not naturally arise in discussions of child labour interventions. However, people in developing countries often live in large integrated families and children and grandparents may effectively compete for resources as dependents within the household. So, if there were pensions for the elderly, resources could be redirected to children. There is some evidence of this in the context of the old Poor Laws in England. Similarly, the extension of the South African pension to black households resulted in improvements in both child health (Duflo 2001) and child labour (Edmonds 2006).

Globalisation, trade, social security

Growth tends to be associated with globalisation which, in turn, often involves expansion of international trade. The popular perception is probably that trade, as currently conducted, aggravates the problem of child labour. The idea is that low wages confer upon poor countries an advantage in international trade which they maintain by exploiting cheap labour which includes the labour of children. This leads to a 'race to the bottom'. Recommended solutions include trade sanctions, consumer boycotts and the creation of core international labour standards. However, these approaches involve 'sticks' and poor children are likely to come out better if international organisations instead use 'carrots'. They also involve the risk that actors in the North arrive at value-based judgements that are then imposed upon the South. The danger is that these recommendations may be motivated by protectionism generated by political pressure from those segments of society in richer countries that find themselves in competition with labour in the South. Perhaps the simplest reason to reject them is that, even if they were undertaken with the best of intentions, they are likely to be ineffective. This is because a ban on the import of goods made with child labour will induce children who are looking to earn to move from the high-wage export sector to the low-wage domestic sector.

International organisations like the World Trade Organisation (WTO) could work instead to improve terms of international trade. While sanctions would cut out the participation of poorer countries, improved terms of trade would encourage their participation and higher prices may be expected to flow back into higher wages and better working conditions. With international labour standards it is not always clear what the level playing field is. There may however be a case for supporting country governments to institute country-wide labour and social security standards. There is very limited, if any, social security in low-income countries. But it is not impossible to afford. Under the old Poor Laws, seventeenth-century England had a sophisticated form of social security that was responsive to economic and demographic shocks including harvest failure, unemployment, illness, widowhood, orphanhood and old age. This was well before the sharp rise in incomes associated with the Industrial Revolution (Slack 1990, Smith 1998, Bhalotra 2001b). The state of Kerala in India and Sri Lanka are amongst contemporary examples of effective public provision of basic services and insurance at relatively low levels of income (Ahmad et al. 1991).

Technological change

A third relevant element of the engine of growth is technological change. The past century has witnessed enormous changes in the production process involving the substitution of machines for labour and of skilled for unskilled labour. Isolated studies suggest that technical change contributed to reducing the demand for child labour, other things being equal. For example, children were needed to work in mines because a man could not stand up in the shaft, it was too narrow. But then a wider shaft was invented and men took over the job from children (Kirby 2003). Peter Kirby has argued that technological change preceded legislation against child labour in engineering the decline of child labour in British history. Similarly, the introduction of machinery for cotton picking in Egyptian farms contributed to the elimination of child labour (Lavy 1985). These examples suggest that a possibility is that relaxing patents could accelerate technological diffusion and thereby social change.

Banning child labour

If child labour were eliminated by a *total* ban, then employers would seek adult labour to fill that space. An increase in the demand for adult labour would lead to higher adult wages, making it unnecessary for (many) parents to send their children to work. As a result, even if the ban were not monitored, children would stay out of work. Working through a labour market in which parents and children are at least partial substitutes, the ban generates a virtuous cycle which can become self-sustaining (Basu and Van 1998). Also, if children are removed from jobs that they are often engaged in – mining, cotton picking, football sewing, or carpet knitting – this will tend to stimulate technical change.

The ban can be conceptualised as effecting coordination across families. The coordination problem arises because it is rational for the individual family to send their child to work if the child's income contributes to subsistence. However, the collective labour supply of all children has the effect of lowering adult wages through competition. So the collectively rational action is to coordinate to keep all children out of the labour market and let the resulting rise in adult earnings cover the income deficit created by taking the children out. Note that the individual family acting alone contributes too small a fraction of the labour on the market to have any effect on the adult wage; this is why coordination is key. So the ban operates equivalently to, say, a village meeting at which all households in the market commit to a coordinated action. This suggests that legislating against child labour may generate a sustainable move away from it.

However, coordinated action can only flip the economy from a 'bad' equilibrium in which children work to an alternative equilibrium in which children do not work if the labour market exhibits multiple equilibria. This, in turn, depends upon assuming that the supply of child labour is decreasing in the adult wage. It is the assumed preference of individual parents to keep their children out of work if they can afford to that generates a potential multiplicity of equilibria at the aggregate level. So if we are looking at a context in which compelling poverty is not the most important problem, but rather poor-quality schooling, then a ban is unlikely to operate as discussed. Also, the adjustment mechanism we described operates in a flexible labour market and an economy populated by family farms and enterprises is not characterised by flexible labour markets. Finally, as discussed in the context of trade sanctions, a *partial* ban of child labour centred on a particular sector of industry is typically a bad idea, because children would just move to the unregulated sector, likely with worse conditions.

An alternative legal intervention would be to institute an adult minimum wage. Then, to the extent that most parents send their children to work because their own wages are too low, the minimum wage should lower child labour. In fact, a minimum wage tends to have two impacts, on different sets of households. It improves wages for those adults that continue to be employed. However, it creates some unemployment as it makes employers less keen to hire workers and workers more keen to work. There may be some increase in child labour from the now unemployed adults. The overall impact of the minimum wage on child labour can be positive or negative (Basu 2000).

It has been argued that wider social and economic development often facilitates adoption of legislation, promoting its political feasibility and incentive compatibility (Doepke and Zilibotti 2005). However, it could be argued that, conversely, legislative action may 'jump start' economic and social development, changing the institutional parameters and altering the configuration of incentives leading to different economic and social choices.

References

Ahmad, E., Dreze, J., Hills, J. and Sen, A. (eds) (1991) *Social Security in Developing Countries* (Oxford University Press).

Baland, J.M and Robinson, J. (2000) 'Is Child Labor Inefficient?', *The Journal of Political Economy* 108(4): 663.

Basu, K. (2000) 'The Intriguing Relation between Adult Minimum Wage and Child Labour', *The Economic Journal* 110(462): 50.

Basu, K. and Van, P. (1998) 'The Economics of Child Labor', *American Economic Review* 88(3): 412.

Bhalotra, S. (2001a) 'Parent Altruism', Discussion Paper 04/562, University of Bristol.

Bhalotra, S. (2001b) 'Growth and Welfare Provisioning: Lessons From the English Poor Laws?', *Journal of International Development* 13(7): 1083.

Bhalotra, S. (2007) 'Is Child Work Necessary?', *Oxford Bulletin of Economics and Statistics* 69(1): 29.

Bhalotra, S. and Heady, C. (2003) 'Child Farm Labor: The Wealth Paradox', *The World Bank Economic Review* 17(2): 197.

Doepke, M. and Zilibotti, F. (2005) 'The Macroeconomics of Child Labor Regulation', *The American Economic Review* 95(5): 1492.

Duflo, E. (2001) 'Child Health and Household Resources in South Africa: Evidence from the Old Age Pension Program', *American Economic Review* 90(2): 393.

Edmonds, E. (2006) 'Child Labor and Schooling Responses to Anticipated Income in South Africa', *Journal of Development Economics* 81(2): 386.

Fiszbein, A., Schady, N. and Ferreira, F. (2009) *Conditional Cash Transfers: Reducing Present and Future Poverty* (World Bank, Washington DC).

Horrell, S. and Humphries, J. (1995) 'The Exploitation of Little Children: Child Labor and the Family Economy in the Industrial Revolution', *Explorations in Economic History* 32(4): 485.

Kirby, P. (2003) *Child Labour in Britain, 1750–1870* (Palgrave MacMillan).

Lavy, V. (1985) 'Cropping Pattern, Mechanization, Child Labor, and Fertility Behavior in a Farming Economy: Rural Egypt', *Economic Development and Cultural Change* 33(4): 777.

PROBE (1999) *Public Report on Basic Education for India* (Oxford University Press).

Slack, P.A. (1990) *The English Poor Law, 1531–1782*, Studies in Economic and Social History (Macmillan).

Smith, R.M. (1998) 'Ageing and Well-Being in Early Modern England: Pension Trends and Gender Preferences Under The English Old Poor Law c.1650–1800', in P. Johnson and P. Thane (eds) *Old Age from Antiquity to Post-modernity* (Routledge).

7
Child labour

An analysis of the nature
of corporate responsibility

SURYA DEVA*

Introduction

This chapter aims to explore the responsibility of corporations regarding child labour. This exploration is done at two levels. First, selected regulatory regimes are reviewed to ascertain the corporate responsibility outlined therein. Under international law generally, the responsibility in relation to human/labour rights was traditionally and primarily conceived with reference to states (Weissbrodt 2005: 59, Fitzgerald 2005: 33). This state-focal nature, though, seems to be undergoing a change in recent years. More importance, for instance, is now being given to states' duty to ensure that non-state actors within their respective jurisdictions comply with the goal of eliminating child labour. In addition to this indirect approach, responsibility for child labour is also being directly imposed on corporations. Moreover, one may notice a voluntary assumption of responsibility on the part of corporations in the form of codes of conduct. An attempt will be made to review some of these diverse regulatory initiatives.

Second, at a normative level, the notion of responsibility is analysed with reference to the idea of being 'responsive' to the state of child labour. 'Responsiveness' is contrasted with 'responsibility' in that the former focuses more on strategy and action rather than outlining what duties

* Associate Professor, School of Law, University of Hong Kong. This chapter is a revised version of a paper presented at the International Conference on 'The Role of Labour Standards in Sustainable Development: Theory in Practice', organised by the University of Bristol and the British Academy, London, on 24–25 April 2009.

corporations have on a given issue (Crane and Matten 2007: 53). Another dimension of being responsive is that one does not have a predefined inflexible response applicable to all situations. The exact contours of the responsibility should rather be determined, to some extent, by what is necessary to achieve the agreed goals. In this sense, responsiveness embodies and reflects a managerial response to social demands (Walker and Parent 2010: 201).

Let us consider an example to understand this proposition better. What should be the responsibility of a corporation operating in developing countries where child labour is a social reality for a number of reasons? One approach could be to predefine the responsibility for all kinds of corporations operating everywhere: that corporations should/shall not hire child labour (in whatever way we define 'child' and 'labour'). However, putting an absolute prohibition on hiring child labour alone may be both insufficient and counter-productive in some cases. In such a situation, one alternative approach could be to contemplate responsibility with reference to the measures that are necessary to accomplish a predefined goal, that is, the effective abolition of child labour in this instance. In other words, corporations should respond as per the demands of the situation. It may then become necessary that the responsibility of corporations in the area of child labour includes elements other than not employing children below the minimum age, e.g., providing education or suitable vocational training, or offering employment to adult members of children's families. Responsiveness, in short, requires that the means employed are robust enough to achieve a given end.

Ascertaining responsibility of corporations

This section reviews a few representative regulatory regimes that outline the responsibility of corporations regarding child labour. In terms of the nature, the regimes reviewed here range from voluntary (codes of conduct) to non-voluntary (UN Human Rights Norms). Whereas some regimes are initiated internally by corporations (codes of conduct), the others owe their origin to external sources and could be part of a multi-stakeholder initiative (ILO Tripartite Declaration, Global Compact). Some regulatory regimes impose responsibility regarding child labour on states (ILO Conventions); others adopt a more direct approach in canvassing the responsibility of corporations (UN Human Rights Norms, OECD Guidelines).

Corporate codes of conduct

A number of corporations, especially the bigger or more prominent ones (Kinley and Tadaki 2004: 953), are increasingly formulating and adopting some kind of voluntary codes of conduct to show their commitment to labour/human rights.[1] The adoption of these codes – which can take various forms in terms of their nature, scope, objective, label, applicability and implementation (Frey 1997: 177–180, Cleveland 1998: 1551, Kinley and Tadaki 2004: 954–955, Picciotto 2003: 141–142) – is driven by several considerations (Anderson 2000: 486). For example, whereas certain corporations might have adopted codes of conduct because it is a 'right' or 'just' way of doing business (i.e., by making a public commitment to respect labour and human rights) (Cassel 1996: 1978–1980), many others might have been forced to respond to market pressure, including the behaviour of consumers, investors, the media, NGOs and unions (Cassel 1996: 177–178, Liubicic 1998: 114–116, Macek 2002: 110–112). Some other corporations might have perceived such codes as a current business fashion statement, or even a means of pre-empting state regulation (OECD 2001: 18), as well as a way of gaining competitive advantage over their business rivals in terms of the solicitation of public support (Lu 2000: 613, OECD 2000: 20–22, Picciotto 2003: 139–140). On the other hand, certain corporations might use the codes as a smokescreen (Engle 2004: 120), or a 'window dressing' device – a human face for inhumane business activities.

To gain a more specific picture of the responsibility assumed by corporations regarding child labour, let us take a closer look at the code adopted by Nike in the mid-1990s in view of the intense public scrutiny that its labour practices in Asia received. The criticism was directed, in particular, against the labour practices adopted by Nike's contractors. One may note that Nike tried to address this issue directly in its code of 1997.[2] The code stated that Nike is 'driven to do not only what is required, but what is expected of a leader' and it expected its 'business partners to do the same'. Under the code, Nike binds 'business partners . . . to specific standards of conduct' outlined therein. The 1997 code contained the following provision regarding child labour: 'Child Labor (Contractor) certifies it does not employ any person under the minimum age established

---

[1] See, for example, the codes available at http://www.codesofconduct.org/company.htm (last visited 5 January 2005).
[2] Available at http://actrav.itcilo.org/actrav-english/telearn/global/ilo/code/nike2.htm

108

by local law, or the age at which compulsory schooling has ended, whichever is greater, but in no case under the age of 14.'

It is clear that Nike's voluntary code of 1997 focused on the *non-employment* of child labour by its contractors. The minimum age for child labour was specified to be fourteen years or higher if so demanded by local laws. The code barely satisfied the requirements of the ILO Convention No. 138 on the Minimum Age for Admission to Employment, but did not respond to a common practice that allowed the employment of children, that is, work being taken and done at home. Nike's 2007 code tried to address this problem and also made improvements in other areas. The provision specific to child labour in the new code reads as follows:

> The contractor does not employ any person below the age of 18 to produce footwear. The contractor does not employ any person below the age of 16 to produce apparel, accessories or equipment. If at the time Nike production begins, the contractor employs people of the legal working age who are at least 15, that employment may continue, but the contractor will not hire any person going forward who is younger than the Nike or legal age limit, whichever is higher. To further ensure these age standards are complied with, the contractor *does not use any form of homework* for Nike production. (Emphasis added.)

In addition to increasing the minimum age limit and prohibiting the use of homework, the code introduced a pragmatic provision: if the contractor has already employed workers above the age of fifteen but less than eighteen, they may continue to work as long as the contractor does not hire workers below eighteen years in future. This provision makes sense because Nike may not always have exclusive contractors to manufacture its products and not all other corporations may have similar policies on child labour. Two other provisions of the 2007 code are worth noting. First, it requires contractors to post the code 'in all major workspaces, translated into the language of the employees'. Furthermore, contractors are obligated to 'train employees on their rights and obligations as defined by [the] code and applicable local laws'. The second improvement that the 2007 code made over the 1997 code was regarding the inspection of documents maintained by contractors showing compliance with the code: the documents could now be inspected by Nike or its designated monitor even without prior notice.

ILO Conventions

Two ILO Conventions directly deal with child labour: the ILO Convention No. 138 and the ILO Convention No. 182 Concerning the Prohibition and Immediate Action for the Elimination of the Worst Forms of Child Labour. It is apparent that both conventions impose responsibility vis-à-vis child labour on member states rather than on corporations (ILO Convention No. 138, Art. 12; ILO Convention No. 182, Art. 10). One may argue though that an effective discharge of responsibility on the part of states will require them to ensure that corporations under their respective jurisdictions comply with the goal of eliminating child labour (ICHRP 2002: 46–52, Reinisch 2005: 79–82, Zerk 2006: 83–91). But this is different from saying that the ILO Conventions impose a *direct* responsibility on corporations to eradicate child labour. As noted before, this practice was consistent with international law's treatment of corporations as its objects.

Nevertheless, it will be useful to compare the two conventions and analyse how the state responsibility in the area of child labour evolved over the years. The ILO Convention No. 138 was underpinned by a desire to establish an overarching and general international instrument regarding a minimum age for employment or work. The Convention required each member state 'to pursue a national policy designed to ensure the effective abolition of child labour' (Art. 1). A review of various provisions of the Convention indicates that the focus or the strategy adopted to abolish child labour was the non-employment of children of a certain age in certain sectors. The Convention seemingly did not consider what other measure states may need to take to achieve this goal, address the root causes of child labour, or respond adequately to the consequences that may follow on account of not employing children.

It also appears that the Convention No. 138 adopted a rights-based approach to child labour (Fyfe 2007: 76–79), which entailed a narrow obligation in terms of not hiring child labour. Although references were made to child labour adversely affecting the physical/mental development or health of children (Arts 1 and 7), this is not how we understand the development discourse now. In other words, the connection between child labour and disempowerment, discrimination or denial of freedoms was not explicitly acknowledged.[3]

---

[3] 'Child labour is work that is damaging to a child's physical, social, mental, psychological and spiritual development ... Child labour deprives children of their childhood and their

In contrast, the ILO Convention No. 182 responded to some of these issues surrounding child labour. The Convention acknowledged, for instance, that poverty was one of the root causes of child labour and that child labour impinged on an important right to basic education. It also took cognisance of the stark reality that the 'needs' of certain families might be adversely affected by prohibiting the employment of children. But most importantly, the Convention required states to take a range of 'effective and time-bound' measures to eliminate the worst forms of child labour. Rather than merely stopping at ensuring the non-employment of child labour, states are obliged to take steps for the 'rehabilitation and social integration' of these children (Art. 7(2)(b)). States should also 'ensure access to free basic education, and . . . vocational training for all children removed from the worst forms of child labour' (Art. 7(2)(c)).

One may conclude that although the ILO Convention No. 182 did not impose any direct responsibility on corporations, it dealt with the issue of child labour (albeit of the worst forms) in a more holistic manner. There was a tacit acknowledgement that the goal of eliminating (the worst forms of) child labour could not be achieved by simply prohibiting the employment of children.

ILO Tripartite Declaration Concerning Multinational Enterprises

The ILO released the Tripartite Declaration of Principles Concerning Multinational Enterprises and Social Policy (ILO Declaration) in 1977. The ILO Declaration was revised in 2000. The Declaration, the result of extensive research and consultation with all interested parties, was an attempt to reach an *'agreed solution in a highly complex and controversial area of social policy* through dialogue and negotiations between governments, employers and workers' (emphasis added). Keeping in mind its 'tripartite' character, the ILO Declaration invited 'governments of state members of the ILO, the employers' and workers' organisations concerned and the

dignity. They are deprived of an education and may be separated from their families. Children who do not complete their primary education are likely to remain illiterate and never acquire the skills needed to get a job and contribute to the development of a modern society.' Global Compact Principle Five, http://www.unglobalcompact.org/aboutTheGC/TheTen Principles/principle5.html (last visited 16 April 2009).

multinational enterprises operating in their territories to observe the principles embodied therein'.

For the purpose of this chapter it is useful to note that the 1977 Declaration did not contain any specific provision concerning the minimum age for work or employment. This is surprising because the Declaration contained several provisions as to various labour rights. This serious gap was, however, filled by the 2000 Revision of the ILO Declaration. The newly inserted paragraph 36 provides: 'Multinational enterprises, as well as national enterprises, should respect the minimum age for admission to employment or work in order to secure the effective abolition of child labour.' This is a welcome step for at least two reasons. First, unlike the ILO conventions, the Declaration imposes a *direct* responsibility on corporations. Second, the responsibility vis-à-vis child labour is deduced with reference to the ILO Convention Nos 138 and 182, thus relying on the existing international standards.

Nevertheless, even the ILO Declaration does not go as far as requiring corporations to take measures other than not employing people below the minimum age. This narrow responsibility might not prove adequate in eliminating child labour.

OECD Guidelines for Multinational Enterprises

The OECD Guidelines, which came into effect on 21 June 1976,[4] were revised in June 2000 and recently updated in May 2011.[5] The Guidelines are the result of the OECD engaging in a 'constructive dialogue with the business community, labour representatives, and non-government organisations' (NGOs).[6] They are recommendations jointly addressed by governments to multinational corporations (MNCs) (Preface, para. 1, para. I.1), and encourage MNCs to observe the principles and standards laid down in the Guidelines in areas such as human rights, disclosure, employment and industrial relations, environment, combating bribery,

---

[4] OECD Declaration on International Investment and Multinational Enterprises, 21 June 1976, reprinted in 15 *ILM* 967 (1976).

[5] OECD Declaration on International Investment and Multinational Enterprises 2000, reprinted in 40 *ILM* 237 (2001).

[6] The OECD Declaration and Decisions on International Investment and Multinational Enterprises: Basic Texts, DAFE/IME(2000)20 (8 November 2000), Foreword, 2–3.

consumer interests, science and technology, competition and taxation (paras II–X).

Similar to the ILO Declaration of 1977, the original text of the OECD Guidelines did not prescribe any responsibility regarding child labour. But this omission was cured by the 2000 Revision. A newly inserted provision reads as follows: 'Enterprises should, within the framework of applicable law, regulations and prevailing labour relations and employment practices: . . . contribute to the effective abolition of child labour' (para. IV.1.b).

Both the ILO Declaration and the OECD Guidelines have used the softer language of 'should' in defining the responsibility of corporations regarding child labour. Two textual differences should be noted though. First, the use of the word 'contribute' in the OECD Guidelines is wider in scope than the term 'respect' in the ILO Declaration. In other words, whereas the ILO Declaration stops at requesting corporations to respect the minimum age for employment, the OECD Guidelines expect corporations to make a contribution (arguably implying taking a range of measures) to achieve the goal of the effective abolition of child labour. Second, unlike the ILO Declaration, the responsibility under the OECD Guidelines is qualified by the 'prevailing labour relations and employment practices', among others. This may result in a dilution of responsibility because prevailing labour/ employment practices in many developing countries might fall short of the goals set in international labour conventions.

Global Compact

While addressing the World Economic Forum in Davos on 31 January 1999, the former UN Secretary-General Kofi Annan proposed the idea of a Global Compact consisting of nine principles in the areas of human rights, labour and the environment.[7] On 24 June 2004, during the Global Compact Leaders Summit, a tenth principle related to 'anti-corruption' was added.[8] It is claimed that the ten principles enjoy 'universal consensus' and 'are derived from' the Universal Declaration of Human Rights (UDHR), the

---

[7] 'Secretary-General Proposes Global Compact on Human Rights, Labour, Environment, in Address to World Economic Forum in Davos', Press Release SG/SM/6881 (1 February 1999), http://www0.un.org/News/Press/docs/1999/19990201.sgsm6881.html (last visited 1 September 2006).

[8] 'The Ten Principles', http://www.unglobalcompact.org/AboutTheGC/TheTenPrinciples/index.html (last visited 29 December 2006).

ILO Declaration of Fundamental Principles and Rights at Work, the Rio Declaration on Environment and Development and the UN's Convention against Corruption.[9]

The Global Compact is a multi-stakeholder initiative involving diverse actors such as governments, corporations, labour and civil society organisations, and the UN (Kell 2003: 37–39). It calls upon business enterprises to 'embrace, support and enact, within their sphere of influence, a set of core values' in the four covered areas: human rights, labour, environment and anti-corruption. The Global Compact 'in its simple form is the dissemination of and adherence to good business practices' (King 2001: 482). At a wider level, the vision of the Global Compact is 'to promote responsible corporate citizenship so that business can be part of the solution to the challenges of globalisation', that is, good corporate citizenship could contribute to establishing a 'more sustainable and inclusive global economy'.[10]

Principle five of the Compact provides that businesses 'should uphold the effective abolition of child labour'. Like other principles, this principle also does not give any clear indication of the responsibility of corporations. Upholding may simply mean complying with the minimum age for employment by not hiring any child labour. It seems, however, that the Global Compact Office expects more than this from its business participants. The following advice as part of a strategy for companies is quite telling:

> If an occurrence of child labour is identified, the children need to be removed from the workplace and *provided with viable alternatives*. These measures often include enrolling the children in schools and offering income-generating alternatives for the parents or above-working age members of the family. Companies need to be aware that, without support, children may be forced into worse circumstances such as prostitution, and that, in some instances where children are the sole providers of income, their immediate removal from work may exacerbate rather than relieve the hardship.[11]

It is apparent from the above advice that merely removing children from employment would not be sufficient; it might, in fact, prove counterproductive in some cases. Therefore, if corporations have to play an important role in abolishing child labour, their responsibility should not

---

[9] Ibid.

[10] 'About the Global Compact', http://www.unglobalcompact.org/AboutTheGC/index.html (last visited 30 October 2006).

[11] 'Global Compact Principle Five', above n. 3 (emphasis added).

primarily be negative in nature. As indicated in the list of actions that business may take, corporations may 'exercise influence on and provide positive incentives for subcontractors, suppliers and other business affiliates to combat child labour'.

UN Human Rights Norms

The Norms on the Responsibilities of Transnational Corporations [TNCs] and Other Business Enterprises with Regard to Human Rights (UN Norms) – which were drafted by the five-member UN Working Group on the Working Methods and Activities of TNCs over a period of four years (Weissbrodt and Kruger 2003: 903–907) – sought to codify the human rights responsibilities of corporations.[12] The UN Norms, coupled with the Commentary appended to them,[13] not only provided the most comprehensive and detailed statement of MNCs' human rights (including labour and environmental rights) obligations, but also outlined the procedure for their implementation (Deva 2004: 493, Nolan 2005: 581, Kinley and Chambers 2006: 447). Although the Sub-Commission on the Promotion and Protection of Human Rights approved the Norms,[14] they lack any 'legal standing'[15] and their future is bleak, in the light of an antagonistic position adopted by Professor John Ruggie, the UN Secretary-General's Special Representative on Human Rights and Transnational Corporations (SRSG).[16]

Nevertheless, as I have argued elsewhere (Deva 2004: 497–501), the UN Norms presented the most promising framework for establishing MNCs' accountability for human rights violations to date (see Rule 2004: 326). First of all, instead of being limited to labour and/or environmental rights, the UN Norms presented a comprehensive list of human rights obligations.

[12] UN Norms on the Responsibilities of Transnational Corporations and Other Business Enterprises with Regard to Human Rights, UN Doc. E/CN.4/Sub.2/2003/12/Rev.2 (13 August 2003).

[13] Commentary on the Norms on the Responsibilities of Transnational Corporations and other Business Enterprises with Regard to Human Rights, UN Doc. E/CN.4/Sub.2/2003/38/Rev.2.

[14] Sub-Commission on the Promotion and Protection of Human Rights, Resolution 2003/16 (13 August 2003), E/CN.4/Sub.2/2003/L.11, 52–55.

[15] Commission on Human Rights, 60th Session, Agenda Item 16, E/CN.4/2004/L.73/Rev.1 (16 April 2004), para. (c).

[16] Commission on Human Rights, Interim Report of the Special Representative of the Secretary General on the Issue of Human Rights and Transnational Corporations and Other Business Enterprises, E/CN.4/2006/97 (22 February 2006), 14–17.

Second, in terms of the nature of obligations also, the Norms clearly made an encouraging advancement vis-à-vis prior regulatory initiatives. As MNCs could violate human rights in several ways (including by failing to act), it is insufficient to draft obligations in conventional 'negative' terms, i.e., that MNCs should or shall not violate human rights. The UN Norms tried to overcome this problem by imposing 'positive' obligations on MNCs (e.g., paras 1 and 12). MNCs shall not only refrain from directly or indirectly contributing to, and benefiting from, human rights violations, but also 'use their influence in order to promote and ensure respect for human rights' (Commentary (b) to para. 1).

Third, the UN Norms proposed specific provisions for the implementation of human rights norms (paras 15–19; see Weissbrodt and Kruger 2003: 915–921). Besides asking corporations to adopt, disseminate and internally implement the obligations laid down therein (para. 15), paragraph 17 of the UN Norms urged states to 'establish and reinforce the necessary legal and administrative framework for ensuring that the Norms' are implemented by MNCs. The Norms also proposed independent and transparent periodic monitoring as well as verification by national and international mechanisms (including those of the UN) (para. 16). This again was a departure from the existing *indirect* mode of implementation in which the responsibility of enforcing corporate human rights responsibilities lies solely and exclusively with states. Note must be taken of another significant provision of the UN Norms which provided for prompt, adequate and effective reparation to persons and communities adversely affected by the failure of MNCs (or other business enterprises) to comply with their responsibilities outlined therein (para. 18).

Let us now turn our attention to the nature of responsibility contemplated by the UN Norms regarding child labour. Two provisions of the Norms are relevant here. Whereas para. 5 provided that corporations 'shall not use forced or compulsory labour', para. 6 required corporations 'to respect the rights of children to be protected from economic exploitation' as forbidden by various international instruments and national legislation. It is noteworthy that the UN Norms did not even use the term 'child labour' – rather, they conceived responsibility in terms of 'economic exploitation of children', a term which is defined to mean employment or work in any occupation before a child completes compulsory schooling, or the employment of children in a manner that is harmful to their health or development (Commentary (a) to para. 6). The Norms, thus, perceived child labour as an obstacle to development.

Similar to the strategies outlined by the Global Compact Office, the Commentary to the Norms contemplated that corporations shall create and implement a plan to eliminate child labour (Commentary (d) to para. 6). Such a plan may include provisions for the suitable education or vocational training of the children removed from the workforce and the employment of parents or older siblings of such children.

Responsibility for responsive corporations

On the basis of the review of existing regulatory initiatives given in the section above, a number of broad conclusions could be drawn regarding the responsibility of corporations regarding child labour. First, although the ILO Convention No. 138 was in place when the OECD Guidelines and the ILO Declaration were being drafted in the mid-1970s, it is surprising that they did not have any specific provision relating to child labour. Second, whereas the initiatives drafted earlier conceived the responsibility of corporations in terms of 'non-employment', the initiatives drafted (or revised) in the last decade go much beyond this in that they envisage corporations taking on additional measures to contribute towards the effective abolition of child labour. Third, some recent regulatory initiatives have imposed a direct responsibility on corporations, though the focus is still on reaching corporations through states. Fourth, the review reveals that most of the initiatives do not specifically outline the responsibility, if any, of a corporation for child labour being hired by its suppliers or contractors. Fifth, if we leave aside the domestic constitutional or legal framework or customary international law, we are still far from having legally binding obligations on corporations on the issue of child labour.

As indicated at the outset in the first section of this chapter, I argue that the responsibility of corporations (as well of states) regarding child labour should be responsive to the needs of fulfilling the goal. The responsibility should entail corporations taking several *core* and *complementary* measures.[17] The core measures could be predefined and common to all corporations, e.g., prohibition on the employment of children in hazardous

---

[17] Archie Carroll has proposed the following four strategies of social responsiveness: reaction, defence, accommodation and proaction, Crane and Matten 2007: 53. The model of responsive responsibility canvassed here focuses only on accommodation and proaction elements.

industries, or the elimination of all practices designated as worst forms of child labour. Taking these measures will satisfy the minimum threshold of corporate responsibility.

However, such core measures might not prove adequate in achieving the goal of eradicating child labour. The core measures should, therefore, be supported by other complementary measures aimed at addressing the root causes of child labour. Such measures – for example, providing education or vocational training, offering childcare and health facilities, offering employment to parents, ensuring alternative sources of income, introducing labelling schemes – may be ascertained in view of the specific needs of a particular sector, corporation or region. Responsive complementary responsibility should also require corporations to ensure that their business partners, contractors and suppliers do comply with the applicable national as well as international child labour laws and standards. By doing so, corporations will not only be acting as good corporate citizens but will also mitigate the adverse effects of their business activities (see Porter and Kramer 2006: 9–10).

As Table 7.1 shows, the existing regulatory initiatives do not generally envisage responsibility in terms of taking robust responsive complementary measures. It is critical that this deficit is cured and that the problem of child labour is dealt with in a holistic manner (Wazir 2002): all stakeholders should be required to assume a range of core and complementary responsibilities. The responsibility of corporations should not be limited to the core responsibility of not employing child labour, on the ground that it is not part of their business or mandate. The reason is simple: duties should be appropriate to secure the realisation of given rights. A narrow negative responsibility not to hire child labour could not fully protect the human rights of children. Although the responsibility of corporations need not be equivalent to that of states, it must also not be insignificant or illusory.

Conclusion

Child labour is a socio-economic cultural reality in many parts of the world. An effective elimination of child labour will require joint efforts on the part of states, civil society and corporations. It is increasingly realised, as reflected in some of the regulatory initiatives surveyed above, that the goal of abolishing child labour could not be accomplished by merely prohibiting

Table 7.1 Nature of responsibility under existing regulatory initiatives

	Core measures	*Responsive measures*	*Nature of responsibility*	*Extent of responsibility*
Codes of conduct (Nike)	Yes (both codes of 1997 and 2007)	Some elements present in the 2007 code	Internal, voluntary, self-regulation	Contractors and business partners bound
ILO Conventions	Yes (in both Convention Nos 138 and 182)	Only in Convention No. 182	Direct responsibility only on states	Not found
ILO Tripartite Declaration	Yes (after the 2000 Revision)	Not found	Direct responsibility	Not found
OECD Guidelines	Yes (after the 2000 Revision)	Arguable but not clearly found	Direct responsibility	Suppliers and business partners are to be encouraged
Global Compact	Yes	Found only in the Commentary to principles	Direct responsibility	Work with suppliers and business partners
UN Human Rights Norms	Yes	Yes (especially in the Commentary)	Both indirect and direct responsibility	Contractors and business partners are bound as independent parties

the employment of children below a certain age limit. Non-employment of child labour has to be complemented with other initiatives aimed at drying up the supply of child labour. At the same time, (dis)incentives might have to be created to reduce the demand for child labour.

I have proposed that corporations have a responsibility beyond not hiring child labour. This responsive approach to ascertain the contents of responsibility may be criticised for giving too much say to public opinion and other actors external to corporations (Tullberg 2005: 261), or for expecting too much from corporations. But it seems that corporations are already responsive actors – they respond to various market variables or conditions all the time while taking business decisions. They should similarly be responsive to the operating social environment in accordance with their nature of business, extent of operations, availability of resources and socio-economic conditions. As to the rising expectations, one may say that the expectations are proportional to the power, influence and activities of corporations.

119

References

Anderson, J.C. (2000) 'Respecting Human Rights: Multinational Corporations Strike Out', *University of Pennsylvania Journal of Labour and Employment Law* 2: 463.

Cassel, D. (1996) 'Corporate Initiatives: A Second Human Rights Revolution?', *Fordham International Law Journal* 19: 1963.

Cleveland, S.H. (1998) 'Global Labour Rights and the Alien Tort Claims Act', *Texas Law Review* 76: 1533.

Crane, A. and Matten, D. (2007) *Business Ethics*, 2nd edition (Oxford University Press).

Deva, S. (2004) 'UN's Human Rights Norms for Transnational Corporations and Other Business Enterprises: An Imperfect Step in the Right Direction?', *ILSA Journal of International and Comparative Law* 10: 493.

Engle, E. (2004) 'Corporate Social Responsibility: Market-Based Remedies for International Human Rights Violations?', *Willamette Law Review* 40: 103.

Fitzgerald, S. (2005) 'Corporate Accountability for Human Rights Violations in Australian Domestic Law', *Australian Journal of Human Rights* 11: 33.

Frey, B.A. (1997) 'The Legal and Ethical Responsibilities of Transnational Corporations in the Protection of International Human Rights', *Minnesota Journal of Global Trade* 6: 153.

Fyfe, A. (2007) *The Worldwide Movement against Child Labour: Progress and Future Directions* (ILO).

International Council on Human Rights Policy (ICHRP) (2002) *Beyond Voluntarism: Human Rights and the Developing International Legal Obligations of Companies* (ICHRP).

Kell, G. (2003) 'The Global Compact: Origins, Operations, Progress, Challenges', *Journal of Corporate Citizenship* 11: 35.

King, B. (2001) 'The UN Global Compact: Responsibility for Human Rights, Labour Relations, and the Environment in Developing Nations', *Cornell International Law Journal* 34: 481.

Kinley, D. and Chambers, R. (2006) 'The UN Human Rights Norms for Corporations: The Private Implications of Public International Law', *Human Rights Law Review* 6: 447.

Kinley, D. and Tadaki, J. (2004) 'From Talk to Walk: The Emergence of Human Rights Responsibilities for Corporations at International Law', *Virginia Journal of International Law* 44: 931.

Liubicic, R.J. (1998) 'Corporate Codes of Conduct and Product Labelling Schemes: The Limits and Possibilities of Promoting International Labour Rights through Private Initiatives', *Law and Policy in International Business* 39: 111.

Lu, S-P. (2000) 'Corporate Codes of Conduct and the FTC: Advancing Human Rights through Deceptive Advertising Law', *Columbia Journal of Transnational Law* 38: 603.

Macek, E.E. (2002) 'Scratching the Corporate Back: Why Corporations Have No Incentive to Define Human Rights', *Minnesota Journal of Global Trade* 11: 101.

Nolan, J. (2005) 'With Power Comes Responsibility: Human Rights and Corporate Accountability', *University of New South Wales Law Journal* 28: 581.

OECD (2000) *Codes of Corporate Conduct: An Expanded Review of their Content*, TD/TC/WP(99)56/FINAL.

OECD (2001) *Corporate Responsibility: Private Initiatives and Public Goals*.

Picciotto, S. (2003) 'Rights, Responsibilities and Regulation of International Business', *Columbia Journal of Transnational Law* 42: 131.

Porter, M.E. and Kramer, M.R. (2006) 'The Link between Competitive Advantage and Corporate Social Responsibility', *Harvard Business Review* (December): 1.

Reinisch, A. (2005) 'The Changing International Legal Framework for Dealing with Non-State Actors', in P. Alston (ed.) *Non-State Actors and Human Rights* (Oxford University Press).

Rule, T. (2004) 'Using "Norms" to Change International Law: UN Human Rights Laws Sneaking in through the Back Door?', *Chicago Journal of International Law* 5: 326.

Tripartite Declaration of Principles Concerning Multinational Enterprises and Social Policy (1977) ILO, 204th Session, 16 November 1977, reprinted in 17 *ILM* 422 (1978).

Tripartite Declaration of Principles Concerning Multinational Enterprises and Social Policy (2000), reprinted in 41 *ILM* 186 (2002).

Tullberg, J. (2005) 'Reflections upon the Responsive Approach to Corporate Social Responsibility', *Business Ethics: A European Review* 14(3): 261.

Walker, M. and Parent, M.M. (2010) 'Toward an Integrated Framework of Corporate Social Responsibility, Responsiveness, and Citizenship in Sport', *Sport Management Review* 13: 198.

Wazir, R. (2002) 'Eliminating Child Labour: Do NGO Interventions Add Up to a Strategy?', *Indian Journal of Labour Economics* 45(3): 615.

Weissbrodt, D. (2005) 'Business and Human Rights', *University of Cincinnati Law Review* 74: 55.

Weissbrodt, D. and Kruger, M. (2003) 'Norms of the Responsibilities of Transnational Corporations and Other Business Enterprises with Regard to Human Rights', *American Journal of International Law* 97: 901.

Westfield, E. (2002) 'Globalisation, Governance, and Multinational Enterprise Responsibility: Corporate Codes of Conduct in the 21st Century', *Virginia Journal of International Law* 42: 1075.

Zerk, J.A. (2006) *Multinational and Corporate Social Responsibility: Limitations and Opportunities in International Law* (Cambridge University Press).

Part IV
Development through trade and / or aid?

8
The very basis of our existence

Labour and the neglected environmental dimension of sustainable development

BEATE SJÅFJELL*

The very basis of our existence

As eloquently put by Advocate General Ruiz-Jarabo Colomer:

> [A]cceptable environment is not the product of social development, but a prerequisite for it to exist, and is a right bound up with human life, without which there is neither mankind nor society nor law.[1]

Sustainable development is an overarching societal goal which encompasses three main dimensions: economic development, social development and environmental protection. The Brundtland Commission defined sustainable development as a development that 'meets the needs of the present without compromising the ability of the future generations to meet their own needs' (World Commission on Environment and Development 1987: 43; for the background to this 'slogan', intended to encompass the whole concept of sustainable development, see Bugge 2008). Sustainable

* Professor, dr. juris, Department of Private Law, Faculty of Law, University of Oslo, and project leader for the research project 'Sustainable Companies'. All comments are welcome: beate.sjafjell@jus.uio.no. Thank you to Tonia Novitz for inviting me to write this chapter and to Stein Evju for helpful comments on the last section. The usual disclaimers apply.
[1] *Opinion of Advocate General Ruiz-Jarabo Colomer in Commission* v. *Council*, Case C-176/03 paras 52–70 with the quote in footnote 51 with reference to Loperena Rota, D., Los derechos al medio ambiente adecuado y a su protección, Revista Electrónica de Derecho Ambiental, No. 3, November 1999.

development has a strong legal position among the ultimate objectives of the European Union.[2] This is underpinned by the growing recognition in the EU of the inextricable entity of humanity, our natural environment and our economic system (Craig 2002). In the search for the balancing that this goal requires within the non-negotiable limits of our planet, the principle of sustainable development is the key. This principle requires the integration of environmental protection requirements in all areas, with the aim of achieving sustainable development.

Conflicts and the search for a balance between conflicting interests are inherent to the quest for a sustainable development. Strong economic interests and lobbying by trade unions ensure that the aspect that gets attention is the challenge of combining economic growth and the socio-economic goal of more jobs, in other words two of the three inter-related dimensions of sustainable development. In that which later became known just as 'the Lisbon Agenda', the European Council set out the new challenge and the new goal of becoming 'the most competitive and dynamic knowledge-based economy in the world'.[3] Although the European Council stated in 2001 that sustainable development is a 'fundamental objective under the Treaties', agreed on a strategy for sustainable development and expressly added an environmental dimension to the Lisbon Agenda,[4] the focus remains on growth and jobs.

The Commission proposes a new start for the Lisbon Strategy, focusing its efforts around two principal tasks – *delivering stronger, lasting growth and creating more and better jobs*.[5] The third dimension, environmental protection, is far too often neglected in practice, in spite of ever stronger warnings from, notably, the IPCC (2008), and an increasingly enhanced position for the objective of environmental protection – as we will see below – in the Treaties of the European Union.

---

[2] As of the Treaty of Lisbon (2007) (OJ 2007 C 306/01), in force 1 December 2009, the European Union replaces and succeeds the European Community. This chapter will therefore only use 'Community' and related terms in their historical context.

[3] Presidency Conclusions of the Lisbon European Council of 23–24 March 2000 (100/1/00) para. 5. The new challenge was that of a 'quantum shift resulting from globalisation and the challenges of a new knowledge-driven economy', to which the Union must react in a manner 'consistent with its values and concepts of society' (para. 1).

[4] Presidency Conclusions of the Gothenburg European Council 15–16 June 2001 (SN 200/1/01 Rev 1) paras 1 and 19–21.

[5] Emphasis in original, see COM(2005)24, Working Together for Growth and Jobs: A New Start for the Lisbon Strategy, available at http://ec.europa.eu/growthandjobs/pdf/COM 2005_024_en.pdf (last visited 2 December 2009).

126

Sustainable development encompasses a complexity of interrelated issues and aspects. Within the social dimension, there is both the risk of conflict and the potential for positive connections between labour interests in developed countries and the developmental and human rights aspects of the situation for workers in developing countries. These aspects have been covered by other contributors to this book. My focus will therefore be solely on the neglected environmental dimension of sustainable development.

The main argument made in this chapter is that ecological sustainable development as the new law is not only supported by normative necessity but also has a legal basis in the law of the European Union.[6] The political and bureaucratic will to carry through the necessary practical implementation is, however, lacking. This does not affect the validity of the legal basis or that of the obligations flowing from the legal basis. Rather, it indicates a need to keep repeating the message until it gets through. This chapter outlines the legal basis and its implications for the prioritisation between the three dimensions in EU law and concludes with some reflections on the possible contribution of labour to the necessary transition to sustainable societies.

Sustainable development and its environmental dimension in EU Law

Environmental protection and sustainable development as general objectives of EU law

The term general objectives of EU law is used here to denote the objectives of the European Union as they are stated in the relevant provisions of the Treaties.[7] These objectives are regarded as objectives of the law of the EU,

---

[6] 'Normative' is used in this article as opposed to 'descriptive', i.e., it refers to how things should be, rather than how they are (although, of course, the two may coincide).

[7] Until 1 December 2009 particularly Article 2 of the former EC Treaty, i.e., the Treaty on the Functioning of the European Union, formerly the Treaty Establishing the European Community (1957), last amended by the Treaty of Lisbon (OJ 2008 C115 (consolidated version)), hereinafter referred to as the EC Treaty in historical contexts and abbreviated TFEU otherwise in accordance with the new reference style of the Lisbon Treaty; as well as the former Article 2 and Article 6 of the Treaty on European Union (1992), last amended by the Treaty of Lisbon (OJ 2008 C115 (consolidated version)), hereinafter referred to as the EU Treaty (abbreviated TEU in accordance with the new reference style of the Lisbon Treaty). Now see notably the new Article 3 TEU (ex Article 2 EU).

based on the premise that the general point of EU law is to facilitate the achievement of the objectives of the EU. Discussing the legislative objectives is important for several reasons. In EU law, with its teleological approach, objectives have a special status. The case law of the European Court of Justice illustrates this with its repeated reference to and emphasis on the objective of the contested legislation or, for example, of the Treaty provision to be interpreted (Sjåfjell 2009a: Part III). Analysing the objectives may tell us the direction that EU law is taking or, should the perception of the objectives have become unclear or out of focus, the analysis may highlight the objectives, indicating the direction that EU law should be taking. The position of environmental protection and sustainable development as general objectives of EU law therefore is highly significant. The general objectives of EU law may be summed up as the ultimate goal of the good society, the achievement of which may be said to consist of five main elements: economic development; social development; environmental protection; the respect for human rights; and contributing to global development (ibid.: Sections 10.3–10.8). Many of these elements are encompassed by the overarching objective of sustainable development.

The underlying motivation of this European project has right from the beginning been peace – the end to all wars.[8] With the forceful support of the European Court of Justice starting decades ago, environmental protection has been elevated from a position of neglect to one of the 'essential objectives' of the European Union.[9] This has been reflected gradually in the Treaties, with environmental protection being promoted to the level of the main objectives' provision of the then EC Treaty by the Treaty of Maastricht, while the Amsterdam Treaty gave us environmental protection as an independent goal, 'rather than an incidental requirement of economic growth' (Craig and De Búrca 2008: 21). The Lisbon Treaty has not changed the terminology of the setting out of the objective concerning environmental protection, namely that of achieving 'a high level of protection and improvement of the quality of the environment' (Article 3(3) TEU). Nevertheless, through the enhanced position of sustainable development

---

[8] Clearer than ever after the implementation of the Lisbon Treaty, see the new Article 3(1) TEU: 'The Union's aim is to promote peace, its values and the well-being of its peoples.'
[9] Which the relevant directive 'must be seen in the perspective of', *ADBHU*, Case 240/83 para. 13. We see here the use of the general goals of the EU in the interpretation of secondary legislation. See *inter alia* Jacobs 2006 and Sjåfjell 2009a: Section 10.5.

as a Treaty goal (and the further strengthening of the *principle* of sustainable development), to which I will return below, environmental protection as a Treaty goal may be said to have an even stronger position after the amendments following the Lisbon Treaty.

Sustainable development, as an objective of EU law, encompasses several of the other general objectives: social and economic development; environmental protection; global development; as well as some aspects of the protection of human rights. For that and other reasons, sustainable development has a special status as an – perhaps even *the* – overarching objective of EU law. The provisions setting out the objectives of the EU in the Treaties pre-Lisbon also mentioned sustainable development, and, from the context and based on other sources, the global aspect of sustainable development as an EU objective was relatively clear.[10] The finally ratified Lisbon Treaty emphasises the position of *global* sustainable development as an overarching objective, while also making clearer its recognition of the three main dimensions of that objective. We can see the latter in Article 3(3) TEU which declares that:

> The Union shall ... work for the *sustainable development of Europe* based on balanced economic growth and price stability, a highly competitive social market economy, aiming at full employment and social progress, and a high level of protection and improvement of the quality of the environment. (Emphasis added.)

The former, the global aspect of sustainable development, is enhanced in an unprecedented manner on Treaty level, in Article 3(5) TEU:

> In its relations with the wider world, the Union shall uphold and promote its values and interests and contribute to the protection of its citizens. *It shall contribute to peace, security, the sustainable development of the Earth, solidarity and mutual respect among peoples, free and fair trade, eradication of poverty and the protection of human rights,* in particular the rights of the child, as well as to the strict observance and the development of international law, including respect for the principles of the United Nations Charter. (Emphasis added.)

This is underlined further in Article 21(2)(d) and (f) TEU dealing with the relationship between the Union and the international community, where the Union expresses its will to work to:

---

[10] Albeit the wording in then Article 2 EC (as opposed to Article 2 EU) was criticised for lack of clarity concerning sustainable development versus sustainable growth (this is indubitably clarified by the Lisbon Treaty's terminology). See Sjåfjell 2009a: Section 10.7.

> foster the *sustainable economic, social and environmental development of developing countries,* with the primary aim of eradicating poverty;
>
> . . .
>
> help develop international measures to preserve and *improve the quality of the environment and the sustainable management of global natural resources,* in order to ensure *sustainable development.*(Emphasis added.)

The enhancement of environmental protection through the principle of sustainable development

The codification of the principle of sustainable development in the environmental integration rule has enhanced the position of sustainable development as an overarching objective and especially that of its environmental dimension. [11] The Maastricht Treaty strengthened this environmental integration rule that had been introduced as a Treaty provision in a somewhat more reticent form by the Single European Act.[12] The Commission later requested that the rule containing the principle be specified in Treaty chapters on various sectors.[13] The interesting result was that the Treaty of Amsterdam promoted the rule to the level of principles in Part one of the EC Treaty, adding the goal of promoting sustainable development and extending its scope from 'policies' to 'policies and activities', giving us the wording in Article 6 EC as it was until the amendment following the Lisbon Treaty. 'Environmental protection requirements *must* be integrated into the definition and implementation of the Community policies and activities referred to in Article 3, in particular with a view to promoting sustainable development.' (Emphasis added.) According to Krämer (2007: 21), this rule 'calls for a permanent, continuous "greening" of all Community policies'. Through the Lisbon Treaty, the environmental integration rule is even further strengthened through the removal of the reference to (then) Article 3 EC, making it applicable for absolutely all of the Union's activities, giving us the following clear legal basis:

---

[11] Ex Article 6 EC, now Article 11 TFEU.

[12] Single European Act version of the principle in Article 130r(2) EC: 'Environmental protection requirements shall be a component of the Community's other policies.' Maastricht Treaty version: 'Environmental protection requirements must be integrated into the definition and implementation of other Community policies.'

[13] Presumably to raise awareness, as the wording of then Article 130r(2) EC applied to all sectors. See Krämer 2004: 34.

> Environmental protection requirements *must* be integrated into the definition
> and implementation of the Union policies and activities, in particular with a
> view to promoting sustainable development.[14]

The Union's emphasis on the principle of sustainable development is
apparent also from the earlier amendment of the Preamble to the EU Treaty
to expressly refer to the 'principle of sustainable development'.[15] The
original Preamble stated that the promotion of economic and social progress was to take place within the context of the internal market and of
'reinforced cohesion and environmental protection', and declared the
determination to ensure that 'advances in economic integration are accompanied by parallel progress in other fields'. The desire to recognise and
promote the principle of sustainable development through amending the
Preamble to expressly include the principle is rather striking. The express
inclusion may also be found in the EU Charter of Fundamental Rights[16] as
well as in the Preamble to the EEA Agreement.[17]

The integration of environmental protection into the Treaties is not a
mere political declaration. The European Court of Justice has repeatedly
sought to strengthen the position of environmental protection as a Treaty
objective, notably in the landmark judgement from 2005 concerning the
Community's competence to mandate criminal penalties on a national
level to enforce environmental protection. The Court referred to the status
of environmental protection as one of the 'essential objectives of the
Community' and added:

> Furthermore, in the words of Article 6 EC [now Article 11 TFEU] '[e]nviron-
> mental protection requirements must be integrated into the definition and
> implementation of the Community policies and activities', a provision which
> *emphasises the fundamental nature of that objective* and its *extension across the
> range of those policies and activities* . . .[18]

---

[14] Emphasis added, Article 11 TFEU.

[15] Done by the Treaty of Amsterdam (1997) (OJ 1997 C 340/1–144), Article 1.

[16] Article 37 of the Charter of Fundamental Rights of the European Union (OJ 2000 C 364/01),
as adapted at Strasbourg, on 12 December 2007: 'A high level of environmental protection
and the improvement of the quality of the environment must be integrated into the policies
of the Union and ensured in accordance with the principle of sustainable development.' The
Charter now has the same legal value as the Treaties, see the new Article 6 TEU.

[17] Agreement on the European Economic Area (OJ 1994 L 1/3–36), which apparently was the
first international legal instrument to use the term. See Sands 2003: 252.

[18] *Commission* v. *Council (criminal penalties)*, Case C-176/03 paras 41–42 (emphasis added),
where the Court went on to demonstrate the scope of that statement in its judgement, paras
47–48.

That the environmental integration rule enhances the position of environmental protection as a general objective (which therefore is relevant for all sectors) is even more clearly expressed by the Court, sitting in the Grand Chamber:

> Moreover, since requirements relating to environmental protection, which is one of the essential objectives of the Community ... must, according to Article 6 EC, 'be integrated into the definition and implementation of ... Community policies and activities', *such protection must be regarded as an objective which also forms part of the common transport policy.*[19]

The Court then went on to say that environmental protection therefore could be promoted with the legal basis concerning the common transport policy.[20] Jacobs (2006: 204) has commented that this judgement is a natural consequence of 'the importance now attached to the protection of the environment because of increasing evidence of environmental deterioration' and adds that, in reaching its conclusion, the Court 'rightly attached importance to the fact that criminal sanctions have come to be seen as necessary means to ensure effective environmental protection' (ibid.: 205).

Further strengthening the position of environmental protection as an objective is the fact that the rule in (now) Article 11 TFEU may be seen as implementing the EU's international responsibilities. Illustrative is *PreussenElektra*, a judgement that has been characterised as 'remarkable'. There the Court refused to extend the definition of state aid to catch the German legislation in question, and even accepted certain discriminatory measures, giving priority to environmental objectives in accordance with international climate change obligations (Thieme and Rudolf 2002: 229). In its analysis of whether the disputed German provisions were nevertheless compatible with the Treaty, the Court started by considering the aim of the contested provisions, linking this to the Community's international obligations:

> The use of renewable energy sources for producing electricity, which a statute such as the amended Stromeinspeisungsgesetz is intended to promote, is useful for protecting the environment in so far as it contributes to the reduction in emissions of greenhouse gases which are amongst the *main causes of climate change which the European Community and its Member States have pledged to combat.*

[19] *Commission* v. *Council*, Case C-440/05 para. 60 (emphasis added).
[20] Ibid. paras 60, 66 and 70. See a further discussion of this aspect of the environmental integration rule in the light of other significant case law, Sjåfjell 2009a: Section 10.5.2.

> Growth in that use is amongst the *priority objectives which the Community and its Member States intend to pursue in implementing the obligations which they contracted by virtue of the United Nations Framework Convention on Climate Change* . . . and by virtue of the [Kyoto Protocol] signed by the European Community and its Member States on 29 April 1998 . . . (Emphasis added.)[21]

The Court further emphasised the obligation to take environmental concerns into consideration with reference to the environmental integration rule, and the contested national provisions were found to be compatible with the Treaty.[22]

The legal significance of the environmental integration rule in Article 11 TFEU

In my earlier work, I have argued that the general objectives entail legal obligations for the EU institutions, in the form, *inter alia*, of an obligation for the EU institutions to seek a balance between the general objectives and a duty to actively work to achieve these objectives.[23] For several reasons, which space does not allow me to go into here, the argument may, generally speaking, be said to be strengthened by the Lisbon Treaty. I will focus solely on the significance of Article 11 TFEU as concerns the legal obligations to promote sustainable development and particularly its environmental dimension.[24]

Article 11 TFEU imposes a legal obligation to integrate environmental protection requirements into all sectors of EU law. The addition of the aim of sustainable development to the environmental integration rule is legally significant. Article 11 strengthens the position of sustainable development as a general objective, and it establishes the direction to be followed when integrating environmental protection requirements into all sectors. When we add this to the very definition of sustainable development, which in itself necessitates the balancing of various objectives, this enhances the argument in favour of the existence of a principle of EU law that requires the balancing of the general objectives (Jans 2000: 18). Further, it reinforces

---

[21] *PreussenElektra*, Case C-379/98 paras 72–74.

[22] Ibid.: para. 76.

[23] See Sjåfjell 2009a: Chapter 10.

[24] These arguments were also valid – and have been put forward – with respect to then Article 6 EC, see ibid.: especially Section 10.7.3. The amendments made by the Lisbon Treaty further reinforce my conclusions.

the view that this balancing must have sustainable development as its ultimate goal, with emphasis given to its environmental protection dimension (Dhondt 2003: 484, Sjåfjell 2009a: Sect. 10.9.3).

Article 11 requires the EU institutions to undertake their activities in a certain way and with a particular goal: in other words, Article 11 requires action. This duty to act is at least in principle enforceable before the Court of Justice (von der Groeben and Schwarze 2003: 644). The action required by Article 11 applies to all stages of a policy or activity, as is apparent from the words 'definition and implementation'. The sustainable development principle is meant to be decisive during the shaping of the policies and activities and integral to their implementation.

Although the Court of Justice has not expressly stated that such obligations flow from the environmental integration rule, its use of, and repeated reference to, the rule as 'a provision which emphasises the *fundamental nature of [the environmental protection] objective* and its *extension across the range of those policies and activities'*[25] underlines the significance of the provision and supports the argument made here.[26] The normative necessity of working towards sustainable development further strengthens the case in favour of a legal duty to act to achieve this overarching goal.

Legal obligations meet political and practical limitations

As early as at the Rhodes Summit of 1988, the heads of government of the European Community, with reference to 'environmental problems of increasing magnitude', declared sustainable development to be 'one of the overriding objectives of all Community policies'.[27] This has been followed

---

[25] E.g., *Commission* v. *Council (criminal penalties)*, Case C-176/03 paras 41–42 (emphasis added).

[26] The opinions of the Advocates General have often been much clearer (see, for example, Opinion of Advocate General Jacobs in *PreussenElektra*, Case C-379/98 and Opinion of Advocate General Léger in *The Queen* v. *Secretary of State for the Environment, Transport and the Regions*, Case C-371/98), perhaps illustrating that sometimes the Opinions are 'jurisprudential racehorses, galloping directly to the finishing line decked out in vivid colours', with the judgements following at a more sedate pace (Arnull 2006: 16).

[27] Presidency Conclusions of the European Council, Rhodes, 2–3 December 1988 (DOC/88/10). At the same Summit, the government heads declared that the completion of 'the Single Market cannot be regarded as an end in itself, it pursues a much wider objective' and in the 'wider international context' the Community and the member states declared their desire to play a leading role in achieving 'a better quality of life for all the peoples of the world' (Annex 1).

up by an abundance of high-level policy documents that emphasise the significance of environmental protection, especially when linked to the goal of sustainable development.[28] The question is, of course, whether this emphasis and the legal obligations flowing from the environmental integration rule have been followed up in practice.

There are indications of a willingness (in principle) to integrate environmental protection properly (COM (1999) 263 final, Krämer 2004: 37). According to the Cardiff process, the Community is to undertake environmental impact assessment, with the aim of integrating environmental protection where necessary.[29] This was followed up by the Commission with its introduction of the Impact Assessment System in 2003.[30] The danger has been mentioned that the impact assessment could turn into a cost-benefit analysis of economic effects for economic operator and, as the environmental effects are difficult to assess precisely, of focus being on the economic costs in the narrow understanding of the term (Krämer 2004: 37–38).

The first external report of the new Impact Assessment System is not encouraging. The report indicates that it is a 'widespread problem' that impact assessment is carried out 'to justify a policy choice already made at the beginning of the process',[31] and that the quality is 'found to be varying and often unsatisfactory'.[32] Further, there may be a danger of more focus on 'reducing administrative burdens on businesses' (through 'better regulation') than on integrating the aim of sustainable development.[33] Not implemented properly, the principle of sustainable development – instead of making environmental law less marginal – may serve to 'subsume

[28] E.g., Presidency Conclusions of the Brussels European Council 15–16 June 2006 (10633/1/06 REV 1).

[29] COM(2002)276 final: Communication from the Commission on Impact Assessment. See Dhondt 2003: 25.

[30] The system is meant to 'replace and integrate all sectoral assessments of direct and indirect impacts of proposed measures into one global instrument', with a twofold aim: achieve the 'balanced and comprehensive assessment of economic, social and environmental impacts' linked to the EU's Sustainable Development Strategy, and facilitate 'Better Regulation'; The Evaluation Partnership, 'Evaluation of the Commission's Impact Assessment System. Final Report – Executive Summary' (report submitted to the Secretariat General of the European Commission, April 2007): 2.

[31] The Evaluation Partnership 2007: 5.

[32] Ibid.: 6. However, the report does point out that the system is still at an early stage (at 2).

[33] See 'Enhancing Impact Assessment', (speech by Catherine Day, Secretary-General of the European Commission, 28 June 2007).

environmental considerations' and 'perpetuate an approach' to economic activities that encourage environmental problems (Sands 2003: 9).

Clearly, there are grounds for criticising the lack of implementation of policies promoting sustainable development. There seems to be a frustrating trend of a lack of cross-sector cooperation combined with the power of vested economic interests that hinder real change. Even in obviously vital sectors for sustainable development such as energy and transport we see forceful speeches and high policy promises of a new approach, ending, after all, with the traditional prioritisations. Nor does there seem to be much of a new approach in the also vital area of agriculture, especially as regards the global aspect of sustainable development (Krämer 2007: 396–400 and 402–410). Dhondt (2003: 479–480) concludes that although there were some integration efforts to be found, there has been 'no true internalisation of environmental costs'. In the traditional core economic area of company and securities law, integration of environmental considerations seems not even to have been considered (Sjåfjell 2009a: Part V).

Nevertheless, we can find examples from more recent years to show that the principle of sustainable development is also making inroads into areas beyond the reach of traditional environmental law, notably the Court's judgements in *PreussenElektra* and *Concordia Bus Finland*. *Concordia Bus Finland* exemplifies Community institutions' compliance with (now) Article 11 in a traditionally economic area of law. The case concerned environmental protection criteria in a process to determine, in economic terms, the most advantageous tender. The objective of the public procurement directive at issue was the elimination of 'barriers to the free movement of services and goods'.[34] Although the directive did not include any references to the protection of the environment or the objective of sustainable development, the Court found, by using the environmental integration principle, that environmental criteria could be included.[35] This has been followed up by the Community legislature in two new public procurement directives, both referring in their Preambles to the case law of the Court of Justice and the environmental integration rule and its aim of sustainable develop-

---

[34] *Concordia Bus Finland*, Case C-513/99 para. 56; see also the Preamble to Directive 92/50/EEC relating to the coordination of procedures for the award of public service contracts (OJ L 209/1–24) with reference to the 'the need to complete the internal market'.

[35] With certain requirements as to transparency and legal certainty and compliance with fundamental principles such as that of non-discrimination, *Concordia Bus Finland*, Case C-513/99 paras 57 and 64.

ment.[36] This does indicate some hope for the future and for the position of sustainable development as an overarching objective and a legal principle of considerable (but, as yet, not always acknowledged) significance.

Yet, the reaction to the so-called financial crisis in Europe has illustrated (again) how quickly legislator focus can switch from contributing to resolving global issues to attending to local demand for economic growth and the preservation of jobs. Sadly, the win-win situation of investing – legislatively and financially – in greening our economies and thereby the labour market seems often to be forgotten in competition with protectionist demands from yesterday's industrial lobbyists. Obviously, the political climate, what the representatives of the member states are willing to agree to, cannot be a relevant restriction of a legal obligation. Of course, the member states can change their legal obligations by amending the Treaty, but as long as they do not do that, the member states are bound by Treaty law.

Although we may safely say that the objective of sustainable development has not yet been integrated properly into all sectors of EU law, this does not detract from the legitimacy and veracity of the legal argument advanced here. Rather, it emphasises the need to spell it out and repeat it until the message gets through.

Labour and the necessary transition

In the long term, and on an aggregated level, there does not have to be a conflict between labour interests and the environmental dimension of sustainable development. This may be put even more strongly: in the long term, satisfying labour interests – both in developed countries and in the

---

[36] 'This Directive therefore clarifies how the contracting entities may contribute to the protection of the environment and the promotion of sustainable development, whilst ensuring the possibility of obtaining the best value for money for their contracts', Recital 12 and Recital 5, respectively, of Directive 2004/17/EC coordinating the procurement procedures of entities operating in the water, energy, transport and postal services sectors (OJ 2004 L 134/1–113) and Directive 2004/18/EC on the coordination of procedures for the award of public works contracts, public supply contracts and public service contracts (OJ 2004 L 134/114–240) (emphasis added); followed up by European Commission, *Buying Green! A Handbook on Environmental Public Procurement* (Luxembourg, Office for Official Publications of the European Communities, 2004). Jans 2000: 19–20, 22, 277 and 292 indicates a number of actual and possible legal consequences of Article 6 (and its predecessor).

complexity of developmental and human rights aspects of poorer regions
– depends on the environmental dimension being properly prioritised. A
fight between labour interests and environmental protection is bound to
end up in a lose-lose situation. Conversely, there is a lot to be won by
focusing on the possibilities that a transition to a sustainable economy with
green jobs entails. The question is not whether we all (including, of course,
those representing labour interests) shall recognise the necessity of taking
care of the environment and respecting the ecological limitations of our
planet. The question is whether we want to do it now while it is still not
too late or whether we want to do it sometime in the future, when the
consequences of ignoring the ecological boundaries make themselves
known too strongly to be ignored. At that stage the costs will be very high,
perhaps too high to be dealt with (see IPCC 2008: 65). It may still be possible
to achieve a relatively peaceful transition to sustainable societies. Certainly
it is not too soon to try – if anything, we are already on overtime. Will
labour cooperate and contribute to a sustainable development or will union
members, like far too many voters in our rich democracies, insist on putting
their own short-term interests first?

Recent changes in Norwegian collective agreements may be a first indication that labour unions are seeing the significance of the environmental
dimension of sustainable development. The Basic Agreement[37] for Civil
Service has a new item in its objectives provision setting out that environmental and climate considerations are to be a part of the cooperation and
co-determination between the parties, with the aim of a sustainable development.[38] This is followed up in the section on consultations to take place
between the parties, where it is now set out that the interests of the
environment and the climate are to be included in discussions concerning

---

[37] 'Basic agreements' typically lay down rules on the relation of bargaining procedures and
relations between national, superior, and local, subordinate, bargaining actors and collective
agreements, also setting out the subordination of the latter to the former, specific rules on
terms and termination of subordinate agreements, on workplace representation and
cooperation, etc. Basic agreements are not a separate type of collective agreement, technically
speaking, but merely one form of (national level) collective agreements (*'tariffavtale'*) in the
general legal sense. The importance of basic agreements lies primarily in that they are included
into and thus form part of the various sector- or branch-specific collective agreements that
are concluded between the basic agreement parties and their affiliated organisations; Evju
2004: 209–210.

[38] The Basic Agreement for Civil Service 2009–2012, Sect. 1(11) (available in Norwegian only
at http://www.regjeringen.no/upload/FAD/Vedlegg/Lønns-%20og%20personalpolitikk/
Hovedavtalen09.pdf (last visited 1 December 2009).

plans for the organisation and how the organisation's budget is to be employed.[39] Although the environment, the climate and the objective of a sustainable development so far are not included amongst the issues to be negotiated between the parties,[40] this is an important first step that shows that objectives other than the traditional labour objectives have made inroads into the area of collective agreements.

No less significant is the inclusion of environmental interests in the Basic Agreement between the Norwegian Confederation of Trade Unions (LO), the largest and most influential workers' organisation in Norway,[41] and the Confederation of Norwegian Enterprise (NHO), the main representative body for Norwegian employers with a current membership of over 19,800 companies ranging from small family-owned businesses to multinational companies.[42] The LO has declared that it has achieved a breakthrough for the inclusion of the environment and the climate in the cooperation between the parties, with insight into the impact of business on the environment to be promoted. The representative for the LO states that 'undoubtedly the environmental responsibility of a business first and foremost rests on the board and management, but the trade union has an important role to play. Information and knowledge is therefore central.'[43] This is implemented in an amendment to the section setting the stage for consultations between the parties, where the wording now underlines that it is 'important to promote understanding of and insight into the financial position of the enterprise *and the effect of the enterprise on the environment*'.[44]

---

[39] Ibid.: Sect. 12(1)(d).

[40] The difference between issues that may be discussed and those that are to be the object of negotiations being that issues to be negotiated between the parties may be referred to a tribunal for resolution in case the parties do not arrive at an agreement themselves.

[41] Also according to its own website, see http://www.lo.no/language/English/?tabid=894 (last visited 1 December 2009).

[42] According to its own website, see http://www.nho.no/english/ (last visited 1 December 2009).

[43] According to the press release concerning the negotiations for the new Basic Agreement, available, unfortunately in Norwegian only, at http://www.lo.no/Presse/Pressemeldinger/Revisjon-av-hovedavtalen-LO-NHO/ (last visited 1 December 2009).

[44] My translation and emphasis. The revised text of the Basic Agreement is not yet available, but the changes agreed upon are set out in a protocol available in Norwegian only at http://www.lo.no/Presse/Pressemeldinger/Revisjon-av-hovedavtalen-LO-NHO/ (last visited 2 December 2009), see also the not yet revised text of the Basic Agreement in an English translation here: http://www.lo.no/Documents/Lonn_tariff/BasicAgreem06-09_1.pdf (last visited 2 December 2009).

Similar changes have also been implemented in other collective agree-ments, both in the sector of the NHO and within that of its sister organisa-tion, the Federation of Norwegian Commercial and Service Enterprises (HSH). HSH is Norway's leading federation of commercial and service enterprises within the private sector.[45] The impact in practice remains to be seen. Certainly the traditionally protectionist and relatively short-sighted interests of national trade unions cannot be expected to change overnight. But this may be the beginning of a sustainable trend of co-operation.

As concerns the contribution of companies, the IPCC has stated that: 'Even though a broad range of cost-effective [greenhouse gas] mitigation technologies exist, a variety of . . . barriers prevent their full realisation in both developed and developing countries' (Bernstein et al. 2007: 476). Why is this so? Probably for a whole range of reasons – amongst them the shareholder primacy drive, the externalisation of the environmental con-sequences of companies' production and the use and discarding of their products, and the fragmentation of responsibility for these consequences. A number of regulatory and other initiatives have been put in place to attempt to make companies sustainable, but as long as the core, the internal decision-making in companies, is ignored in this process, the effect of what we may call the external regulation will tend to be limited and the scope for 'greenwashing' is wide open. I have elsewhere made the argument that changes need to be implemented in company law (Sjåfjell 2009a and 2009b).

Labour's focus on environmental protection can probably not substitute the, in my opinion, necessary redefinition of the purpose of companies and of the role and position of the board. Nevertheless, the contribution of labour is definitely not to be underestimated.[46] Companies need the incen-tive of environmental pressure from the labour side in their internal decision-making to become truly sustainable. Time will show whether this, together with other initiatives, will be sufficient. The attitude of labour may turn out to be decisive for the way forward and for whether the necessary transition to a sustainable economy and sustainable societies is carried through without societal upheaval and unnecessary costs in the interrelated terms of human suffering, loss of biodiversity, as well as financial impact.

---

[45] See HSH's website http://www.hsh-org.no (click the UK flag for English; last visited 2 December 2009).

[46] This is reflected in the research project 'Sustainable Companies', where company law, labour law and accounting law constitute the core areas.

References

Arnull, A. (2006) *The European Union and its Court of Justice*, 2nd edition (Oxford University Press).

Bernstein, L. et al. (2007) 'Industry', in B. Metz, O.R. Davidson, P.R. Bosch, R. Dave and L.A. Meyer (eds) *Climate Change 2007: Mitigation. Contribution of Working Group III to the Fourth Assessment Report of the Intergovernmental Panel on Climate Change* (Cambridge University Press).

Bugge, H.C. (2008) '1987–2007: "Our Common Future" Revisited', in H.C. Bugge and C. Voigt (eds) *Sustainable Development in International and National Law* (Europa Law Publishing).

Craig, P. (2002) 'The Evolution of the Single Market', in C. Barnard and J. Scott (eds) *The Law of the Single European Market* (Hart Publishing).

Craig, P. and De Búrca, G. (2008) *EU Law: Text, Cases, and Materials*, 4th edition (Oxford University Press).

Davies, P.G.G. (2004) *European Union Environmental Law* (Ashgate).

Dhondt, N. (2003) *Integration of Environmental Protection into other EC Policies: Legal Theory and Practice* (Europa Law Publishing).

Evju, S. (2004) 'Norway', in R. Blanpain (ed.) *The Actors of Collective Bargaining: A World Report (Bulletin of Comparative Labour Relations* 51: 207–218) (Kluwer Law International).

IPCC Core Writing Team, Pachauri, R.K and Reisinger, A. (eds) (2008) *Climate Change 2007: Synthesis Report. Contribution of Working Groups I, II and III to the Fourth Assessment Report of the Intergovernmental Panel on Climate Change* (IPCC).

Isoard, S. and Henrichs, T. (2005) 'European Environment Outlook', European Environment Agency, Report 4/2005, reports.eea.europa.eu/eea_report_2005_4/en/outlook_web.pdf (last visited 6 October 2007).

Jacobs, F. (2006) 'The Role of the European Court of Justice in the Protection of the Environment', *Journal of Environmental Law* 18: 185.

Jans, J.H. (2000) *European Environmental Law*, 2nd revised edition (Europa Law Publishing).

Krämer, L. (2004) 'The Genesis of EC Environmental Principles', in R. Macrory (ed.) *Principles of European Environmental Law* (Europa Law Publishing).

Krämer, L. (2007) *EC Environmental Law*, 6th edition (Sweet & Maxwell).

Magraw, D.B. and Hawke, L.D. (2007) 'Sustainable Development', in D. Bodansky, J. Brunnée and E. Hey (eds) *The Oxford Handbook of International Environmental Law* (Oxford University Press).

Sands, P. (2003) *Principles of International Environmental Law* (Cambridge University Press).

Sjåfjell, B. (2009a) *Towards a Sustainable European Company Law. A Normative Analysis of the Objectives of EU Law, with the Takeover Directive as a Test Case* (Kluwer Law International).

Sjåfjell, B. (2009b) 'Internalizing Externalities in EU Law: Why Neither Corporate Governance nor Corporate Social Responsibility Provides the Answers', *The*

George Washington International Law Review 40(4): 977–1024 (available at ssrn. com/paper=1139584).

Thieme, D. and Rudolf, B. (2002) 'International Decisions: PreussenElektra AG v. Schleswag AG. Case C-379/98', *The American Journal of International Law* 96: 225.

Voigt, C. (2008) *Sustainable Development as a Principle of Integration in International Law. Resolving Potential Conflicts between Climate Measures and WTO Law* (Martinus Nijhoff Publishers).

von der Groeben, H. and Schwarze, J. (2003) *Kommentar zum Vertrag über die Europäische Union und zur Gründung der Europäischen Gemeinschaft* [*Commentary to the Treaty on the European Union and the Treaty Establishing the European Community*], 6th edition (Nomos).

World Commission on Environment and Development (1987) *Our Common Future* (Oxford University Press).

9

Development, the movement of persons and labour law

Reasonable labour market access and

its decent work complement

ADELLE BLACKETT*

Introduction

The discussion in this chapter is intimately linked to what it means to think about 'work' in global, territorial terms; terms that move us beyond an assumption that our justifiable starting point is the nation state in which we live (Pogge 2008, 2010, Fraser 2009).

It is widely accepted that labour law is at a crossroads. Globalisation in the form of the 'New Economy' has been a readily observable phenomenon for at least twenty years (Arthurs 1996). The effectiveness of labour regulatory structures in many developing countries has long been understood to be out of sync with the vast majority of the workforce of the South (Sidibe 1999, Cook 2006, Meknassi 2010).

Recently, the impact of new economy changes has been felt in industrialised market economies of the North, with great urgency (Supiot 2001). Non-traditional, precarious, but increasingly typical forms of work are flourishing outside of the purview of existing labour regulatory structures (Fudge and Owens 2006: 77–97). Strikingly, pre-industrial forms of work, workplaces and regulatory responses also proliferate (Stone 2004). The new economy no longer simply coexists with Fordist workplace

* Associate Professor and William Dawson Scholar, Faculty of Law, McGill University. The historical framing and discussion of adjustment costs build, with permission, upon reflections in Blackett 2010.

paradigms; it supplants them as the norm, and challenges domestic regulatory responses.

Scholarship rethinking labour law abounds (Conaghan, Fischl and Klare 2002, Conaghan and Rittich 2005, Arup et al. 2006, Davidov and Langille 2006, Teklè 2010) and analyses situating the challenge of footloose capital and porous yet restrictive borders for labour (Sassen 1998) resolutely in a development framework are not only timely but critical.

In this chapter, I argue that rethinking the boundaries of labour law must include considering a broad range of public policy measures that not only intersect with labour law, but shape it. In particular, trade liberalisation and restrictions to the movement of persons influence our understandings of how labour is meant to be regulated. This chapter offers a brief historical framing and a discussion of some of the contemporary empirical literature, to capture employment effects of an asymmetrical liberalisation that has fundamentally called into question the embedded liberal compromise made by industrialised market economies. It argues that efforts to rethink the boundaries of labour law must engage with trade law and immigration law. In the process, it challenges the binary between trade *versus* aid. It suggests that it is neither acceptable nor strategically wise to resist the movement of persons for work and its development implications; rather it is time to focus carefully on the terms of that movement. It suggests that support for a notion of 'reasonable labour market access for migrant workers' must be accompanied by a 'decent work complement', which might take the form of a 'reverse' social clause. This chapter offers the most preliminary engagement with the idea, suggesting that it is one way to begin to think seriously about re-embedding the social in the economic in a manner that takes transnational movement of persons seriously.

Historical framing – trade theory, embedded liberalism and the South

For many of the industrialised nation states of Europe entering the General Agreement on Tariffs and Trade (GATT) at the end of World War II, colonial preferences enabled them to continue a pattern of exchange (or unidirectional trade) between the colonies and the metropolitan territories. Through the extraction of raw commodities – and through the commodification of the labour power of colonial peoples – these nations could afford to build up hard-won embedded liberal policies domestically (Polanyi 1944), including the social welfare systems that have been an integral part of our public policy for work for over 50 years, but that are now under significant intellectual and political challenge.

When colonialism formally ended, trade preferences accorded to former colonies continued through grandfathering mechanisms; although they ensured some level of preferential access for exports from former colonies to industrial markets, these policies became perceived as trade-based aid policies to promote development through secured market access on the basis of which some countries could construct particular social schemes. This was the case in many of the Caribbean Community (CARICOM) countries, whose secured access for primary crops like bananas and sugar cane enabled them to reorganise production. In the case of bananas, this entailed a move away from plantation-style economies that typified the slave relationship toward cooperative-style small banana productions that seemed more socially palatable modes of production upon which to construct post-colonial social relationships that strove to be equitable (Levitt 2005: 35–39 and 57). This was meant to include ensuring workers a living wage and a superior quality of life (Blackett 2002a: 913–916). Yet the Caribbean region joins other developing countries in existential questioning about whether contemporary trade arrangements continue to permit them to promote or even retain a particular vision of social development (Girvan 2009, Blackett 2010, Antoine 2011).

Certainly, when multilateral trade was negotiated at Bretton Woods in the immediate post-war period, the broader logic of liberalising access to markets was also anchored in a vision of growth and development. Moreover, a relationship between employment and trade policies was 'widely appreciated' in policy circles (Gardner 1956: 104–106), and explicitly contemplated in the Havana Charter. Even a 'social clause' was envisaged in Chapter III (US Department of State, Pub. No. 3117, 1948). The Havana Charter specifically embraced standards of living and ensured full employment and a large and steadily growing volume of real income (see GATT, Preamble). However, the Havana Charter and the International Trade Organisation (ITO) that it would have created were not adopted. Rather, the multilateral trade system was put in place through a self-executing agreement between 'contracting parties', the GATT, without a permanent secretariat or a clause on unfair labour conditions. What the GATT brought was a system that privileged 'non-discrimination' between trading nations to ensure access to foreign markets in the absence of major colonial ties. Non-discrimination was critical to the US, a major post-WWI major exporter of mass produced industrial products. (See further Blackett 1999: 5–8.)

Embedded liberalism ensured that economic liberalisation could occur progressively, through trade liberalisation beyond state borders, while redistributive policies on labour and social security would take place within the confines of the sovereign industrialised nation state. For Europe, this compromise is reflected in the original Treaty of Rome.

At the moment of the establishment of the European Economic Communities, a report commissioned of a group of experts of the International Labour Organisation (ILO), led by Swedish trade economist and Nobel Laureate, Bertil Ohlin (the Ohlin Report of 1956), became the basis upon which the Treaty of Rome was constructed. The report, although prepared in respect of European economic cooperation, focused on the 'social implications of freer international trade' and concentrated 'principally on problems arising out of the liberalisation of trade' (Ohlin Report 1956: 100). Amongst the social problems that it identified were (ibid.: 99–100):

1   The question whether international differences in labour costs and especially in social charges do or do not constitute an obstacle to the establishment of freer international markets;
2   The question of what can be done to reduce to a minimum the hardships that closer economic cooperation may involve for persons engaged in particular industries;
3   The question whether, if a freer international market were established, it might be necessary for the countries of Europe to shape and carry out their social policies with a greater degree of international consultation and cooperation than at present; and
4   The social problems connected with freer international movement of labour.

The experts accepted that there are particular industries in high-wage and low-wage countries that cannot compete with foreign products, but argued that '[i]t is precisely the fact that there are such cases in every country that makes international trade mutually advantageous' (ibid.: 105). The experts distinguished between differences in general levels of labour costs as opposed to exceptionally low labour costs relative to the general cost of labour in the same country. The latter might constitute a form of subsidisation or 'unfair competition'. While the Ohlin Report noted that there may

146

be an abstract economic advantage to importing countries even in the case of low-cost subsidised imports, it considered that 'there are serious objections to demanding sacrifices on the part of employers and workers in the competing industries of other countries facing such "unfair competition"' (ibid.).

The experts approached the question of harmonisation cautiously, by asking whether 'a particular element in social conditions or policy results in a pattern of labour costs such that the level of wages and social charges in one industry is significantly lower than that prevailing in other industries of the same country' (ibid.: 106). They considered that the cases where harmonisation might be necessary are 'neither very numerous nor, from the point of view of competition in international trade, very essential'; they were considered not a prerequisite for trade liberalisation in Europe, but rather as matters to be undertaken 'during the period of transition' (ibid.).

There was one 'unjustified inter-industrial wage difference' that according to the experts needed to be eliminated lest it 'substantially distort international trade': 'differences in the extent to which the principle of equal pay for men and women is applied in different countries' (ibid.: 106–107). The experts based their assessment on the existing normative framework, notably Article 2 of the then draft European Social Charter of the Council of Europe, 'which aims at the establishment of wages that would provide equal pay for equal work and ensure to the worker and his family a decent existence'[1] (ibid.: 107), as well as relevant international labour conventions on minimum wage fixing and the Equal Remuneration Convention, 1951 (No. 100). They recommended that '[i]f countries agreed to implement certain of these principles, consideration might be given to the adoption of an international labour Convention designed to be applied on a regional basis in Europe' (ibid.: para. 160). For this reason, the original Treaty of Rome contained Article 119, reflecting a compromise for France,

---

[1] See e.g., 'Paris's illegal immigrants fight to live openly', *Globe and Mail* (Toronto) 7 December 2009, available at http://www.theglobeandmail.com/news/world/pariss-illegal-immigrants-fight-to-live-openly/article1392094/. In Quebec, the Union of Agricultural Producers (UPA) in a 2005 report on the vegetable farms, noted that employers considered the physical demands of the job (43% of farms questioned), the poor remuneration (35%) and the poor working conditions (23%) as the leading factors explaining why it is difficult to recruit workers. Yet, the large-firm employers responded that to resolve these recruitment difficulties, the majority took measures to hire foreign employees (50%); another 23% of respondents used intermediaries to find workers. Only 13% considered mechanisation, and an even smaller number (barely 11%) considered offering better working conditions.

which was the only member of the original Treaty of Rome in 1957 to have specific legislation requiring equal pay, and which feared a competitive disadvantage chiefly with Italy's significant female labour force notably in the textile industry (Hepple 2009: 138). But it is crucial to recall that no magic line was drawn in the sand in terms of what trade theory requires (Unger 2007, Blackett 2010). The shift was a normative one, reflecting the importance ascribed to what is now one of the fundamental principles and rights at work.

The significance of the normative line drawing may be understood better in historical perspective. The embedded liberal compromise, alongside greater economic liberalisation at the regional level, has been characterised as an 'unstable chemical compound', unable to retain the equilibrium of 'Keynes at home and Smith abroad' that prevailed when 'the circulation of capital was *effectively* limited and contained' (Giubboni 2006: 18–19) and that led to the 'eclips[ing] of national sovereignty in social matters' once increased economic and monetary regulatory capacity were effectively constitutionalised at the supranational level of the European Union (EU) (ibid.: 25).

In this regard, the Ohlin Report contains what in retrospect is a most significant separate note by Mr Maurice Byé, who identified as a principal conclusion on which the report, in his view, should have been based, the 'danger that more capital will move from certain countries to existing industrial centres in other countries than would be desirable from the point of view of the capital-exporting countries' (Ohlin Report 1956: 122). Although he acknowledged that the report considers this matter with reference to existing underdeveloped southern regions, Mr Byé considered that the phenomenon 'might also apply to those regions that are now developed, if their growth were to slow down or be reversed' (ibid.). He argued for measures that would orient capital movements to harmonise growth, including (ibid.):

> the establishment of a reconversion fund and of a fund to promote the adaptation of the labour force, the establishment of a fund to promote investment in developing regions and the establishment of a bank for granting temporary assistance to undertakings in areas threatened with stagnation.

In other words, he recognised the need for measures of labour market distribution beyond the nation state, in the form of adjustment mechanisms, a matter which the EU has had to address at various historical moments, and which others have advocated in respect of multilateral trade liberalisation as they consider the internal limits of liberal trade. Chairman

Ohlin noted that certain of the proposals were briefly mentioned in the main report, although some experts doubted the feasibility of establishing new institutions 'for the foreseeable future' (ibid.). Giubonni (2006: 45) discusses the more constructivist approach captured in the ensuing Spaak Report, which sought to liberalise the migration of labour and optimistically assumed that a consequence rather than a precondition of liberalisation would be higher levels of social conditions through a strengthening of individual member states' capacity to regulate in the social field.

Internal limits of liberal trade, adjustment costs and the movement of persons

Despite the optimistic assumptions regarding social policy in both multilateral and European trade liberalisation, deep contradictions were to be borne out in the way the principles of non-discrimination are applied. The most familiar sectoral examples have been clothing manufacturing, until the GATT multi-fibre agreement was phased out, and persisting protection of agriculture in the EU and the US. These elements have come to epitomise the managed trade character of the multilateral system. They have been highlighted notably by civil society groups like OXFAM in the debate in favour of trade *versus* aid, as reflecting the apparent hypocrisy of the position taken by major industrial powers.

It is true that the heavily protected sectors ensured that workers who are citizens of industrialised market economies had decent working conditions, conditions that provided them with a stable livelihood, some leisure and access to a range of social welfare mechanisms. They have historically preserved a standard of living for agricultural producers (the citizens) that respected what economist Max Corden (1997) characterises as the 'conservative social welfare function'. Ironically, these protectionist state policies in industrialised market economies had also been at the core of aid in the form of sending surplus food supplies that may impede local production in developing countries rather than trade in the form of liberalised market access. (Two of the starkest examples are captured in two 2005 World Trade Organisation (WTO) reports: EU-Sugar Report and the US-Cotton Report.)

Hoekman and Winter (2005: 8 and 15) suggest that, with due regard to deficits in the existing literature, the following conclusions hold. First, 'greater trade with developing countries will adversely affect the low wage

149

workers in industrialised nations by "effectively" expanding the stock of unskilled labor, thus lowering wages'. Second, 'unskilled labor has seen its relative remuneration fall generally. Moreover, the skill premium has risen in *both* developing and OECD countries – rising inequality between the skilled and unskilled is a global phenomenon.' Labour market segmentation occurs across borders, and across the North-South divide to capture what may be referred to as the South in the North. The South in the North is intimately related to trade liberalisation.

The movement of persons is part of this picture of labour market segmentation across borders, and it can be a grim one. In 2005, for example, 6,000 people desperate to leave sub-Saharan Africa died in their treacherous attempt to cross over the narrow strip of sea between Morocco and the Spanish Canary Islands, in search of work. The lucky 23,000 who make it alive every year, and get through the many entry barriers to Fortress Europe's clandestine labour market (Senate Standing Committee 2007), perform a wide range of poorly paid, precarious work in heavily protected and heavily trade-exported sectors like agriculture, and like what remains of the textiles and clothing industry in post-industrial market economies, as well as in the informal, under-regulated European care economy. Both documented and undocumented temporary migrants are said to be absolutely indispensable for the remaining viability of industries that are at a competitive disadvantage vis-à-vis many of the developing countries from which these workers flee (Simard and Mimeault 1999). Yet the workers may live in insalubrious conditions and face harsh working conditions,[2] systemic racial and gender discrimination, harassment and segregation,[3] and perennial precariousness, including the ultimate risk: expulsion under the strictures of immigration rule enforcement.

We have grown deeply accustomed to thinking about migration policy – both permanent and temporary – as 'domestic policy' whose justifications are local, and largely determined by political 'realities', realities that are ostensibly shaped by the concerns of labour locally. The line of il/legality drawn between documented and undocumented migration remains the

---

[2] The shocking 2005 Quebec human rights tribunal case of *Centre Maraîcher Eugène Guinois*, Quebec Human Rights Tribunal (14 April 2005) J.E. 2005-779; D.T.E. 2005T-399; [2005] R.J.Q. 1315; [2005] R.J.D.T. 1087; [2005] R.R.A. 68, sanctions direct, blatant racial discrimination and segregation, although it overlooks the systemic character of the discrimination.
[3] See ILO-WTO, 'Trade and Employment: Challenges for Policy Research', 19 February 2007, available online at http://www.wto.org/english/res_e/booksp_e/ilo_e.pdf

defining characterisation upon which many rights are considered to rest. Yet the workers' relentless border-crossing and sustaining labour market participation mock the boundary drawing exercise, and compel regulatory response.

The mobility of labour as a factor of production is one of the starting assumptions of liberal trade. Respected economic analyses of the relationship between trade and employment suggest an interchangeability between low-skilled labour migration to work under conditions of the South in industrialised market economies of the North, and the import of goods produced by that low-skilled labour in developing countries of the South.[4] Moreover, as Sir Bob Hepple QC (2005: 5) astutely points out, '[a]n obvious solution to the inequalities between poor and rich countries would be free migration'. But even talking about free labour migration is seen as utopian, or nightmarish, depending on one's perspective. The heavily mediatised flows of migrants who are forced to leave under conditions of political instability and economic need capture the imagination more than past liberalisation experiences suggesting that workers do not generally pick up and leave their homelands en masse when restrictions on labour mobility are relaxed. Migration and development are intertwined.

Trade policy on labour mobility post-Uruguay Round is subsumed by Mode 4 (the movement of persons supplying services) of the existing General Agreement on Trade in Services. It encapsulates highly limited disciplines with few requirements for members to accept foreign labour along familiar liberal trade principles like most favoured nation status and national treatment. This is in contrast with the significant movement on liberalisation of temporary migration through the invariably asymmetrical exchanges between specific labour sending and labour receiving countries, including bilateral agreements and memoranda of understanding (MOU).

Analyses of migration policy do not sufficiently consider the South within the North, or its impact over time on the unravelling of labour

---

[4] According to the Caribbean Trade and Adjustment Group assessing the viability of the industry it was expected that only Belize could retain banana production subject to some restructuring, because 'its non-unionised industry, largely dependent on Central American migrant labour, is considered internationally competitive, and capable of substantial expansion'. See Caribbean Trade and Adjustment Group, 2001, 'Improving Competitiveness for Caribbean Development'. Report prepared at the request of the Regional Negotiating Machinery and the Caribbean Community Secretariat, Doc. No. CRNM/CTAG/FINAL REPORT/Rev2/08/01, Washington, DC.

regulatory systems both in the South and in the North. This is not simply a development policy concern; we cannot talk about the state of crisis faced by state labour regulation and stable employment policies in the North and in the South without contemplating how fortified but infinitely – and necessarily – permeable national borders in industrialised market economies collide with the particular places in developing countries that have an abundance of low-cost labour. Through this form of labour mobility, migrant workers become the ultimate representation of the commodification of labour.

Beyond trade versus aid: adjustment policy-based distributive justice within and beyond borders

To be clear, I do not think that the international community is prepared to endorse a multilateral regime for the free movement of persons from developing countries to industrialised market economies any time soon, although I do think that those concerned with sustainable development should avoid waging a rearguard operation that emphasises closed borders and a return to a past that sealed out distributional concerns beyond the borders of industrialised market economies. In addition to the terribly important work of denouncing deplorable working conditions and lack of citizenship at work of temporary migrants in construction, agricultural and paid care, labour and development scholars should be at the forefront of establishing proactive responses that at once problematise the public policy shift and reconstruct existing global responses to the re-commodification of labour under trade law.

Part of the problematisation must entail considering the impact of labour migration under conditions of 'unfreedom' – the absence of a normative baseline that can meaningfully be enforced, the constant threat that expulsion will frustrate labour rights claims, as well as the persistence of conditions of the South in the North for those 'racialised' workers who may have permanent resident status but face pernicious occupational labour market segmentation (Sharma 2006: 64). The impact on the integrity and maintenance of existing labour regulatory frameworks may too easily be overlooked. While historically attention has been placed on the impact of immigration on wage levels, labour relations specialists should consider the impact on the organisation of work, and the ability of actors to unionise and retain unionisation in sectors other than the 'lowest' wage sectors. In the Canadian context of targeted temporary migration schemes, the impact on decertification amongst formerly heavily unionised ski-lift operators, on unionisation rates in the hotel and tourism industry, and even on the organisation of work in the pharmaceutical industry (from owners of capital to employees), warrants closer attention. Rethinking the boundaries of labour law entails assessing systemic impacts on existing labour relations frameworks, and assessing spaces for reconstruction.

One space for reconstruction is to reshape the terms of transnational labour market access. Labour, migration and trade should be considered in tandem with development. In this light, what might the progressive realisation of 'reasonable labour market access' for migrant labour look like under a multilaterally-negotiated system that builds within it conditions for the non-commodification of that labour power through decent working conditions? This chapter suggests in the following section that it could take the form of a 'reverse' social clause for labour receiving countries, understood as a decent work complement to reasonable labour market access. In other words, the reasonable nature of the labour market access is understood in relation to the fundamental decency of the working conditions. This preliminary linkage proposal is meant to offer a framework that is at least complementary – if not ultimately pareto superior – to the individually agreed temporary migration schemes prevalent in bilateral agreements, MOU and regional trade agreements. The framework would in particular seek to palliate the attractiveness of treacherous clandestine movements that characterise the asymmetrical, exclusionary mobility, too often disconnected from an integrated labour rights framework, and removed from any notion of citizenship at work. It seeks to challenge the labour market dislocations of 'global care extraction' (Parreñas 2005) associated with this labour mobility, without regulatory coherence, by offering a degree of transnational labour regulatory coherence (Blackett 2011).

By granting and disciplining reasonable labour market access, the income maintenance justification for preserving citizens' standard of living – so central to Corden's work – is not overlooked, but addressed seriously. Even when it entails maintaining trade tariffs for more than a temporary period, the justification resides in the view that it is 'unfair' to allow real income to be reduced significantly without unavoidable or particularly compelling justification (Corden 1997: 74–77). As we focus on a development policy that emphasises meaningful trade access by developing countries to markets of the global North, it should be recalled that Corden argued that we should prefer adjustment assistance over protectionist policies (Corden and Vousden 2001). Indeed, Corden acknowledged that some protectionist policies introduced in response to the conservative social welfare function had a trade diversionary and redistributive function that privileged regions in the North over those in the South. Under the classic vision, states are responsible for ensuring the welfare of their citizens. Sovereign territory is a crucial part of this understanding.

It should be flagged as an aside that Corden's approach, although it is supportive of economic liberalisation policies, reflects a very different vision of workers and their entitlement to particular standards of living than the literature emanating from international financial institutions (notably the World Bank's *Doing Business* series – available at www.doing business.org), which recasts formal sector workers in both industrialised and developing countries as vested interest groups or societal elites collecting unrealistically high rents that stifle employment promotion and liberalised trade (see the critique offered by Santos 2006). Those reports thereby challenge a vision of labour market regulation that sees certain entitlements as characteristics of a form of social citizenship. Instead, they attempt to provide the moral grounds for re-regulating to promote economic liberalisation.

The contemporary, persisting financial crisis makes the need for an intellectual challenge to liberal trade from a labour perspective that grapples with the maintenance of an acquired standard of living particularly timely and compelling. This shift would deepen the movement in the literature in industrialised market economies away from an abstract social clause debate around a problematic assertion of 'social dumping'. The case for trade liberalisation less frequently entails acceptance of the claim (rather than the empirics) from trade policy that the pain of trade liberalisation resulting in the loss of certain inefficient sectors is ultimately global growth maximising in the aggregate, with little attention to the impact across differentiated state spaces. As Roberto Unger (2007: 51) so evocatively affirms, there is a 'remarkable paradox . . . [that] the political division of humanity is both the premise of trade theory and a fact to whose significance, transmutations, and possible functional equivalents . . . the theory is, and has always been, blind'. Attention has moved beyond a level playing field analysis, through an invocation of basic social standards that make trade fair and sustainable. The inherent linkage between trade and labour policy and the need for an intellectually appropriate stopping point, theorised in a path-breaking paper by Brian Langille (1996), may not so readily be sidestepped, but rather is deepened through a growing recognition of a comparable claim for another 'factor of production', the environment. The nature and limits of the structural social bargain represented by embedded liberalism at the national level increasingly requires considered attention.

Trade and development scholar Yong-Shik Lee (2007) – who is unsympathetic to including labour standards in trade agreements and who makes the case for reasonable labour market access for migrant workers – considers that social dislocation should be accepted by industrialised market economies, but dealt with through trade adjustment via social welfare or social protection systems. Alongside Supiot's (2001) call for concentric spheres of social drawing rights partly disembedded from the standard employment relationship, Lee provides a renewed call from the trade literature for adjustment assistance – that is, social welfare programmes – to offset the temporary impacts of the trade dislocations, to facilitate rather than postpone structural change and to compensate labour. Although likely to take the form of active labour market policies (Ashiagbor 2005), I would like to suggest that an analysis from trade law and policy provides an important justification for maintaining – if significantly redesigned – public social protection measures as necessary components of ensuring that the outcomes of trade are fair, and that social justice and social peace are maintained in industrialised market economies.

As concerns developing countries, John Gerard Ruggie reminds us that developing countries rarely had the 'privilege of cushioning the adverse domestic effects of market exposure' (Ruggie 2003: 94). 'The majority lack the resources, institutional capacity, international support and, in some instances, the political interest on the part of their ruling elites.' (Ibid.) The WTO constituency itself has declared this to be a 'new era of global economic cooperation, reflecting the widespread desire to operate in a fairer and more open multilateral trading system for the benefit and welfare of their peoples' (Marrakesh Declaration 1994). If trade liberalisation is justified through its benefit for the welfare of peoples, then aggregate welfare gains are important but only a starting point. Trade entails that at least in the first instance the pie is not only divided nationally (anymore, if ever it was), but globally. Yet the distributional consequences of trade, including trade adjustment, are overlooked for developing countries.

The case of CARICOM member states is instructive. The mostly micro island states with open economies and relatively high standards of living (many are not even classified as least developed countries (LDCs)) face the impact of the removal of trade preferences through the combined effect of the WTO's EC-Bananas decisions (and ongoing disputes) and recent end to the European Union-African, Caribbean and Pacific Group of States (EU-ACP) preferential trade arrangements on Belize, Jamaica and several Eastern Caribbean countries (the Windward Islands). In myriad panel and appellate body trade reports of significant technical complexity, the WTO's Dispute Settlement Body (DSB) found the EC (as it then was) to be in breach of its GATT obligations. This was by reason of the non-reciprocal trading arrangement that allowed preferential entry of bananas of former colonies of primarily Britain and France into the EC over the generally less costly 'dollar bananas' produced primarily by US multinational corporations based in countries like Colombia and Guatemala under more 'competitive', but problematic, labour and environmental conditions. The DSB is far from being willing or able to imagine a 'like products' or 'competitive products' analysis that would account for the difference between 'dollar bananas' and bananas produced under socially and economically stable production processes espoused by small-scale family and cooperative Caribbean banana producers.

But beyond an internal critique of the way in which trade law identifies efficient distribution, there is a complementary redistributive consideration necessary if the aggregate welfare enhancement rationale is to make sense across the diversity reflected in the existence of state borders, the *raison d'être* for trade law. It is to think about adjustment costs beyond national borders. The decisions have simply crippled Caribbean economies, so much so that they have garnered the outrage of some of the most ardent anti-linkage free trade economists, like Jagdish Bhagwati (2000: 203), who insists that 'nothing in the doctrine of free trade requires that we ride rough-shod, at breakneck speed and with reckless disregard, over the economies of the small and poor nations'. CARICOM nation states have not been able to undertake the trade adjustment on their own. Bhagwati would have international institutions (albeit the international financial institutions (IFIs)) assume that responsibility, as a form of global distributive justice, or embedded liberalism beyond national borders. Currently, no mechanisms are embedded in the multilateral liberal trade system or international institutions that could coordinate to provide policy coherence, to ensure that the adjustment toward greater liberalisation is compensated.

To bring the story full circle, there are two telling developments. First, the industry is no longer viable in the CARICOM with one exception: the CARICOM member state geographically situated in Central America, Belize. It might just remain competitive because its geographical base enables it to approximate the conditions of employment of its neighbours, by relying heavily on low-wage, non-unionised migrant labour from neighbouring Central American countries.[5] Second, rather than promote social adjustment, the EU has recently negotiated at breakneck speed the first of a different kind of trade agreement with former ACP countries – a reciprocal trade agreement with strong investment rights – with the slightly differently constructed Caribbean Forum (CARIFORUM) countries (Girvan 2009).

The Cambodian Better Factories case study may provide an important counter-example. In brief, this war-ravaged country transformed itself from an agrarian state barely able to feed its population to a leading indirect beneficiary of the Multi-Fibre Agreement's (MFA) export quotas that were still in place through 2004, to become a key producer of apparel through mainly Chinese and other Asian foreign direct investment (FDI), with preferential access to the US consumer market. Although labour law reform remains an important part of the picture, the US as a major industrialised trading partner combined accrued market access with ILO-enabled continuous improvement in the effectiveness of local labour law to foster a comparative institutional advantage for Cambodia that stood it in good stead for reciprocal trade with the US after the MFA expired, although there is little reason to believe it has not been spared the impact of the current financial crisis (Hall 2000, Elliott and Freeman 2003, Kolben 2007).

Both examples suggest that it is not necessary to assume that individual states should be the (only or main) source of their own systems of social adjustment: bilateral, regional and international action can be targeted, and drawn upon to build local capacity both to weather social dislocation and to readjust and develop a comparative advantage.

To engage in this discussion does not have to lead to a nihilistic vision of labour standards in the North. Instead, it entails putting policies together, that is, to tease out the implications of what is ultimately a far more 'open' approach to global trade, labour and development policy; and to take seriously the recognition that many people would much rather live in the land where they and their ancestors were born if only they had the employment opportunities to do so. It builds on an understanding that the focus of the right to development is as much international as it is national (Marks 2010). In so doing, we can think about how to construct a multilateral trade system that embraces distributive justice across borders. This entails thinking about institutional structures that can help to cushion and

---

[5] The notion of a decent work complement would seek to address this challenge through a panoply of remedial measures, as discussed in the next section.

promote developing country industries and decent work both in the South and the North. This is at once a form of trade policy and aid policy: trade provides increased market access including for labour; aid entails adjustment assistance through global distributive justice.

Putting trade, labour and development together: preliminary reflections on a reverse social clause?

By putting trade, labour and development together, we are forced to reflect both on the South and on the North, including the perpetuation of conditions of the 'South in the North' that this chapter has addressed. The notion of a (classic) social clause has been significantly debated in an overwhelming volume of literature. But what would be the implication of imagining a social clause that under carefully circumscribed conditions would aim to promote decent conditions for migrant workers? The counterbalance for reasonable labour market access, a reverse social clause would require states, employers and other business actors that avail themselves of migrant workers to ensure that working conditions protect (states) and respect (employers and business actors) migrant workers' human rights, including their fundamental principles and rights at work, while ensuring a panoply of state judicial, state non-judicial, and non-state remedies (Ruggie 2008, 2010, 2011). A fundamental principle of decency at work has been argued to underpin domestic labour standards legislation, and may be considered a counterbalance to principles like market efficiency.[6] A proposal built upon the interplay between such normative international and national starting points to harness the duty to enforce domestic remedies with international monitoring mechanisms might be referred to as a 'reverse' social clause, or a 'decent work complement' to reasonable labour market access.

In reviewing the existing literature in English to identify whether this notion has already been theorised, the contemporary use of the notion that I identified was by Justice Mark Fernando of the Supreme Court of Sri Lanka. Questioning whether it is right to impose a social clause amongst unequals, he asks, 'Does social justice require instead what I might call

---

[6] See Federal Labour Standards Commission, 'Fairness at Work: Federal Labour Standards for the 21st Century' (Harry Arthurs Report), Ottawa 2006 at X, available at http://www.rhdcc-hrsdc.gc.ca/eng/labour/employment_standards/fls/pdf/final_report.pdf

"reverse social clauses" limiting the unfair competitive advantages possessed by producers in the developed world? Would this be more especially the case if it would safeguard not only conditions of labour in the developing world but living standards everywhere?' (Fernando 1994: 97). Fernando's short text (four pages), directly attacks any form of wage inequity at a global level, irrespective of where the work is performed (ibid.: 99). In this regard, Fernando calls for far more than current trade policy supports, but perhaps not more than that to which the radicalisation of liberal trade theory ultimately aspires.

Admittedly, at one level, I invoke the language of a reverse social clause rhetorically, to emphasise the receiving countries, often in the global North, who rely on migrants; the language challenges the assumption implicit in much of the literature that social clauses are meant to apply in developing countries. The assumption may well be thin, however, as the experience with the North American Free Trade Agreement (NAFTA) (both its side agreement on labour, the North American Agreement on Labour Cooperation (NAALC), and its investment chapter incorporating tough investor protections and transnational arbitral dispute resolution mechanisms) confirms. Both Canada and the United States have been subject to NAALC submissions alleging a failure to enforce labour standards, and NAFTA Chapter 11 suits challenging important regulatory features of their laws (see Blackett 2002a). Far from presupposing a developing country decent work deficit, the notion of a decent work complement to reasonable labour market access builds on an appreciation for the structural causes of inequitable global labour market participation. It accepts and seeks to be responsive to the injustice and infeasibility of '[a] system that imposes burdens on poor countries but does not require rich countries to share these burdens' (Barry and Reddy 2008: 25). In this regard, the decent work complement builds on Barry and Reddy's compelling affirmation that a constructive linkage:

> should be unimposed, transparent, and rule-based; involve adequate burden sharing; incorporate measures that ensure that appropriate account is taken of viewpoints within states; and be applied in a context-sensitive manner.
>
> (Ibid.: 79; see also Ruggie 2011: Principles 25–31)

The decent work complement seeks to reconcile trade theory with state-centred assumptions about the appropriate locus for distributive justice. It draws on the normative ruminations in the Ohlin Report that underpinned the reference to equal pay for work of equal value on the basis of gender in the Treaty of Rome in respect of the broader question of labour market inequities on the basis of grounds of discrimination identified in Convention No. 111. It insists upon and problematises the importance of the place of production to the project of trade across borders. It considers the movement of persons within trade theory in as serious a manner from a non-discrimination perspective as one would be forced to consider the conditions under which products enter national territory. If liberal trade is state-centred and interested in the conditions of trade not only at borders but within them, then an inquiry into labour market conditions when reasonable labour market access is advocated as a logical corollary of liberal economic policy-making becomes essential.

Migrants may be either permanent or, as promoted by the OECD and international financial institutions, temporary. Not only is the movement of persons heavily gendered, but in industrialised market economies migrants tend also to be members of racialised communities from the global South. Members of racialised, immigrant communities may be differently situated in the labour market, with restricted access – either formally, through temporary migrant worker schemes that tie employment to one employer or one industry, or informally, through labour market segmentation on the basis of race for those who hold permanent resident status or political citizenship. In both cases, traditional access to justice mechanisms may be under-utilised or under-enforced, thereby replicating the conditions of the South in the post-industrialised countries of the North. This has the convenient effect of fostering price competitiveness of locally produced products with products imported from the South (Blackett 2007). This relationship complicates trade theory assumptions of labour market substitutability (Thomas 2011).

A reverse social clause invokes the prospect that the conditions of migrant workers in the North would be subjected to international scrutiny through a careful mix of domestic (state and non-state) and multilateral oversight mechanisms. While a classic, formally negotiated social clause may initially be received with the hostility surrounding proposals for a classic social clause, and while raising both prospects could conceivably cancel them both out entirely, debates on recognising and operationalising constructive linkages between trade and labour have become increasingly refined (see, for example, Barry and Reddy 2008). The focus in this work is not on the rigidity of a 'clause' but rather on a measure that seeks policy and regulatory complementarity, that recognises and promotes reflective, international deliberative spaces for interpretation (Young 2000, Brunnée and Toope 2010, Johnstone 2011) and that strives for policy coherence across governance levels for the social.

As I have argued elsewhere, there is an inherent linkage between labour as a factor of production and trade (Blackett 1999). While the WTO dispute settlement body is hardly the most effective or desirable mechanism for promoting labour rights (Blackett 2003, Hepple 2005), and while other mechanisms should be cultivated (Kinley 2009), much is needed in multi-level regulatory policy to address meaningfully the North–South dimensions of labour in trade as a global public policy concern (Blackett 2002b: 372). The invocation of a reverse social clause would condition the terms of entry of migrant workers onto domestic space to fundamental decency. It would focus on the formal, hard law that may erroneously be presumed to function well in rule-of-law states of the post-industrial North. It would also focus on the kind of low visibility practices that contribute to labour market precarity, and that prevail in the global North; those practices have the potential to undermine the effectiveness of the hard labour law on the books. A decent work complement in the form of a reverse social clause could be as simple as a requirement ensuring the 'effective enforcement' of existing local labour law compliant at least with core international human rights and international labour law principles, applicable to citizens and permanent residents who work in the domestic economy vis-à-vis migrant workers, with monitoring mechanisms (preferably engaging the ILO or decentralised in regional governance mechanisms) and reports that could be granted a degree of probative value in WTO dispute settlement mechanisms. Specific regulatory instruments contemplating migrant workers' international human rights including the new Decent Work for Domestic Workers Convention (No. 189) and its accompanying Recommendation (No. 201), 2011, would remain crucial benchmarks.

Consider, for example, the importance of a recent British Columbia human rights tribunal decision in a case involving discrimination against temporary migrant workers from the South, as compared with temporary migrant workers from Europe. Substantially lower salaries were paid to perform the same or similar work, and the workers faced inferior living conditions, accommodations and expense arrangements.[7] This was not a

---

[7] See *C.S.W.U. Local 1611* v. *SELI Canada and others (No. 8)*, 2008 BCHRT 436, available online. The claim of discrimination is characterised as follows at para. 9:
- Lower salaries, with the Latin Americans being paid substantially less than the Europeans for performing the same or similar work;
- Adverse housing, with the Latin Americans residing at the 2400 Motel on Kingsway, and most of the Europeans being housed in condominiums rented by the Respondents in the False Creek area, close to the worksite;

minimum wage case, although there was some evidence suggesting that the wages of those from Latin America were effectively below provincial minima. Both groups were recognised to have earned more in Canada than they earned in their countries of origins, and the employer attempted to justify the differentials between them in part on the basis of countries of origin. A factual situation involving wage differentials reflecting country of origin (which seems to reflect the basic assumptions of trade law if the workers were to remain in their country of origin and the owner of the capital, the employer, relocated), becomes deeply problematic when it takes place within the confines of the same nation state. International labour standard setting does not focus on establishing international minimum wages. Rather, under liberal trade resting on the embedded liberalism bargain, domestic labour law is meant to apply domestically, irrespective of the national origin of the worker. The Ohlin Report's reflections on relative rather than general wages reflect the policy reasons underscoring this concern about significant internal wage disparity. The B.C. Human Rights Tribunal found that the complainant had established a prima facie case of discrimination that was not rebutted by the respondent, and ordered the employer to pay both the average salary differential and compensation for injury to the Latin American workers' dignity.

The B.C. Human Rights Tribunal's decision puts squarely the distributive justice questions that are at the heart of determining the asymmetrical, but persistently territorial, scope of labour law. Although a thorough analysis of the implications of the case for trade law is beyond the scope of this chapter, it is worth noting briefly a few elements that relate to a decent work complement to reasonable labour market access in the interplay between the national and the international. First, the decision as framed within human rights mechanisms relies on the assumption of equal treatment for migrant workers. The language of 'discrimination' so familiar and arguably robust in the trade law context is employed in respect of the

- Adverse meal arrangements, with the Latin Americans being given money for breakfast, and tickets redeemable at two restaurants chosen by the Respondents for lunch and dinner, and most of the Europeans being given money for breakfast and dinner, and tickets for lunch only; and
- Adverse expense arrangements, with the Latin Americans being required to submit expenses for reimbursements, receiving an average reimbursement of about $76 per month, and the Europeans being given allowances of $300 per month, regardless of actual expenses incurred.

I thank Judy Fudge for drawing my attention to this case.

162

movement of persons. The case compares two categories of migrants, from the South and the North, as the issue of domestic standards was addressed, somewhat questionably, by the British Columbia Labour Relations Board.[8] Second, the decision focuses on labour in the construction industry, which unlike textile production or off-shore call centre service work, but like care work, cannot easily be re-located. Its focus is the investment nexus of trade, or trade in services through the movement of persons, rather than the movement of goods. As students of the European Posted Workers' Directive know, it is not a coincidence that most of the regulatory tension over the movement of persons under globalisation accompanies work that cannot easily be dislocated.[9] But the B.C. Human Rights Tribunal builds on understandings both of territory and equality of treatment to re-centre the appropriate regime for labour governance (cf. Mundlak 2009). It captures the places of globalisation, texturing the perception of its footloose character with attention to the demands of particular sectors and following through with a regulatory logic applicable to place.[10] The human rights approach grounds abstract understandings of comparative advantage, forcing us to be clear about the terms of exchange: is it labour scarcity, as migration schemes suggest, or the search to contain labour costs below industry standards, or even below statutory minimum wages, or, more fundamentally, a broader flexibilisation of labour regulatory mechanisms through the fragilisation of the labour force? The very call for clarity may be an important part of the regulatory complementarity, forcing decision-

[8] The matter of alleged discrimination between Latin American workers and Canadian residents was submitted by the labour union, the Construction and Specialized Workers' Union, Local 1611 (CSWU), to the British Columbia Labour Relations Board, alongside a submission that the Board should also look at the differences in the rates of pay between Latin American and European employees. The Labour Relations Board considered the former, but considered that the latter was a matter for the Human Rights Tribunal. In deciding upon the former question, it compared ranges of wages between the two groups, but included the cost of accommodation, meals and airfare for the Latin American migrant workers within the 'wages'. As a result, it concluded that the Canadian residents and Latin American migrant workers were paid comparable wages, based on aggregate wage ranges. It considered that insufficient evidence had been submitted to allow it to determine whether the Latin Americans, who the CSWU argued were more skilled than the Canadian residents, suffered adverse treatment in individual pay. See *Seli Canada Inc.* v. *Construction and Specialized Workers' Union Local* 1611, 2007 CanLII 5090 (BC L.R.B.) paras 95–113.
[9] See Posted Workers Directive (96/71/EC); see also Deakin 2008.
[10] The Quebec Human Rights Commission's recent position on foreign domestic workers' (aides familiales) right to access to occupational safety and health benefits in Quebec follows similar reasoning. See http://www.cdpdj.qc.ca

makers to be forthcoming about the bases upon which assessments of the regulation of labour in an era of liberalised trade are made.[11] And it should be no surprise that the interface between trade, labour and development becomes clearer too. As with the historical framing, the importance of establishing normative baselines is underscored to avoid subsuming the social in the economic.

The focus of my ongoing research on this topic is to identify how the decent work complement would harness reporting on the human rights conditions of migrant workers to monitoring and compliance institutions of international organisations including the ILO Committee of Experts and possibly special procedures mandate holders of the United Nations Human Rights Council. While a decent work complement could ultimately contemplate ways of informing contextualised interpretation under the WTO DSB, the proposed linkage would embrace a broad range of international informational, deliberative and incentives-based opportunities – including the WTO's own Trade Policy Review Mechanisms – to consider how institutional linkages between international institutions can be engaged cooperatively to improve the terms under which migrants travel and work.

Conclusion

This chapter has contended that trade liberalisation and the movement of persons fall within the boundaries of labour law. An implication of the chapter is that those concerned with development are hard pressed to see development policy within the dyad of trade *versus* aid, which has long been understood in the literature to be relatively interchangeable (Böhning and Schloeter-Paredes 1994), even though trade policies can actually increase labour migration (Thomas 2011). It argues for trade and aid, but sees them as interrelated, and tied to a distributive justice framework, or embedded liberalism beyond national borders.

A further implication of this chapter is that enquiries into the boundaries of labour law cannot simply entail the South, as the North is intimately

[11] In Canada, see the recently released Report of the Auditor-General of Canada to the House of Commons, Chapter 2, selecting foreign workers under the Immigration Program, Fall 2009. Main points of Chapters 1–8 available at http://209.71.218.213/internet/docs/parl_oag_200911_00_e.pdf, and Chapter 2 available at http://textsfornothing.com/blog/wp-content/uploads/22072340-Chapter-2-Selecting-Foreign-Workers-Under-the-Immigration-Program.pdf

connected to it and the effects on labour regulation both in the North and the South extend beyond states' porous borders. Trade and labour law both fundamentally engage distribution and redistribution. They depend on territory and the relationship between spaces, as well as the factors of production that tie them together. And they both require us to approach them not only by radicalising their theoretical frames, but also by reintroducing the normative – that is, the normative baselines upon which to make work decent. A critical site for this rethinking is the terms under which migrant labour travels. It sketches the beginnings of an argument for reasonable labour market access for migrant labour, coupled with a 'reverse' social clause.

Incorporating these considerations into rethinking labour law entails shifting paradigms. There is little room for the illusion that the kind of linkage proposed in this chapter will come easily. But then, why should it? Even the original embedded liberal compromise was itself the result of a long and hard battle.

References

Antoine R.-M. (2011) 'Rethinking Labor Law in the New Commonwealth Caribbean Economy: A Framework for Change', *Comparative Labor Law & Policy Journal* 32: 343.

Arthurs, H. (1996) 'Labour Law Without the State', *University of Toronto Law Journal* 46: 1.

Arup, C., Gahan, P., Howe, J., Johnstone, R., Mitchell, R. and O'Donnell, A. (2006) *Labour Law and Labour Market Regulation* (Federation Press).

Ashiagbor, D. (2005) *The European Employment Strategy: Labour Market Regulation and New Governance* (Oxford University Press).

Barry, C. and Reddy, S. (2008) *International Trade and Labor Standards: A Proposal for Linkage* (Columbia University Press).

Bhagwati, J. (2000) *The Winds of the Hundred Days: How Washington Mismanaged Globalization* (MIT Press).

Blackett, A. (1999) 'Whither Social Clause? Human Rights, Trade Theory and Treaty Interpretation', *Columbia Human Rights Law Review* 31: 1.

Blackett, A. (2002a) 'Toward Social Regionalism in the Americas', *Comparative Labor Law & Policy Journal* 23: 901.

Blackett, A. (2002b) 'Mapping the Equilibrium Line: Fundamental Principles and Rights at Work and the Interpretive Universe of the World Trade Organization', *Saskatoon Law Review* 65: 369.

Blackett, A. (2003) 'Defining the Contemporary Role of the State: WTO Treaty Interpretation, Unilateralism, and Linkages', in C. Carmody, Y. Iwasawa and

S. Rhodes (eds) *Trilateral Perspectives on International Legal Issues: Conflict and Coherence* (American Society of International Law).

Blackett, A. (2007) 'Situated Reflections on International Labour Law, Capabilities, and Decent Work: the Case of Centre Maraîcher Eugène Guinois' hors série', *Quebec Journal of International Law*: 223.

Blackett, A. (2010) 'Trade Liberalization, Labour Law and Development: A Contextualization', in T. Teklè (ed.) *Labour Law and Worker Protection in Developing Countries* (Hart Publishing).

Blackett, A. (2011) 'Introduction: Regulating Decent Work for Domestic Workers', *Canadian Journal of Women and the Law* 32: 1.

Böhning, W.R. and Schloeter-Paredes, M. (1994) *Aid in Place of Migration?* (ILO).

Brunnée, J. and Toope, S. (2010) *Legitimacy and Legality in International Law: An Interactional Account* (Cambridge University Press).

Conaghan, J., Fischl, R.M. and Klare, K. (eds) (2002) *Labour Law in an Era of Globalization: Transformative Practices and Possibilities* (Oxford University Press).

Conaghan, J. and Rittich, K. (2005) *Labour Law, Work, and Family* (Oxford University Press).

Cook, M.L. (2006) *The Politics of Labor Reform in Latin America: Between Flexibility and Rights* (Pennsylvania State University Press).

Corden, W.M. (1997) *Trade Policy and Economic Welfare*, 2nd edition (Oxford University Press).

Corden, W.M. and Vousden, N. (2001) 'Paved with Good Intentions: Social Dumping and Raising Labor Standards in Developing Countries', in Z. Drabek (ed.) *Globalisation Under Threat* (Edward Elgar).

Davidov, G. and Langille, B.A. (eds) (2006) *Boundaries and Frontiers of Labour Law: Goals and Means in the Regulation of Work* (Hart Publishing).

Davidov, G. and Langille, B.A. (eds) (forthcoming) *The Idea of Labour Law* (Oxford University Press).

Deakin, S. (2008) 'Regulatory Competition after Laval', *Cambridge Yearbook of European Legal Studies* 10: 581.

Elliott, K.A. and Freeman, R.B. (2003) *Can Labor Standards Improve Under Globalization?* (Institute for International Economics).

Fernando, M. (1994) 'Towards International Social Justice', in ILO *Visions of the Future of Social Justice: Essays on the Occasion of the ILO's 75th Anniversary* (ILO).

Fraser, N. (2009) *Scales of Justice: Reimagining Political Space in a Globalizing World* (Columbia University Press).

Fudge, J. and Owens, R. (eds) (2006) *Precarious Work, Women, and the New Economy: The Challenge to Legal Norms* (Hart Publishing).

Gardner, R. (1956) *Sterling-Dollar Diplomacy: Anglo-American Collaboration in the Reconstruction of Multilateral Trade* (Clarendon Press).

Girvan, N. (2009) 'Some Lessons of the Cariforum-EU EPA', *Trade Negotiations Insights* 8, available online at http://ictsd.org/i/news/tni/57509/

Giubboni, S. (2006) *Social Rights and Market Freedom in the European Constitution: A Labour Law Perspective* (Cambridge University Press).

Hall, J.A. (2000) 'Human Rights and the Garment Industry in Contemporary Cambodia', *Stanford Journal of International Law* 36: 119.

Hepple, B. (2005) *Labour Laws and Global Trade* (Hart Publishing).

Hepple, B. (2009) 'Equality at Work', in B. Hepple and B. Veneziani (eds) *The Transformation of Labour Law in Europe: A Comparative Study of 15 Countries 1945–2004* (Hart Publishing).

Hoekman, B. and Winter, L.A. (2005) 'Trade and Employment: Stylized Facts and Research Findings', World Bank Policy Research Working Paper No. 3676, available at http://www.un.org/esa/desa/papers/2005/wp7_2005.pdf

Johnstone, I. (2011) *The Power of Deliberation: International Law, Politics and Organizations* (Oxford University Press).

Kinley, D. (2009) *Civilising Globalisation: Human Rights and the Global Economy* (Cambridge University Press).

Kolben, K. (2007) 'Integrative Linkage: Combining Public and Private Regulatory Approaches in the Design of Trade and Labor Regimes', *Harvard Journal of International Law* 48: 203.

Langille, B. (1996) 'General Reflections on the Relationship of Trade and Labour (or: Fair Trade is Free Trade's Destiny)', in J.N. Bhagwati and R.E. Hudec (eds) *Free Trade and Harmonization* (MIT).

Lee, Y.-S. (2007) *Reclaiming Development in the World Trading System* (Cambridge University Press).

Levitt, K. (2005) *Reclaiming Development: Independent Thought and Caribbean Community* (Ian Randle Publishers).

Marks, S. (2010) 'Obligations to Implement the Right to Development: Philosophical, Political, and Legal Rationales', in B. Andreassen and S. Marks (eds) *Development as a Human Right: Legal, Political and Economic Dimensions*, 2nd edition (Intersentia).

Meknassi, R. (2010) 'The Effectiveness of Labour Law and Decent Work Aspirations in the Developing Countries: A Framework for Analysis', in T. Teklè (ed.) *Labour Law and Worker Protection in Developing Countries* (Hart Publishing and ILO).

Mundlak, G. (2009) 'De-Territorializing Labor Law', *Law & Ethics of Human Rights* 3, available at http://www.bepress.com/lehr/vol3/iss2/art4

Ohlin Report (1956) Group of Experts, 'Social Aspects of European Economic Co-operation', Studies and Reports, New Series, No. 46 (ILO), in *International Labour Review* 74: 99.

Parreñas, R.S. (2005) *Children of Global Migration: Transnational Families and Gendered Woes* (Stanford University Press).

Pogge, T. (2008) *World Poverty and Human Rights*, 2nd edition (Polity Press).

Pogge, T. (2010) *Politics as Usual: What Lies Behind the Pro-poor Rhetoric* (Polity Press).

Polanyi, K. (1944) *The Great Transformation* (Beacon Press).

Ruggie, J. (2003) 'Taking Embedded Liberalism Global: The Corporate Connection', in D. Held and M. Koenig-Archibugi (eds) *Taming Globalization: Frontiers of Governance* (Polity Press).

Ruggie, J. (2008) 'Promotion and Protection of all Human Rights, Civil, Political,

Economic, Social and Cultural Rights, Including the Right to Development', United Nations Human Rights Council, 7 April 2008, A/HRC/8/5.

Ruggie, J. (2010) Remarks by Special Representative of the Secretary-General John Ruggie, 'The Protect, Respect and Remedy Framework: Implications for the ILO', International Labour Conference, Geneva, 3 June 2010, available online at http://www.ilo.org/wcmsp5/groups/public/-ed_emp/-emp_ent/-multi/documents/genericdocument/wcms_142560.pdf

Ruggie, J. (2011) Report of the Special Representative of the Secretary-General on the issue of human rights and transnational corporations and other business enterprises, 'Guiding Principles on Business and Human Rights: Implementing the United Nations "Protect, Respect and Remedy" Framework', United Nations General Assembly, 21 March 2011, A/HRC/17/31.

Santos, A. (2006) 'The World Bank's Uses of the "Rule of Law" Promise in Economic Development', in D. Trubek and A. Santos (eds) *The New Law and Economic Development* (Cambridge University Press).

Sassen, S. (1998) *Globalization and its Discontents: Essays on the New Mobility of People and Money* (The New Press).

Senate Standing Committee on Foreign Affairs and International Trade (2007) 'Overcoming 40 Years of Failure: A New Roadmap for sub-Saharan Africa', February 2007, available at http://www.parl.gc.ca/39/1/parlbus/commbus/senate/Com-e/fore-e/rep-e/repafrifeb07-e.htm#FOREWORD

Sharma, N. (2006) *Home Economics: Nationalism and the Making of 'Migrant Workers' in Canada* (University of Toronto Press).

Sidibe, O. (1999) 'Réalités Africaines et Enjeux pour le Droit du Travail' ['African Realities and Challenges for Labour Law'], *Bulletin de Droit Comparé du Travail et de la Sécurité Sociale* [*Bulletin of Comparative Law of Labour and Social Security*]: 130–141.

Simard, M. and Mimeault, I. (1999) 'Exclusions Légales et Sociales des Travailleurs Agricoles Saisonniers Vehiculés Quotidiennement au Québec' ['The Daily Vehicles of Legal and Social Exclusion of Seasonal Agricultural Workers in Quebec'], *Industrial Relations* 54: 388.

Stone, K. (2004) *From Widgets to Digits: Employment Regulation for the Changing Workplace* (Cambridge University Press).

Supiot, A. (2001) *Beyond Employment: Changes in Work and the Future of Labour Law in Europe* (Oxford University Press).

Teklè, T. (2010) *Labour Law and Worker Protection in Developing Countries* (Hart Publishing).

Thomas, C. (2011) 'Migration and Social Regionalism: Labour Migration as an Unintended Consequence of Globalization in Mexico, 1980–2000', in A. Blackett and C. Lévesque (eds) *Social Regionalism in the Global Economy* (Routledge).

Unger, R. (2007) *Free Trade Reimagined: The World Division of Labor and the Method of Economics* (Princeton University Press).

Vosko, L. (2010) *Managing the Margins* (Oxford University Press).

Young, I.M. (2000) *Inclusion and Democracy* (Oxford University Press).

Part V
Achieving development through social dialogue, corporate social responsibility and other participatory strategies

10
Corporate social responsibility

Its potential and its limits for labour participation

CHARLOTTE VILLIERS*

Introduction

Large corporations are crucial to sustainable development. They have considerable financial and political power. The corporate social responsibility (CSR) dimension of their activities gives rise to an expectation that they will also participate in sustainable development activities, since CSR and sustainable development are closely linked, the two terms frequently being treated as interchangeable. The potential role of corporations through their CSR activities in sustainable development is significant for workers and trade unions because sustainable development is widely considered to include recognition of the needs and relevance of labour. CSR might thus be considered to provide an open door for a more participatory role for workers and their representatives and for achieving better and stronger labour standards. However, I will argue in this chapter that CSR is unlikely to bring about sustainability in this way and is in fact more likely to exclude labour participation. In the next part of the chapter, I address the links that can be made between CSR and labour rights. In the third part, I highlight the limitations of CSR and seek to explain why its promises are likely to be unfulfilled. In part four, I argue that an alternative approach is required. Workers and trade unions need to collaborate with other social movements to establish a countervailing power to that enjoyed by large corporations. A stronger accountability regime is also required that will ensure real responsibility of corporations for their actions.

* Professor of Company Law, University of Bristol.

The relevance of CSR for labour standards and worker participation

Two key links exist between CSR and labour standards: definitions of CSR that include recognition of the needs of stakeholders and not just of shareholders; and relevance of the role of trade unions in shaping the sustainable development agenda to which CSR is connected.

Definitions of CSR

There are many available definitions of CSR. Dahlsrud, for example, presents an analysis of 37 definitions (Dahlsrud 2008). Two definitions frequently cited include those of the European Commission and the World Business Council for Sustainable Development. The European Commission has defined CSR as:

> A concept whereby companies integrate social and environmental concerns in their business operations and in their interaction with their stakeholders on a voluntary basis.[1]

Similarly, the World Business Council for Sustainable Development defines CSR as:

> the commitment of business to contribute to sustainable economic development working with employees, their families, the local community and society at large to improve their quality of life.[2]

US-based global business organisation Business for Social Responsibility (BSR), tells us that CSR means:

---

[1] See Communication from the Commission concerning Corporate Social Responsibility, March 2006, Implementing the Partnership for Growth and Jobs: Making Europe a Pole of Excellence on CSR (March 2006) (COM(2006)136 final); Communication from the Commission concerning Corporate Social Responsibility, July 2002, A Business Contribution to Sustainable Development (July 2002) (COM (2002)347 final of 2.7.2002); Official Consultation on CSR, July 2001, Corporate Social Responsibility Green Paper, Promoting a European Framework for Corporate Social Responsibility (July 2001) (COM (2001)366 final of 18.7.2001), all available at: http://ec.europa.eu/enterprise/policies/sustainable-business/documents/corporate-social-responsibility/index_en.htm

[2] The World Business Council for Sustainable Development (2002) *The Business Case for Sustainable Development: Making a Difference Toward the Johannesburg Summit 2002 and Beyond* at p. 6, available at http://www.wbcsd.org/DocRoot/rZNj49UF0okxGvdLfDte/business-case.pdf

> ... operating a business enterprise in a manner that consistently meets or exceeds the ethical, legal, commercial, and public expectations society has of business.[3]

Other related terms include corporate citizenship and triple bottom line.

A key feature of CSR is stakeholder involvement (ibid.: 4) and employees are typically regarded as major stakeholders. In a seminal article on CSR, Carroll (1991: 46) describes the orientation of CSR towards stakeholders and the moral aspiration of CSR: 'Employees are a human resource that must be treated with dignity and respect. Goal [*sic*] is to use a leadership style such as consultative participative that will result in mutual confidence and trust. Commitment is a recurring theme. Employees' rights to due process, privacy, freedom of speech and safety are maximally considered in all decisions. Management seeks out fair dealings with employees.'

Highlighting this moral aspiration, Daugareihl (2008: 96) observes that the definition of CSR supplied by the European Commission 'should lead to respect for the methods of worker participation, where these exist by virtue of applicable positive law, and to defend them where the law does not do so'. Such observations might indicate that CSR is a potential friend to the trade union movement and is likely to result in the establishment of and protection of labour standards and labour participation. This interpretation of CSR is supported by the link between CSR and sustainability, given the trade union movement's recognised influence on the sustainable development agenda.

Trade union links to sustainability

CSR is frequently linked to sustainable development. The two concepts are often used interchangeably, and CSR definitions usually include references to sustainable development (Moon 2007: 297). Indeed, not only is CSR related to the concept of sustainable development, but, also, it has been argued that 'the most significant source for the current CSR concept comes from concern for the environment' (Justice 2002: 2).

Why might these observations be relevant for trade unionists? Importantly, Dwight Justice (ibid.: 2–3) notes that trade unionists played a major role in linking the environmental with the social during the development of the idea of sustainable development. In particular, trade

---

[3] BSR, *Online Introduction to CSR*, available at http://www.bsr.org

unions succeeded, according to Justice, in obtaining recognition that there was a social dimension to sustainability.

At the institutional level, the UN Department of Economic and Social Affairs, Division for Sustainable Development document *Agenda 21*, adopted at Rio de Janeiro in 1992, makes clear the link between sustainable development and trade union actions. Thus *Agenda 21* encourages active participation of workers and their trade unions. For example, paragraph 29.1 states:

> trade unions are vital actors in facilitating the achievement of sustainable development in view of their experience in addressing industrial change, the extremely high priority they give to protection of the working environment and the related natural environment, and their promotion of socially responsible and economic development. The existing network of collaboration among trade unions and their extensive membership provide important channels through which the concepts and practices of sustainable development can be supported.

At paragraph 29.2, *Agenda 21* states:

> The overall objective is poverty alleviation and full and sustainable employment, which contribute to safe, clean and healthy environments – the working environment, the community and the physical environment. Workers should be full participants in the implementation and evaluation of activities related to *Agenda 21*.

These efforts are to be implemented by promoting freedom of association and strengthening participation and consultation. *Agenda 21* includes the statement at paragraph 29.5 that:

> Governments, business and industry should promote the active participation of workers and their trade unions in decisions on the design, implementation and evaluation of national and international policies and programmes on environment and development, including employment policies, industrial strategies, labour adjustment programmes and technology transfers.

Clearly, *Agenda 21* suggests that trade unions have a role to play in sustainable development and that business and industry also play a crucial role in a country's social and economic development.

A major concern in the debate is whether trade unions and workers have really managed to attain a full role or whether, instead, the notion of sustainable development has been effectively hijacked by business and industry. Springett and Foster (2005), for example, note that there has been a tendency for hegemonic elites, comprising representatives chiefly from the administrative state and corporate bodies, to take power over decision-making and non-decision-making so that the agenda is framed by silences as well as a largely managerial perspective on sustainable development. Springett and Foster (ibid.: 272) advocate an alternative approach, observing that the 'good life' would rely upon the development of local sustainable development initiatives and the empowerment of people through deliberative democracy and a more inclusive discourse. Similarly, Söderbaum (2004) argues that sustainable development builds on an assumption that normal imperatives of democracy can be relied on. It is this democratic feature that offers a potential role to trade unions, since unions are seen as vital actors in a deliberative democracy setting, not least because they tend to be identified as leaders in democracy. Gallin (2000: 27), for example, describes a 'typical trade union' as 'a democratic organization in which the members have a sense of citizenship and ownership'. He notes, moreover, that,

> at the beginning of the twenty-first century, the trade union movement remains *the only democratically organized movement at the world level* that is defending, explicitly or implicitly, the vision of a society organized to serve the common welfare and based on the values of social justice, equality and co-operation.
>
> (Ibid.: 8, emphasis added)

In summary, the definitions of CSR and the links between CSR and sustainable development make possible the argument for CSR to have the potential to strengthen labour standards and for labour participation in corporate decisions. CSR does at least appear to consist of recognition of the impact of companies on the environment and on labour conditions. In addition, the rhetoric of stakeholder engagement gives rise to the possibility of trade union and worker input.

Despite the links and the potential strengths, CSR also has its limits from the perspective of labour participation and protection. I will turn next to the limits of CSR more generally in this regard.

Limits of CSR for labour protection

CSR appears to have the potential to be a positive influence on corporate actions and labour interests. However, numerous features of CSR expose such positive claims to doubt. These include the vague definitions available for CSR and the emphasis upon voluntary action and management discretion as well as the broad range of stakeholders with whom workers and trade unions would have to compete under a CSR umbrella. Further problems are identified with the company law structure that frames the CSR agenda.

Definitions

The first problem to note is that there is a variety of available definitions for CSR. This variety has the potential to make CSR ultimately meaningless as a concept unless a particular definition is adopted broadly. Some specific definitions are in themselves significantly vague. For example, BSR, a US-based global business organisation describes CSR, as noted above, as 'operating a business enterprise in a manner that consistently meets or exceeds the ethical, legal, commercial, and public expectations society has of business'.[4] This definition tells us neither what those expectations are nor how consistent they might be.

The definitions favoured by both the European Commission and the European Parliament emphasise the voluntary nature of CSR which is most worrisome. The European Commission, for example, defines CSR as a 'concept whereby companies decide *voluntarily* to contribute to a better society and a cleaner environment' (emphasis added). CSR is regarded as 'a concept whereby companies integrate social and environmental concerns in their business operations and in their interaction with their stakeholders *on a voluntary basis*' (emphasis added). The European Commission's definition highlights the voluntary nature of CSR as a business activity because it goes beyond the law. If CSR is voluntary this is problematic for trade unions on two levels. First, there is no guarantee of what corporations will do in order to meet their CSR aspirations. As their actions are voluntary this does not entail obligations but rather treats CSR as good behaviour, almost as charity, philanthropy, or even kindness, all of which companies are under no legal duty to offer. There is nothing mandatory about CSR. Therefore, competing demands on a corporation may affect how it regards its CSR requirements. Thus, for workers, their interests have no guarantee of being accommodated. Second, the voluntary nature of CSR renders it a subject for managerial discretion. Whilst trade unions or workers might seek to

---

[4] http://www.bsr.org

influence the exercise of that discretion the reality is that the corporate managers are able to make their CSR decisions with or without the input of trade unions or workers. The managerial discretion and the voluntary nature of CSR limit its potential effect. In reality, without the input of trade unions, corporate managers are likely to narrow the practical impact of CSR.

This narrow perspective of management has been noted by commentators in the context of sustainable development. Springett and Foster (2005: 272), for example, claim that the trade union movement adopts a strong conception of sustainable development focusing on institutional, social, environmental and economic imperatives, whereas the corporate bodies and state representatives adopt a weak conception based on ecological modernisation and reliance upon strong economic growth. These observations are supported by Peter Söderbaum (2009) who notes that CSR and sustainable development tend to be viewed in ideological terms and so are influenced by neoclassical and neo-liberal ideologies: 'Neoclassical trade theory focuses on one dimension, i.e., the price at which a commodity can be delivered, and is extremely narrow in cutting off a large number of other considerations about impacts on employment in different parts of the world, on the environment and on culture. Ethics is not part of this idea of rationality. The international trade theory is rather of a cynical kind.' Söderbaum identifies the features of neoclassical economics and neo-liberalism as including: focus on markets; economic growth in GDP terms; the only type of organisation seriously considered is a business, firm or corporation; consumers have priority; narrow focus on one commodity at a time; analysis is largely monetary in kind; efficiency refers to monetary cost; simplistic nature of international trade theory that supports export-oriented production at the expense of local self-reliance; and belief that unrestricted capital movements across borders are good for efficiency in a global perspective. Söderbaum notes that in the development dialogue, economic growth is still the dominant objective. In contrast, trade unions see a link between some of the sustainability aspects and the principles championed by the trade union movement: equity; emancipation; health and safety; secure and meaningful jobs free from exploitation; and protection of the environment. The trade union view of sustainable development includes the three pillars of social, economic and environmental responsibility as well as a cultural dimension (Springett and Foster 2005: 278). It is clear from these observations that trade unionists are likely to be disappointed with a managerial prerogative over CSR as that will restrict its possibilities to less than those imagined by the trade unions.

Workers and other stakeholders

Workers and employees have struggled to get recognition within company law. They tend to be regarded as outsiders rather than as insiders within the company and so are forced to rely on labour law protections rather than be integrated into the corporate law system. The notorious failure of the Draft Fifth European Company Law Directive highlights the difficulties for employees in attaining participation in corporate decision-making (Villiers 1998). A CSR agenda does not ensure greater integration for employees or their representatives.

CSR does not give to workers a priority over other stakeholder groups. Rather, they are forced to compete with other stakeholder interests. Indeed, for employees in particular, this has been an unfortunate development in UK company law with the implementation of section 172 of the Companies Act 2006. Before that section was introduced, and prior to the existence of the currently prevailing CSR agenda, employees had, within company law, section 309 of the Companies Act 1985 to protect them. That section required company directors, when fulfilling their management duties, to take into account the interests of employees. The provision was frequently criticised as mere lip-service to employee interests. Much was made of the fact that the old section 309 did not provide employees with standing to challenge managers in the courts when they felt that the managers had failed to take their interests into account. The provision was largely seen as no more than window dressing (Villiers 2000). Nevertheless, employees stood more chance of their interests being considered than they do now under section 172 which is a more broadly inclusive provision, requiring managers to take into account the interests of other stakeholder groups as well as those of employees, though primarily with the aim of meeting the long-term interests of the shareholders.

Compared to the previous common law duty of directors to act in the company's interests, section 172 appears to be more supportive of a stakeholder perspective. The common law duty did not preclude directors from having regard to various stakeholders as part of their duty to act bona fide in the best interests of the company, but, as Goddard (2008: 471–472) remarks, 'section 172 goes further: it posits a relationship between the pursuit of shareholder wealth maximisation and the obligation to consider the impact of decisions on various stakeholders'. Goddard quotes a government minister who said that section 172 'marks a radical departure in articulating the connection between what is good for a company and what is good for society at large' (ibid.).

Section 172 is widely regarded as a statutory manifestation of CSR requirements (Yeoh 2007). Yet for employees, at least, section 172 is problematic because its potential effect is to dilute the importance attributed to the interests of the employees. Indeed, none of the interests listed are to be given primacy since the directors need only 'have regard to' such interests. Nor does this preclude directors from taking decisions that are inconsistent with any such interests.[5] Section 172 could have the effect of increasing the discretion enjoyed by directors without exposing them to challenge by the stakeholders where they feel their interests have not been given due or sufficient consideration. Without *locus standi* to challenge them, the directors have nothing to fear from the employees. If their interests should conflict with those of the shareholders it would be unlikely that the shareholders would make a challenge on their behalf. Conversely, the shareholders might complain also that such a provision makes their own challenges more difficult because the need to consider other stakeholders increases the discretion of the directors and equips them with a defence against a shareholder challenge. In section 172 directors are to act in good faith and to give regard to such interests in a way that they believe will promote the company's success. The good faith element is relatively easy to satisfy and may therefore legitimise the decisions that directors make rather than expose them to further challenge. Within such discretion, the wording of the section indicates to the directors that their overriding aim is to satisfy the interests of the members as a whole over the long term. In practice, directors are going to continue to feel constrained to look after the interests of their shareholders.

The next section will highlight some of the limiting factors that might be imposed on the CSR agenda by this narrow company law framework more generally.

Company law obstacles to effective CSR

The UK company law system is, in reality, likely to present obstacles to effective use of the CSR agenda for trade unions. Key problems include the emphasis on profit maximisation and shareholder interests, as well as

---

[5] This interpretation is suggested by Clifford Chance in a report submitted to the UN Special Representative of the Secretary-General on the Issue of Human Rights: Corporate Law Tools Project, September 2009, available at http://www.reports-and-materials.org/Corporate-law-tools-reports-UK-Sep-2009.pdf

fundamental corporate law principles of limited liability and separate personality.

Shareholder primacy and profit maximisation

In the UK and in the US the primary focus of company law is shareholder satisfaction. This arises first because shareholders are generally treated as owners of the company (cf. Ireland 1999) and second because of the implications of larger companies being structured by a separation of ownership and control. That separation makes possible the opportunity for self-serving behaviour by those in control at the expense of the shareholders' interests (Fama and Jensen 1983). A number of scholars and observers from both left and right of the political spectrum point to examples of the push towards shareholder value arising from more fluid capital markets, widespread institutional investment and regulatory competition. (See La Porta et al. 1998, 1999, 2000)

The corporate disasters at Enron and Worldcom and the collapse of the stock market during the early 21st century revealed the limitations and flaws in the shareholder-centred vision and encouraged a renewed impetus for the stakeholder model of corporate law. The Company Law Review that the New Labour Government began in the UK in 1998 and completed with the enactment of the Companies Act 2006 concluded that an enlightened shareholder vision (ESV) should prevail that accommodates other interests in a company's operations.

ESV was explained succinctly in a lecture by Professor Paul Davies (2005), who had participated in the Company Law Review as a member of the review group steering committee:

> The aim is to make it clear that although shareholder interests are predominant (promotion of the success of the company for the benefit of its members), the promotion of shareholder interests does not require riding roughshod over the interests of other groups upon whose activities the business of the company is dependent for its success. In fact, the promotion of the interests of the shareholders will normally require the interests of other groups of people to be fostered. The interests of non-shareholder groups thus need to be considered by the directors, but, of course, in this shareholder-centred approach, only to the extent that the protection of those other interests promotes the interests of the shareholders.

What is clear from Professor Davies' explanation is that enlightened shareholder value gives rise to a tamer pursuit of shareholder interests – a long-term profit maximisation that requires other interests to be given recognition.

According to Andrew Keay (2007: 590), the ESV approach 'was clearly based on shareholder value and involved directors having to act in the collective best interests of shareholders, but it eschewed an exclusive focus on the short-term financial bottom line and sought a more inclusive approach that valued the building of long-term relationships'. The enlightened shareholder value approach 'envisaged directors taking a balanced approach and that the long-term view should not be paramount over the short term or vice versa' (ibid.).

A consequence of this legal model of the company is that CSR, regarded as a stakeholder-oriented issue, is given less attention than the primary objective which is to increase profits for the shareholders. Indeed, company law arguably actually *mandates* profit maximisation and thereby sits in direct conflict with 'any incurrence of uncompensable costs for socially desirable action' (Parkinson 1993: 260). One major protection that company law provides for shareholders is the privilege of limited liability and this principle has significant consequences for CSR.

The problem of limited liability
A major privilege given to shareholders in company law is that of limited liability. Limited liability is a prominent feature of the facilitative business environment objective of company law, allowing shareholders to be responsible for only a limited amount of their company's debts in the case of insolvency; the paid-up value of their shares. This has potentially devastating consequences for CSR because shareholders are encouraged to sanction more risky activities in the hope that their profits will grow but also secure in the knowledge that if the risk fails and things go wrong their own liability will be limited to the sum of money they invested. As is expressed by Plesch and Blankenburg, 'the company is designed to provide [the shareholders] with money, while protecting them from the responsibility for their actions or inactions in relation to it. A company can be prosecuted or sued if it sells defective products, destroys the environment or sells weapons to the enemy, but its shareholders are immune . . . Shareholders have regulated protection, at a time when other regulation is being swept away in their favour' (Plesh and Blankenburg 2007: 7). Paddy Ireland (2010: 845–846) describes the corporate legal form, combining limited liability and separate legal personality, as providing for shareholder *ir*responsibility, whereby shareholders 'schizophrenically identify themselves very closely with the companies in which they hold shares for some purposes, while seeing themselves as completely separate from them for

others'. He argues (ibid.: 848) that the corporate legal form provides a 'shareholders' paradise': a body of law able to combine the ruthless pursuit of 'shareholder value' without any corresponding responsibility on the part of shareholders for the losses arising out of corporate failure or the damage caused by corporate activities or malfeasance.

This emphasis on protecting shareholders may have a limiting effect on CSR because shareholders are unlikely to pursue a CSR course actively against their managers. Ireland (ibid.: 845) notes, for example, the silence of shareholders with regard to dangerous working practices of Railtrack that were implicated in the Hatfield rail disaster in the UK in 2000. The shareholders had neither spoken up nor campaigned against the company's safety record. Yet they continued to draw dividends without feeling any responsibility for the actions of their company. However, they did challenge, unsuccessfully, a decision by the then Secretary of State, Stephen Byers, to force the company into administration, a decision which reduced the value of their shares.

Separate legal personality
Company lawyers are familiar with the separate personality theory as a concept arising from the fictional personhood of the company. This fiction also limits the possibility of connecting the company to an obligation based on moral responsibility. Morality and moral responsibility are features of natural personhood associated with the ability to think and the possibility of free will. As a fictional entity the corporation's personhood is inherently limited as is the ability of the company to think for itself. It is difficult to attribute responsibility to something that is not a fully moral person (Quigley 2004). The difficulty of connecting human rights to corporate entities is also apparent when companies are viewed as artificial entities or as complex contractual associations. Corporate social responsibility is then apparently removed from a notion of the moral responsibility of the company.

Other features of company law in the UK, and in the US and other countries that would support arguments against reliance on company law for CSR, include examples of corporate attempts to reduce their tax obligations and the possibility of tax avoidance (McBarnet 2003: 229), creative or even bad accounting practices (McBarnet and Whelan 1999), corporate governance failures (Clarke 2010), and scandals of excessive executive remuneration (Villiers 2010). These examples do not suggest a deep commitment to corporate ethics or distributive justice, both arguably vital elements of an effective CSR system. Such a barren ground for the potential growth of CSR leads us to wonder why CSR has in fact been embraced by many corporations. The characteristics of the phenomenon go some way towards explaining this enthusiasm by companies for CSR.

CSR's attractions for corporations and its problems for trade unions
and workers

CSR has been warmly embraced by companies. This is perhaps because its recent development has been much more as an ameliorative device than as a transformative phenomenon (Ireland and Pillay 2010: 12). Contemporary CSR emphasises partnership and advocates of the 'triple bottom line' argue that maximisation of shareholder value is good for society as a whole (Dolan and O'Pondo 2005, Prieto-Carrón et al. 2006: 984). Thus CSR does not present any real challenge to the shareholder primacy model that dominates at least Anglo-American company law. In some ways corporate managers have effectively hijacked CSR and turned it into a paternalistic force that enables them to engage in stakeholder management and to impose their own corporate goals onto the regulatory agenda. By adopting CSR corporations can effectively co-opt NGOs and stakeholders and also ensure that state regulation will not be imposed upon them. This point is highlighted by Prieto-Carrón et al. (ibid.) who note the dominating discourse of the business case for CSR and the lack of discussion on power issues. In stakeholder management these points need to be recognised particularly since 'some stakeholders are often missing from lists of stakeholders, or physically absent from stakeholders' meetings and forums' (ibid.). They are precisely those in developing countries who do not have a voice in society: farmers, children, workers – especially home based workers and women workers. They note that 'even if these groups occasionally have a voice in multi-stakeholder initiatives, power relations between stakeholders continue to shape the issues that are raised, the alliances that are formed and the successes that are identified' (ibid., quoting Dolon and O'Pondo 2005). These inequalities are reproduced further in codes of conduct and practices that are created by companies or by international bodies such as the OECD or the ILO. The effect is to create market dependence rather than market enablement (Meiksins Woods 1999). This point is further illustrated by Crane, Matten and Moon (2004: 112): 'Corporations have a strong influence on the administration of social rights of their employees, including aspects of health and safety, fair wages, education, etc. This is particularly the case in developing countries where governments have proven unwilling or unable to protect such rights, leaving it open to the discretion of corporations. This raises questions about the mechanisms of influence open to employees to shape this provision, including models of employee participation and "co-determination".'

The strong influence that corporations have on the shaping and development of CSR has the effect that, despite its rhetoric of emancipation, and its promise of discourses of corporate citizenship, in reality social responsibility and sustainability are defined by narrow business interests and serve to curtail the interests of external stakeholders (Banerjee 2008: 51). Ultimately CSR may be regarded as an agenda that seeks to preserve a particular social order rather than as a force for change (Harvey 2006).

Having presented a rather pessimistic view of CSR and its limited promises, what might be an alternative route for employees and trade unions to get their voices heard in large corporations and to be able to influence corporate actions for sustainable development?

Alternatives

Trade unions are not irrelevant to corporate or political action. However, to seek influence through CSR is likely to leave trade unions and their members disappointed and workers insufficiently protected from the external costs of corporate action. Singh and Zammit (2000) argue for an alternative managed world trade that is less divisive (between the Northern and Southern hemispheres) and that is focused on reducing poverty and on promoting participation and labour standards. They note also that it is imperative that we address the increase in informal labour. Trade unions need to find ways to represent those workers in informal sectors.

The key to effective protection is power. At present big business has enormous economic and political power nationally and internationally. A necessary step is as Banerjee (2008: 75) suggests: 'to question the autonomy or corporate law and focus attention on the power dynamics between different groups in society'. Importantly, Banerjee (ibid.), citing Frank (2001: 143), argues that: 'restoring a sense of social justice and equity cannot be achieved through some final triumph of the corporation over the body and soul of humanity, but some sort of power that confronts business'.

Corporations have been described both as a 'giant that can mobilise vast resources to gain influence' and as a 'medusa' (Utting 2008: 973). The effect has been to alter the course of activism and for corporations to be able to

184

co-opt NGOs and CSR institutions. What is necessary is to find a force that will confront business. This requires collective action between trade unions and NGOs (Gallin 2000) as well as utilising states and international institutions. For example, the European Trade Union Confederation (ETUC) notes a need to take into account fundamental ILO standards, ILO Tripartite Declaration and OECD Guidelines as the bases for the conduct of European companies with regard to their direct or indirect interests in the South.

Utting (2008: 971) argues for corporate accountability as an alternative to CSR. He suggests that corporate accountability brings issues of conflict, redistributive politics, counter hegemonic struggles and structural change back into the equation. These are concepts that lie at the foundations of the trade union movement. With their democratic functions trade unions have the potential to use the accountability movement to generate a counter-vailing power. Only then might corporations behave more responsibly and labour be given an opportunity to protect itself and to find a true participatory role.

References

Banerjee, S.B. (2008) 'Corporate Social Responsibility: The Good the Bad and the Ugly', *Critical Sociology* 34: 51.

Carroll, A.B. (1991) 'The Pyramid of Corporate Social Responsibility: Toward The Moral Management of Corporate Stakeholders', *Business Horizons* 34: 39.

Clarke, T. (2010) 'Recurring Crises in Anglo-American Corporate Governance', *Contributions to Political Economy* 29(1): 9.

Crane, A., Matten, D. and Moon, J. (2004) 'Stakeholders as Citizens? Rethinking Rights, Participation and Democracy', *Journal of Business Ethics* 53: 107.

Dahlsrud, A. (2008) 'How Corporate Social Responsibility is Defined: An Analysis of 37 Definitions', *Corporate Social Responsibility and Environmental Management* 15: 1.

Daugareihl, I. (2008) 'Employee Participation, Ethics and Corporate Social Responsibility', *Transfer: European Review of Labour and Research* 14: 93.

Davies, P.L. (2005) 'Enlightened Shareholder Value and the New Responsibilities of Directors', Lecture delivered at the University of Melbourne Law School (the inaugural WE Hearn Lecture), 4 October 2005.

Dolan, C. and O'Pondo, M. (2005) 'Seeking Common Ground: Multi-Stakeholder Processes in Kenya's Cut Flower Industry', *Journal of Corporate Citizenship* 18: 1.

Fama, E. and Jensen, M. (1983) 'The Separation of Ownership and Control', *Journal of Law and Economics* 26: 301.

Frank, T. (2001) *One Market Under God: Extreme Capitalism, Market Populism and the End of Economic Democracy* (Anchor).

Gallin, D. (2000) 'Trade Unions and NGOs: A Necessary Partnership for Social Development', Civil Society and Social Movements Programme Paper Number 1, (June 2000, UN Research Institute for Social Development).

Goddard, R. (2008) 'Directors' Duties', *Edinburgh Law Review* 12: 468.

Harvey, D. (2006) *A Brief History of Neoliberalism* (Oxford University Press).

Ireland, P. (1999) 'Company Law and the Myth of Shareholder Ownership', *Modern Law Review* 62: 32.

Ireland, P. (2010) 'Limited Liability, Shareholder Rights, and the Problem of Corporate Irresponsibility', *Cambridge Journal of Economics* 34: 837.

Ireland, P. and Pillay, R. (2010) 'Corporate Social Responsibility and the New Constitutionalism', in P. Utting (ed.) *Corporate Social Responsibility and Regulatory Governance: Towards Inclusive Development?* (UNRISD/Palgrave Macmillan).

Justice, D. (2002) 'Corporate Social Responsibility: Challenges and Opportunities for Trade Unionists', Cornell University ILR School, Paper available at http://digitalcommons.ilr.cornell.edu/codes/9 (last accessed 22 September 2010).

Keay, A. (2007) 'Tackling the Issue of the Corporate Objective: An Analysis of the United Kingdom's "Enlightened Shareholder Value" Approach', *Sydney Law Review* 29(4): 577.

La Porta, R., Lopez-De-Silanes, F., Schleifer A. and Vishny, R. (1998) 'Law and Finance', *Journal of Political Economy* 106: 1113.

La Porta, R., Lopez-De-Silanes, F., Schleifer A. and Vishny, R. (1999) 'Corporate Ownership Around the World', *Journal of Finance* 54: 471.

La Porta, R., Lopez-De-Silanes, F., Schleifer A. and Vishny, R. (2000) 'Investor Protection and Corporate Governance', *Journal of Financial Economics* 58: 3.

McBarnet, D.J. and Whelan, C. (1999) *Creative Accounting and the Cross-eyed Javelin Thrower* (Wiley).

McBarnet, D. (2003) 'When Compliance is not the Solution but the Problem: From Changes in Law to Changes in Attitude', in V. Braithwaite (ed.) *Taxing Democracy: Understanding Tax Avoidance and Evasion* (Ashgate).

Meiksins Woods, E. (1999) 'The Politics of Capitalism', *Monthly Review* 51 (available at http://monthlyreview.org/999wood.htm).

Moon, J. (2007) 'The Contribution of Corporate Social Responsibility to Sustainable Development', *Sustainable Development* 15: 296.

Parkinson, J. (1993) *Corporate Power and Responsibility* (Oxford University Press).

Plesch, D. and Blankenburg, S. (2007) *Corporate Rights and Responsibilities: Restoring Legal Accountability* (Royal Society of Arts) (see www.rsa.org.uk).

Prieto-Carrón, M., Lund-Thomsen, P., Chan, A., Muro, A. and Bhushan, C. (2006) 'Critical Perspectives on CSR and Development: What We Know, What We Don't Know and What We Need to Know', *International Affairs* 82: 977.

Quigley, W. (2004) 'Catholic Social Thought and the Amorality of Large Corporations: Time to Abolish Corporate Personhood', *Loyola Journal of Public International Law* 5: 109.

Singh, A. and Zammit, A. (2000) *The Global Labour Standards Controversy: Critical Issues for Developing Countries* (United Nations).

Söderbaum, P. (2004) 'Democracy, Markets and Sustainable Development: The European Union as an Example', *European Environment* 14: 342.

Söderbaum, P. (2009) 'Making Actors, Paradigms and Ideologies Visible in Governance for Sustainability', *Sustainable Development* (online publication).

Springett, D. and Foster, B. (2005) 'Whom is Sustainable Development *For*? Deliberative Democracy and the Role of Unions', *Sustainable Development* 13: 271.

Utting, P. (2008) 'The Struggle for Corporate Accountability', *Development and Change* 39: 959.

Villiers, C. (1998) *European Company Law: Towards Democracy?* (Ashgate).

Villiers, C. (2000) 'Section 309 of the Companies Act 1985: Is it Time for a Reappraisal?', in H. Collins, P. Davies and R. Rideout (eds) *Legal Regulation of the Employment Relation* (Kluwer).

Villiers, C. (2010) 'Controlling Executive Pay: Institutional Investors or Distributive Justice?', *Journal of Corporate Law Studies* 10(2): 309.

Yeoh, P. (2007) 'The Direction and Control of Corporations: Law or Strategy?', *Managerial Law* 49: 37.

11
Corporate social responsibility meets traditional supervision of fundamental labour rights

Why CSR needs social dialogue to fill the governance gaps

DAVID TAJGMAN*

The International Labour Organisation's (ILO) 1998 Declaration on Fundamental Principles and Rights at Work prioritised four core labour standards' principles and led to a burst of new ratifications of the international treaties that are the subject of those principles.[1] Complementing the states' ratifications, the prioritised four principles – compellingly authoritative since the Declaration was adopted in the uniquely tripartite and globally representative specialised UN agency – have become the cornerstone of labour principles reflected in private social responsibility initiatives. Scores of voluntary company- and industry-level codes of conduct and related corporate social responsibility (CSR) initiatives name either the 1998 Declaration, the four fundamental principles, or the under-

---

* External Lecturer, Aarhus University School of Law, Aarhus, Denmark. Principal Consultant, Labour in Development.
[1] The terms 'core labour standards' and 'fundamental labour standards' are used interchangeably in this chapter to mean the four subject matter areas identified in the 1998 Declaration. The term 'principle' is used to mean an unspecified essential content of the international norms in these four areas. The term 'Convention' is used to mean the ILO Conventions – their 'specific rights and obligations' – that are subject to international supervision, under various provisions (Articles 19, 22, 24, 26, 33, 37, etc.) of the ILO Constitution. For a further discussion of the unclear relationship between core labour standards principles and core labour standards conventions, see Alston 2004b: 490–495.

lying eight core labour standards ILO Conventions directly as the labour standard norms to which the initiative owners hold themselves accountable. Numerous commentators have discussed the Declaration's development and content (Kellerson 1998, Trebilcock 2004) and impact (Alston 2004a, N'Diaye 2004, Langille 2005, Maupain 2005).

Ten years on there are important identified gaps in state implementation of the ratified Conventions that are the subject of the four principles. These gaps leave important holes in public policy and legislation. In a number of important substantive areas, these gaps have the effect of leaving it to private actors to figure out what would amount to fulfilling the norms of fundamental labour principle inspired codes of conduct. Inescapably left on their own to figure out approaches, CSR-respecting enterprises are subject to criticism levelled on the basis of interpretations of these principles given by civil society organisations and labour rights' campaigners. In the absence of proper and internationally-compliant labour standards governance, and motivated at least to minimise reputational risk by avoiding misinterpretation of the principles, enterprises can find it advantageous to use social dialogue mechanisms to assert pressure to fill these gaps.

This chapter details this situation. The first part provides the necessary background information. The second part gives concrete examples of how this governance gap raises challenges to implementing CSR initiatives. It is suggested in the third part that – perhaps ironically, considering the arguable origins of CSR in neo-liberal deregulatory fervour – social dialogue and reform by non-compliant state actors is the only sustainable solution.

The ILO's role as maker of international labour standards

As readers of this chapter are most likely well aware, for ninety years the ILO has been the only international organisation with a membership of both global scope and tripartite character – representatives of governments, employers' and workers' organisations – in the business of making international labour standards treaties. To date, some 188 Conventions have been adopted and 7,650 ratifications – binding only on the relevant ILO member state – have been made.[2]

---

[2] As of 21 November 2009. These gross figures disregard a handful of pure denunciations, *de jure* denunciations arising from ratification of revising Conventions, and the results of the

Before 1998 the ILO made standards on different subjects, each more or less on par with each other in terms of the policy importance to be attached to them (Alston 2004b: 484). The International Labour Conference adopted Conventions and Recommendations; Conventions were ratified; international supervision monitored application and prompted eventual change by the state actors bound by the instruments (Boivin and Odero 2006). Spectacular cases arose (Blanchard 2004), but knowledge of the field and its standards were generally relegated to the niche market of specialists whose job it was to deal with this system of standards (Maupain 2005). It was with modern, post-1989 globalisation that the desirability of categorising standards was recognised (Servais 2004) and the need to prioritise or, to use Alston's term, 'privilege' core labour standards (Alston 2005) acknowledged.

Global changes prompts prioritising and promotion of principles

With the results of the global changes wrought by structural adjustment activities of the international financial institutions under the Washington Consensus in developing countries, the demise of an alternative model for social and economic development offered by the Soviet Union and its allied communist bloc, and the closure of the Uruguay round and the creation of the World Trade Organisation – to name a few of the upheavals in the closing two decades of the last century – the call for the social justice promised to result from the ILO's system of standards became louder. Indeed, the Organisation needed to modernise as a result of these developments; this happened eventually with the adoption in 2008 of the Declaration on Social Justice for a Fair Globalisation (2008 Declaration), with a way station stop at the 1998 Declaration.

But back in the 1990s, on the standards front, the then-Director-General Michel Hansenne started a campaign in 1994 to promote states' universal ratification of the core labour standards Conventions. Proposals were concurrently put forward to deal with allegations of the states' breach of fundamental equality and forced labour principles, regardless of ratifica-

Cartier Working Group (Chigara 2007) establishing that some 70 Conventions continue to be relevant, up to date and subject to promotion for ratification. The magnitude, breadth and acceptance of the ILO's standards remain nevertheless prodigious.

190

tion of the relevant ILO Conventions. The idea was to model the treatment of allegations in respect of these subjects on the way allegations dealing with freedom of association have been treated since 1951. The idea was resisted and ultimately defeated by the ILO's government and employer groups.[3] Some kind of approach that did not depend on ratification was needed. The idea was developed for a Declaration on Fundamental Principles and Rights at Work, with a twinned message of *prioritisation* through reaffirmation of an obligation to respect, and *promotion* through technical assistance (Kellerson 1998).

What has been the result for state and private actors under the 1998 Declaration?

For many governments, the adoption of the Declaration was a final nudge towards ratification. During the period from June 1994 to the present date, the International Labour Office has been able to top up the number of ratifications of fundamental labour standards Conventions. Figures 11.1 and 11.2 show that over three time periods – prior to the start of the Director-General's ratification campaign in June 1994, from June 1994 to the adoption of the promotional 1998 Declaration, and since the adoption of the 1998 Declaration – there has been a significant number of new ratifications. Regular periodic international supervision begins soon after each new ratification and a number of mechanisms for treating ad hoc allegations of inadequate implementation of the standards becomes possible.[4] Through this traditional mechanism of binding states and supervising them internationally, the campaign for universal ratification has been welcomed by at least some of the ILO's constituents concerned that the Organisation's system of standards should be strengthened.[5]

---

[3] See ILO Governing Body documents GB.267/9/2 and GB/267/LILS/5 (November 1996).

[4] Reports on newly ratified Conventions become due one year after the coming into force of the instrument for that country, and this happens one year after the ratification is registered with the Secretary-General of the United Nations. Representations under Article 24 and complaints under Article 26 of the ILO Constitution, in addition to the possibility for workers' and employers' organisations to give information and comments to the Committee of Experts on the Application of Conventions and Recommendations (CEACR) and to bring particular cases up for public discussion at the International Labour Conference in June each year. For further details on supervision, see *Handbook of Procedure Relating to International Labour Conventions and Recommendations*, (ILO, Geneva, revised 2006).

[5] See ILO Governing Body documentation, in particular reports of the GB Committee on Legal Issues and International Labour Standards, for discussion of the subject of 'ratification and promotion of fundamental ILO Conventions' at: http://www.ilo.org/global/What_we_do/Officialmeetings/gb/GBSessions/GB.306/lang—en/commId—LILS/index.htm

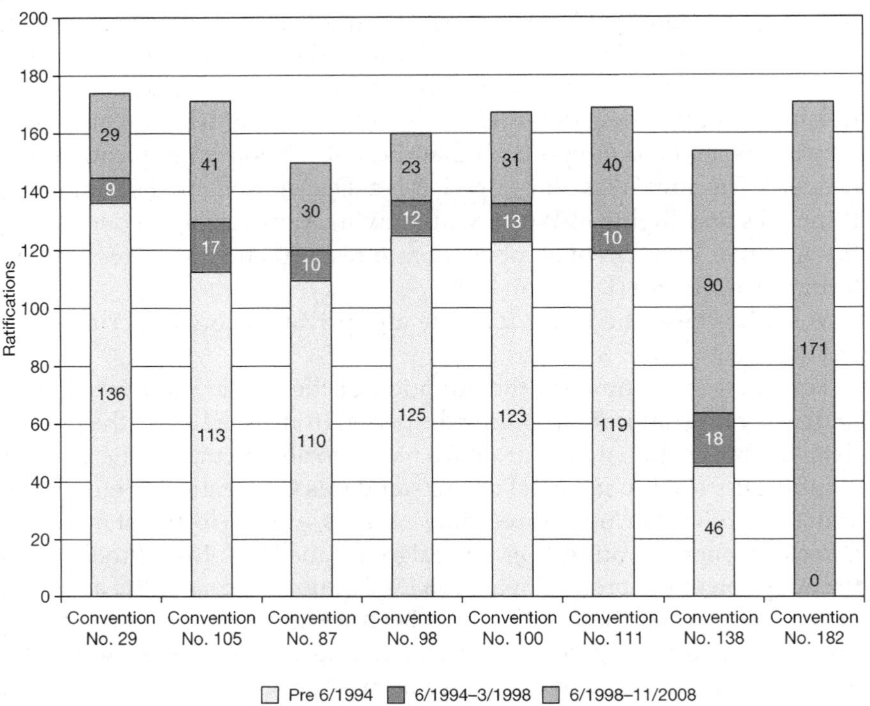

Figure 11.1 Ratification of core labour standards Conventions in three periods

For private actors, the Declaration prioritised four labour standards principles above all others, which have in turn become the cornerstone of most labour principles as reflected in private social responsibility initiatives. Scores of voluntary company- and industry-level codes of conduct and related corporate social responsibility initiatives either name the Declaration, the four fundamental principles, or the underlying eight core labour standards Conventions directly as the labour standard norms to which the initiative owners would hold themselves accountable (OECD 2001, World Bank 2003). The core labour standards have been 'mainstreamed' in this same way into unilateral trade arrangements and bilateral trade agreements, loan and investment terms of international financial institutions, operational arrangements for regional development banks and bilateral development agencies (Bakvis and McCoy 2008).

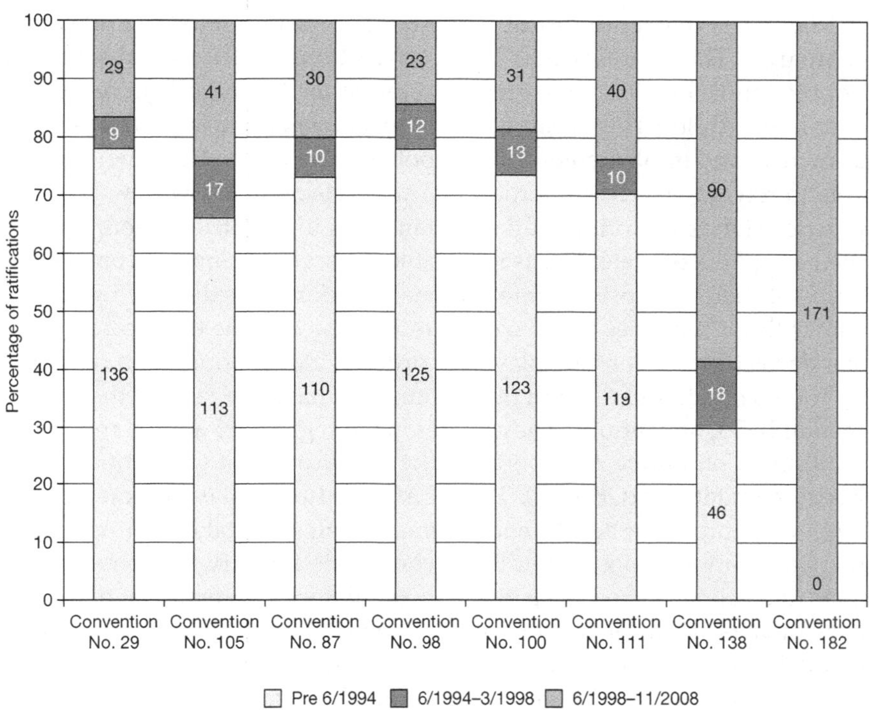

Figure 11.2 Percentage of current ratifications achieved during three periods

The implication of ratifications for supervision and due diligence in applying CSR

The result of the broad success of the prioritisation and promotion of the core labour standard Conventions and principles, and the ratification campaign, is that today CSR-respecting enterprises and governments are under pressure to actually achieve the norms of the 1998 Declaration. For governments, this means implementing the standards set out in the ILO Conventions that were originally meant for them, or working toward realising their principles under the 1998 Declaration. For the private actor, this means respecting the international standard-conforming national standard or complying with one's own private international standard-based code, monitoring and enforcing it along the supply chain. Three caveats condition this situation today.

The first is that a number of large states are resistant to the ratification campaign. The result is that large proportions of the global working population lie outside the system of international standards in respect of certain principles. This is bad news for promoters of social justice, as well as owners and implementers of CSR policies and codes, since they are not able to rely on objective international supervision to know how law and practice stands up to international standards in countries where they or their suppliers operate. Nor is it possible to assess the law and practice in terms of their own private international standard-based code. Table 11.1 shows those countries that have not ratified each of the eight core labour standards Conventions, displayed in order of global population ranking.

The second has to do with those countries that have ratified the fundamental ILO Conventions. These states make regular tri-annual reports to the ILO's Committee of Experts on the Application of Conventions and Recommendations (CEACR). The CEACR in turn makes comments asking, for example, for additional information on steps taken to implement the Conventions. Most often these comments identify implementation gaps that call for remedy in legislative, regulatory or practical action. CSR code owners and implementers are able to turn to this supervision of these countries to gauge state compliance with the fundamental labour standards Conventions. With this information about state implementation in hand, social auditors and others involved with CSR compliance mechanisms are able to focus their often limited resources on enterprise-level compliance.

The caveat here is that on the basis of this system of reporting and supervision, the CEACR has, in fact, comments pending on the application of virtually every country's ratified fundamental labour standard Conventions.[6]

Figure 11.3 shows the situation for the 129 countries that have ratified all eight core labour Conventions and the 54 countries that have not; the

---

[6] The ILO's APPLIS database displays all pending comments at the URL: http://web fusion.ilo.org/public/db/standards/normes/appl/Art22byConv.cfm?hdroff=1&conv=C029 &Lang=EN, where the phrase can be changed to match the relevant three-digit convention number, i.e., 105, 087, 098, 100, 111, 138 and 182. Since governments sometimes report irregularly, a researcher needs to also search country by country the area called 'Archive of comments made by the CEACR' in this real-time public website to assure fully accurate global results. The data presented in this chapter is current as of just prior to the CEACR meeting in December 2009.

Table 11.1 Countries where fundamental Conventions are not ratified (black), population rank (as of 25 June 2011)

		Forced labour		Freedom of association		Equality		Child labour	
	Pop. Rank	C29	C105	C87	C98	C100	C111	C138	C182
China	1	■	■	■	■				
India	2			■	■			■	■
United States	3	■		■	■	■	■	■	
Brazil	5			■					
Bangladesh	7							■	
Japan	10		■				■		
Mexico	11				■			■	
Viet Nam	13		■	■	■				
Iran	17			■	■			■	
Thailand	21			■	■		■		
Myanmar	24		■	■		■	■	■	■
Korea	26	■	■	■	■				
Kenya	32			■					
Sudan	33			■					
Canada	36				■			■	
Morocco	38			■					
Iraq	39			■					
Nepal	40			■					
Malaysia	43		■	■			■		
Afghanistan	44	■		■	■				
Uzbekistan	45			■	■				
Saudi Arabia	46			■	■				
Australia	52							■	
Cuba	75								■
Somalia	89			■	■			■	■
Laos	104		■	■	■			■	
Jordan	105			■	■				
Turkmenistan	113			■	■			■	
Eritrea	114			■	■				■
Singapore	115		■	■	■		■		
United Arab Emirates	117			■	■	■	■		
New Zealand	123				■				
Lebanon	124			■	■			■	
Liberia	130					■	■		
Kuwait	137			■	■	■	■		
Oman	138			■	■	■	■	■	
Guinea-Bissau	148			■				■	
Qatar	150			■	■	■	■	■	
Timor-Leste	155		■	■	■			■	
Bahrain	159			■	■	■			
Solomon Islands	166	■	■	■	■	■	■	■	
Suriname	167			■	■			■	■
Brunei Darussalam	172	■	■	■	■	■	■	■	■
Maldives	176	■	■					■	
Vanuatu	178							■	■
Saint Lucia	182	■						■	
Marshall Islands	200	■	■	■	■	■	■	■	■
Tuvalu	215	■	■	■	■	■	■	■	■

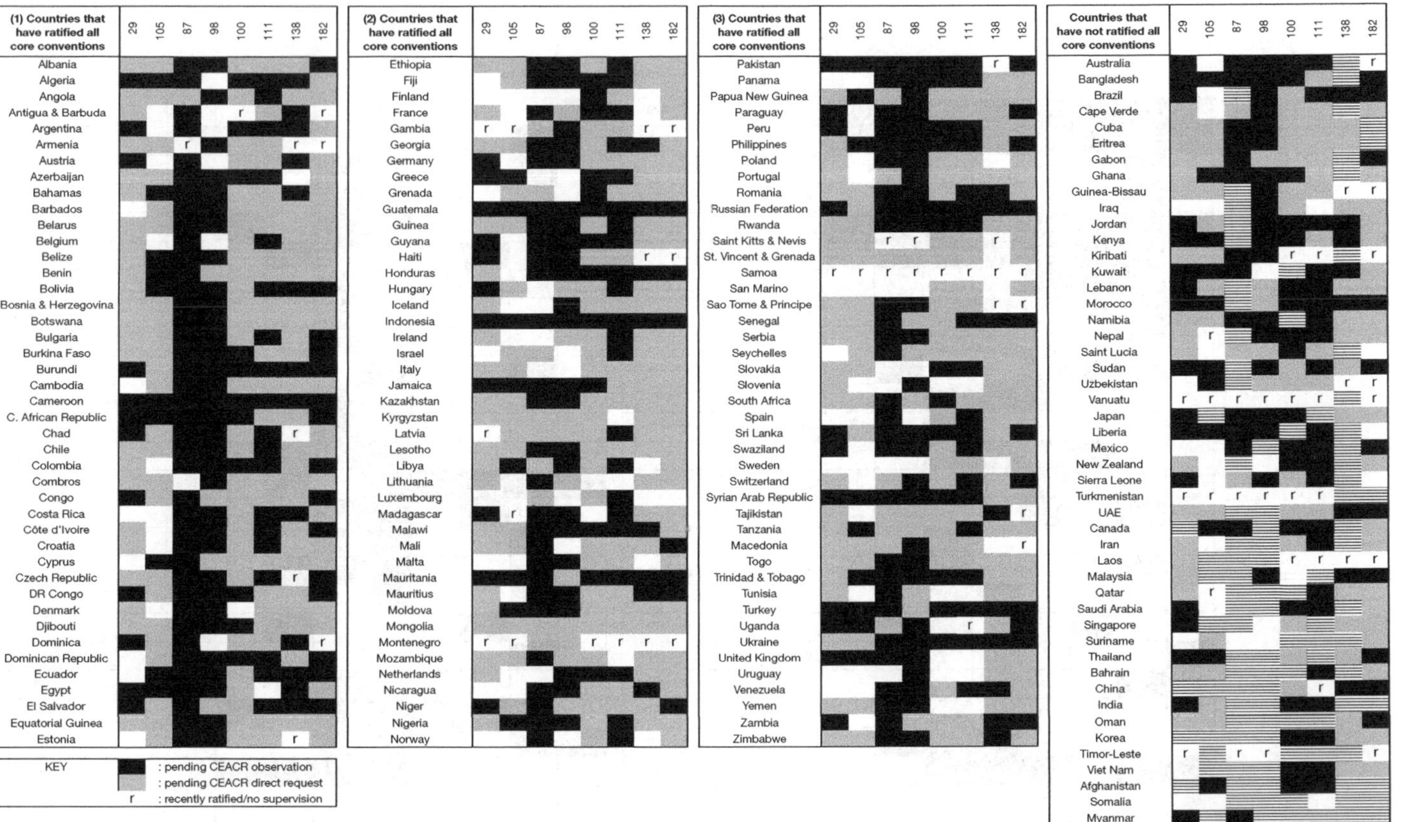

Figure 11.3 CEACR comments pending for 129 countries that have ratified all the core labour Conventions and the 54 that have not

few empty cells are cases where the CEACR has no comments pending.[7] While comments may ask only for further information or even express satisfaction in new developments, the vast majority identify implementation gaps. Some of these deal with matters that have little impact on employment in the private sector, but many expose governance gaps that have the effect of raising very practical concerns for implementing private codes of conduct.

The third has to do with the fact that the ILO's core labour standards Conventions do not always yield for the private actor a principle that can be used as a prescriptive guide for behaviour in response to a factory or field situation. This is because they are set to be universal standards flexible enough for all ILO states to comply with (Humblet and Zarkas-Martres 2004). This is where CSR meets traditional supervision of international labour standards, and why states' governance gaps cause direct problems for enterprises that want to exercise due diligence in implementing their CSR codes and policies along their supply chains.

The effect of state governance gaps on implementing private actors' CSR principles

Leaving aside the not insignificant debate about the actual meaning of the forty words used to enunciate the core labour principles in the 1998 Declaration and in the private initiatives that have adopted them per se (Alston 2004b, Alston 2005), do state governance gaps have a deal-breaking significance for CSR implementation? Is it not possible for a private actor to simply improve upon national standards by meeting the level of the international – and thus its own private – standard? Knox is quite right in

---

[7] Each horizontal row represents the situation of the country named to its left. *In each of the four graphics*, the eight tinted columns represent the eight core labour standard Conventions. The black cells are pending observations or observations with direct requests for the country; the grey cells are pending direct requests (no observation); 'r' indicates that the Convention has been recently ratified or that no first report from the country on the application of the standard has yet been provided and thus ILO supervision has not begun. *For the three graphics to the left*, countries are presented in alphabetical order. *For the graphic to the right*, countries are presented according to the number of core Conventions each has ratified, starting with 7 for Australia, 0 for Tuvalu. Cells with horizontal lines indicate the Convention concerned has not been ratified.

positing that 'to be meaningful labor protections [in international instruments] must address not only governments, but also private employers [and] thus, labor agreements typically specify duties that state parties are required to impose on private actors' (Knox 2008: 24). Indeed, he has pointed out that ILO Conventions are a type of international law that specifies 'the private duties that governments are obliged to impose ... [and which] imposes private duties indirectly, as a secondary effect of the duties it places directly on states' (Knox 2008: 18). Ruggie has suggested, after all, 'ILO conventions ... basically say what private actors are supposed to do'.[8] Yet, both these commentators overlook the fact that the flexibility required to make ILO standards universal among *states* leaves qualitative gaps that make them less than fully appropriate for direct transposition to the shop floor. The standards set in important aspects of fundamental Conventions are often not on a two-dimensional, 'higher' and 'lower' plane. Where this is the case, private actors simply cannot do better than the national standard because something other than 'better' is required of the *state* for compliance.

For example, assuring (as Convention No. 87 requires) 'that workers ... without distinction whatsoever, have the right to establish and ... join organisations of their own choosing without previous authorisation' in practice means a kind of qualitative compliance that answers practical questions about, at a minimum, how organisations secure and retain legal personality. Only the state can establish rules in this regard. Virtually all states have, in fact, complied with this standard in ways that establish all types of conditions and requirements for these organisations. The CEACR finds some of these inconsistent with its understanding of the standard established by the few words of Convention No. 87. This situation can make it impossible for a CSR-respecting enterprise to comply with the international standard.

In sum, states' governance gaps can cause a variety of challenges for implementing CSR-respecting enterprises. Examples of these challenges are considered in detail in this section.[9] These situations can give concerned

---

[8] John Ruggie, presentation to Carnegie Council, 28 October 2008, Business and Human Rights: Achievements and Prospects, transcript at: http://www.cceia.org/resources/transcripts/0074.html

[9] Citations are made to comments of the CEACR in the form: *Country O[bservation]* or *D[irect]R[equest] C[onvention Number] Year of publication.* The cases cited here are representative and not exhaustive.

198

enterprises an incentive to press the state to do the kind of qualitative compliance that is needed to respond to ILO supervision.

Freedom of association and the effective recognition of the right to collective bargaining

The core labour standards' principles are reflected in the Freedom of Association and Protection of the Right to Organise Convention 1948 (No. 87) and the Right to Organise and Collective Bargaining Convention 1949 (No. 98). Perhaps more so than the other three core labour standards areas, freedom of association and the effective recognition of the right to collective bargaining are negative rights where the practical focus is on constraining states' restrictions on exercise of the rights. For states, this is the core labour standards area plagued most by political concerns about the ways in which workers and employers are able to give effect to their rights (Elliot and Freeman 2004). States thus regulate rather heavily in this area and not always in ways that conform to international standards. Consideration is given below to how this might effect the implementation of CSR and codes of conduct.

State legislated monopolies and other basic restrictions

What is a company to do when it wants to afford its workers freedom of association but domestic law prevents it? In the case of China, Vietnam or Brazil where ILO Convention No. 87 has not been ratified and where legislated monopoly organisations exist contrary to international standards, there are no CEACR pronouncements upon which to justify private non-compliance. The violation of workers' rights by the states' imposition of mandated organisations is so flagrant and acknowledged that, in these cases, private actors have a known excuse for not complying with international standards. The cases of ratifiers, such as Cuba, Syria, Nigeria, Panama, Libya and Belarus,[10] are at least being supervised. De facto monopoly situations also exist and have been identified by the CEACR.[11] Associations can be prohibited in various sectors, such as agriculture[12] and

---

[10] Cuba O C87 2008, Syrian Arab Republic O C87 2009, Nigeria O C87 2009, Panama O C87 2009, Libyan Arab Jamahiriya C 87 2009, Belarus O C87 2009.

[11] Moldova O C87 2009.

[12] Pakistan O C87 2009, Canada O C87 2008, Bangladesh O C87 2008, Bolivia O C87 2009, Honduras O C87 2008, Cape Verde DR C87 2009.

home work, or in areas, such as export processing zones (EPZs).[13] Where government has explicitly excluded workers in EPZs from being in a trade union, how does a CSR-respecting brand or employer behave, and particularly where activists call for upholding the international and not the national standard? In all such cases, it is difficult to imagine a viable private sector option for respecting the principle without directly violating the national law. Alternative representative bodies – works councils, worker/management committees, etc. – created by the employer either on its own or in compliance with national law open channels of communication but do not amount to expressions of freedom of association.

Representatives' access to workers and facilities for representation
There is no reference in either ILO Conventions Nos 87 or 98 to access of worker representatives – internal or external to the enterprise – to workers; the Workers' Representatives Convention 1971 (No. 135) and its accompanying Recommendation (No. 143) do give guidance. The possibility of access is essential if organisation is to take place in the first place and if representation is to be effective once workers are organised; many codes of conduct recognise as much. The CEACR has identified governance gaps in respect of the area, for example where minimum requirements must be met before certain facilities are to be made available to workers' representatives,[14] access is completely banned in certain facilities,[15] and other types of limitations are imposed.[16] This is an area where a CSR-respecting enterprise or its code-respecting supplier may be able to informally waive the preferences given to its property rights by national laws in order to assure the access of workers' representatives. Recommendation No. 143 gives real, sufficiently specific factory-level guidance in respect of a number of matters for which national legislation may not have set standards, including the issues of facilities for workers' representatives, time off for representation purposes, permission for taking time for representational work, remuneration while doing representational work, access to workplace facilities for representational purposes, posting of notices, distribution of pamphlets and documents, access to management officials and

---

[13] Bangladesh O C87 2008, Pakistan O C87 2009, Togo O C87 2009.
[14] Botswana O C87 2008, Lesotho O C87 2009.
[15] Democratic Republic of the Congo O C87 2008, Nigeria O C87 2009.
[16] Australia O C87 2009, United Kingdom DR C87 2009.

collection of dues on the employer's premises.[17] Unfortunately, on the issue of access for workers' representatives who are not employed in the enterprise, the Recommendation points back to the making of national rules, either in law, regulation or collective agreements.[18] State governance gaps on this point may cause practical difficulties, particularly in the context of trade union organising. Indeed, it might be a contributing factor at the root of practical difficulties complained of by trade unions in fully realising workers' rights to organise. As long as code owners and implementers accept the guidance in Recommendation No. 143 as their own standard, it is difficult to imagine situations where the absence of rules made by the state actor, even where Convention No. 135 is ratified,[19] will impede the good faith implementation of private initiatives.

Inadequate protections

The idea that an employer should not harass workers for exercising associational rights is essential to this fundamental principle; it is also easy to distil into a private obligation. The problem is that enterprises and their managers usually find it difficult to admit that personnel actions are taken because of the exercise of rights.[20] An impartial fact finder with binding decision-making authority is needed and Convention No. 98 clearly obliges the state to assure this. In this area as well, unfortunately, international supervision has exposed extensive weakness. Where the remedy is not dissuasive,[21] the procedures take too long or seem suspiciously inactive suggesting practical inadequacy,[22] mixed motivations are not considered discriminatory,[23] the scope of protection is limited,[24] or there is a complete

---

[17] Recommendation No. 143, paragraphs 9–16.

[18] Recommendation No. 143, para. 17.

[19] Burundi DR C135 2005.

[20] The ILO has noted that allegations of anti-union discrimination are now the single largest category of complaints brought to the attention of its Committee on Freedom of Association. International Labour Office 2008b: para. 30.

[21] Eritrea O C98 2008, Honduras O C98 2008, Kiribati O C98 2009, Nicaragua O C98 2009, Switzerland O C98 2009, China, Macau Special Administrative Region Direct Request C98 2008, China (Hong Kong Special Administrative Region) O C98 2009, Cambodia O C98 2008.

[22] Indonesia O C98 2008, Sri Lanka O C98 2009, Costa Rica O C98 2008.

[23] United Kingdom O C98 2009.

[24] Eritrea O C98 2008, Georgia O C98 2008, Iraq O C98 2008, Kiribati O C98 2009, Liberia C98 Observation 2009, Togo O C98 2009.

absence of protective provisions,[25] a potential private answer to this governance problem is a fact finder with binding authority. The recent high-profile case involving the allegedly anti-union motivated closure of Russell Corporation's Jerzees de Honduras factory – operating in a country cited by the CEACR as not having adequate protections from anti-union discrimination – is an example of the possibility for a private fact-finding and remediation solution. In that case, the Fair Labor Association Board of Directors could be seen as having served a type of non-binding adjudicatory role working on the basis of multiple special audit reports.[26] The case, as well as other similar cases,[27] also demonstrates the potential limitations of private actions – the difficulty of identifying violations through audits, the high costs of investigation and conclusion making, and the condition precedent of NGO outcry.

Right to strike
The right to strike is the holy grail of freedom of association, without which collective bargaining is reduced to collective begging. How can a private enterprise properly assure this incentive instilling aspect of the collective bargaining principle where the state itself unduly hampers it? Would a private enterprise voluntarily respect its workers' right to down tools that is more liberal than one offered by the state when an impasse has been reached at the bargaining table – or even before, in cases where the state has arranged binding arbitration as collective negotiation's terminus? Prohibition or limitation of the right to strike in EPZs,[28] one-party referral to strike-enjoining conciliation or compulsory binding arbitration,[29] restrictions that limit or weaken the right to strike,[30] extra-large majorities needed to call strikes,[31] complex or slow conciliation/mediation procedures that

[25] Ethiopia O C98 2009, Haiti O C98 2009, Iraq O C98 2008, Montenegro O C98 2009, Nepal O C98 2009, Paraguay O C98 2009.
[26] See http://www.fairlabor.org/news_releases_a1.html, for full details of the case.
[27] Taiway Sports (China), Jaqalanka Group (Sri Lanka).
[28] Bangladesh O C87 2009, Mozambique O C87 2009, Panama O C87 2009.
[29] Antigua and Barbuda C87 Observation 2009, Jamaica O C87 2009, Kuwait O C87 2009, Madagascar O C87 2009, Malta O C87 2009, Nicaragua O C87 2009, Pakistan O C87 2009, Romania O C87 2009, Ukraine O C87 2009, Montenegro DR C87 2009.
[30] Australia O C87 2009, Bolivia O C87 2009, Colombia O C87 2009, United Kingdom O C87 2009, Mozambique O C87 2009, Nigeria O C87 2009.
[31] Bolivia O C87 2009, Ethiopia O C87 2009, Kazakhstan O C87 2009, Nigeria O C87 2009, Peru O C87 2009, Sao Tome and Principe O C87 2009, Seychelles O C87 2009, Trinidad and Tobago O C87 2009, Kyrgyzstan O C87 2009.

make a lawful strike impossible,[32] and notification of the duration of a strike prior to its start[33] are the most common limitations found by the CEACR to be contrary to the fundamental right.

The elimination of forced or compulsory labour

The core labour standards' principles are reflected in the Forced Labour Convention 1930 (No. 29) and the Abolition of Forced Labour Convention 1957 (No. 105).

Overtime amounting to forced labour

The CEACR has delineated those situations where overtime work is tantamount to forced labour.[34] In this case the CEACR's discussion of the principle should enable a code owner to know where there is a risk of its violation. It is striking how the CEACR meticulously focuses its comments in this area on state action to prevent abuses despite the fact that the complaints it has received concern the conduct of private actors.[35] What happens where there is no legislated or collectively bargained limit to

---

[32] Kiribati O C87 2009, Mauritania O C87 2009, Zambia O C87 2009, Libyan Arab Jamahiriya DR C87 2009.

[33] Russian Federation O C87 2009, Tunisia O C87 2009, Syria O C87 2009, Yemen ObC C87 2009, Kyrgyzstan O C87 2009, Macedonia O C87 2009, Mongolia DR C87 2009.

[34] General Survey on Forced Labour, International Labour Office 2007: para. 132–134. The imposition of overtime is not forced labour so long as it is within the limits permitted by national legislation or collective agreements. Above those limits, the CEACR considers it appropriate to examine the circumstances in which there may be a link between an obligation to perform overtime work and the prohibition of forced labour. The CEACR examined different arrangements governing the imposition of work outside normal daily working hours where in some cases fear of dismissal drives workers to work overtime hours well beyond what is allowed under national legislation. In other cases, where remuneration is based on productivity targets, workers may be obliged to work beyond normal working hours, as only in so doing can they earn the minimum wage. The CEACR has observed that although workers may in theory be able to refuse to work beyond normal working hours, their vulnerability means that in practice they may have no choice and are obliged to do so in order to earn the minimum wage or keep their jobs, or both. The Committee has considered that, in cases in which work or service is imposed by exploiting the worker's vulnerability, under the menace of a penalty, dismissal or payment of wages below the minimum level, such exploitation ceases to be merely a matter of poor conditions of employment and becomes one of imposing work under the menace of a penalty and calls for the protection of the Convention.

[35] See Guatemala O C29 2008, Peru O C29 2008, El Salvador O C29 2009. This goes to the need of international supervisory machineries to deepen their setting of obligations for private actors under international instruments like the ILO Conventions. See Knox 2008.

working hours, or where there are no standards for minimum earnings? In such cases would it be impossible to judge where long working hours have ceased to be merely a case of poor working conditions and have become forced labour? A governance gap here could well impede CSR implementation.

Prison labour hired to private enterprises

Some states have established systems that make common prison inmates available to private individuals or companies for work.[36] This is contrary to the principle reflected in Convention No. 29 as understood by the CEACR. Even where the state supervises the working prisoners,[37] or where the law requires that prison labour for private individuals or companies be voluntary,[38] the CEACR insists that such prisoners must have conditions of service and benefits on par with ordinary workers, to assure conditions approximating a free employment relationship.[39] The well-meaning code owner will meet these conditions even if not required by the public scheme. Yet the combination of the widespread private use of non-conforming prison labour under publicly sanctioned programmes and arguments positing rehabilitation and other benefits for prisoners – arguably a form of corporate social responsibility in and of itself – might make it difficult for code owners to resist non-compliant states' offers of labour at below-market rates (Atkinson 2002).[40] A useful additional discipline for code owners in this area is the rule in the international trade regime that permits governments to restrict imports 'relating to the products of prison labour' (Article XX of the General Agreement on Tariffs and Trade 1994). Any risk-averse enterprise will steer far afield from any use of prison labour anywhere in

[36] Poland DR C29 2008, Germany O C29 2009, Jamaica O C29 2009, Bulgaria DR C29 2009, Belarus DR C29 2009, Botswana DR C29 2009, Dominica DR C29 2009, Gabon DR C29 2009, Ireland DR C29 2009, Namibia DR C29 2009, Peru DR C29 2009, Russian Federation DR C29 2009, Slovakia DR C29 2009.

[37] Australia O C29 2009, Hungary O C29 2009, Guinea DR C29 2009.

[38] France DR C29 2009.

[39] Any labour that is voluntarily offered is not forced or compulsory labour as defined by Convention No. 29. The CEACR does not accept that prisoners can give voluntary assent to an employment relationship where the terms do not approximate free employment relationship. New Zealand's arrangements for voluntary prisoner employment are acceptable to the CEACR (New Zealand DR C29 2009).

[40] A number of major brands and retailers are alleged to have taken advantage of China's offer in this respect. See http://www.humanevents.com/article.php?print=yes&id=16577 ; http://www.david-kilgour.com/2008/Dec_17_2008_06.php

the supply chain. States' failure to meet international standards in this area can nevertheless burden the implementation of private standards.

It is difficult to imagine circumstances where gaps in states' application of Convention No. 105 can confuse private actors' application of its principles. This is so because the Convention's prohibitions are largely of actions only the state can make. Where Convention No. 29 calls for the general abolition of forced labour – a standard a private actor has the ability to understand and the power to comply with – Convention No. 105 requires the abolition of forced labour only in five particular cases.[41] For private actors, these five cases are already covered by the principle of 'no forced labour' in Convention No. 29; the practical focus of Convention No. 105 is these types of forced labour as they arise as a result of a prison sentence, which is generally excluded from the definition of forced labour in Convention No. 29. (See the explanation in Javillier et al. 2004: 67.) But can a state's application gap in respect of Convention No. 105 nevertheless cause difficulties for private code implementation?

Pursuing non-compliant remedies
One example where private action could be seen as complicit in breaching the principle of this international norm is where the private actor pursues a remedy that includes forced labour contrary to the prohibitions of Convention No. 105. Consider forced labour as a punishment for having participated in a strike. In Bolivia, the advocacy of lockouts, strikes or stoppages declared illegal by the labour authorities is punishable by imprisonment of one to five years, including the possibility of forced prison labour.[42] Where, as in this case, the restrictions placed on calling a strike are excessive in terms of Convention No. 87, any possibility for a prison term with forced labour runs counter to Convention No. 105. If a private actor relied on these provisions to have a strike declared illegal and then pursued criminal penalties including the possibility of forced prison labour, a case could be made that the private actor is acting contrary to a private code based on fundamental forced labour principles. Seeking a state's

---

[41] These are: (a) as a means of political coercion or education or as a punishment for holding or expressing political views or views ideologically opposed to the established political, social or economic system; (b) as a means of mobilising and using labour for purposes of economic development; (c) as a means of labour discipline; (d) as a punishment for having participated in strikes; and (e) as a means of racial, social, national or religious discrimination.
[42] Bolivia O C105 2009. See also CFA Case No. 2007 (GB.277/9/1).

authority to requisition workers in order to keep private operations open in the case of a strike would likewise be problematic.[43]

Benefiting from the labour of prisoners being punished in contradiction of the standard

A private actor that benefits from the prison labour of a prisoner of conscience – the forced labour of a political dissident – could be justifiably seen as acting in contradiction of the core labour standards' principles reflected in Convention No. 105. In Algeria, the CEACR has seen that the punishment for expressing political views includes forced prison labour and that the labourers can be put at the disposal of private individuals or companies.[44] A company would not want to benefit from such labour if it wants to comply with a private code based on fundamental forced labour principles. If China had ratified Convention No. 105, enterprises operating and being supplied there would have the benefit of the CEACR's opinion of labour education (*laogai*) schemes and would shun any contact with products produced with the labour of its inmates.

Benefiting from forced labour for economic development

The forced labour in Myanmar could probably be considered labour exacted for purposes of economic development as prohibited by Convention No. 105. That Convention is not ratified by Myanmar, and thus we have no pronouncement on the point from the CEACR or an ILO Commission of Inquiry, but Uzbekistan has ratified Convention No. 105 and concern has been expressed that labourers are forced to work for purposes of economic development – picking cotton there.[45] These are not cases where gaps in state implementation create confusion for private actors; these standards are clear and there is no gap needing to be filled in that respect. The challenge for a code-respecting enterprise is at least to avoid benefiting directly from the states' breaches of the standard. The Total Group attempts to make this point in its response on its presence in Myanmar by saying that 'all forms of forced labour in the area where Total operates have been eradicated ... there is no forced labour in the villages in the [Yadana]

---

[43] Senegal DR C105 2008.
[44] Algeria O C105 2008.
[45] Uzbekistan O C105 2009.

pipeline area',[46] and that it 'has made it abundantly clear that everyone employed by Total E&P Myanmar, its affiliates and its subcontractors to build and operate the pipeline was a paid, voluntary adult with a written contract, and underwent a physical examination prior to hiring and received safety training'.[47] Unfortunately for the company, doubts remain on the international stage (Earth Rights International 2009). Even in a case like Uzbekistan, where the tainted raw material may be several links removed on an international buyer's supply chain, concerned companies nevertheless act to avoid appearing to benefit from non-conforming state practices.[48] Indeed, the Uzbeki government took pains to point out that 'government officials cannot impose compulsory labour on the population for the profit of private employers',[49] perhaps with a view to protecting the market for the Uzbeki 'white gold'.

The abolition of child labour

The core labour standards principles are reflected in the Minimum Age Convention 1971 (No. 138) and the Worst Forms of Child Labour Convention 1999 (No. 182). The foci of these two instruments are very different; care needs to be taken in distilling their principles for use by private actors.

Convention No. 138 tells the state actor to establish minimum ages for admission to work or employment that comply with a range offered in the instrument. The minimum for normal work cannot be lower than fifteen (or fourteen for a developing country); not lower than thirteen (or twelve for a developing country) for light work (if the country wants to permit light work); and not lower than eighteen for hazardous work (although states can establish schemes with safeguards that would permit persons aged sixteen to do hazardous work).[50] The first challenge for the private actor then is to identify the equivalent minimum standard for its operations

---

[46] See 'Total's response on its presence in Myanmar' at http://burma.total.com/

[47] See http://burma.total.com/en/controverse/p_4_1.htm. The more difficult question in such a case is whether a company can ethically justify investment in a country where the state exacts forced labour; this question is beyond the scope of this chapter.

[48] Tesco, Asda Walmart, Marks & Spencer and Gap 'pulled out from the central Asian state'. 'Uzbekistan forced to stop child labour', the *Observer*, Sunday 24 May 2009, Business News & Features: 3.

[49] Government response in Uzbekistan O C105 2009.

[50] Under Article 3, paragraph 3, of the Convention, national laws or regulations or the competent authority may, after consultation with the organisations of employers and workers

under a CSR scheme. For hazardous work the relevant minimum is eighteen; a risk-adverse enterprise would avoid attempting to operationalise the safeguards offered to the state actor where it had not actually made use of them.[51] For normal work, the standard would be fifteen years of age. Even where the state has not complied with these basic provisions by, for example, not clearly setting the minimum age,[52] not making the prohibition of employment or work absolute,[53] not having a prohibition applicable to all employment and work[54] or only in some sectors of economic activity,[55] a private actor should have no difficulty identifying and upholding the higher, international standard compliant minimum. Even where the state had failed to identify, as required, the types of work deemed to be hazardous and therefore subject to the higher, eighteen-year minimum,[56] the risk-averse enterprise should be able to orient practices to avoid any type of work that might be seen as hazardous.

concerned, where such exist, authorise employment or work as from the age of sixteen years on condition that the health, safety and morals of the young persons concerned are fully protected and that the young persons have received adequate specific instruction or vocational training in the relevant branch of activity. Several countries have these schemes, including Netherlands DR C138 2008, Republic of Korea DR C138 2008, Kenya O C138 2009, Turkey O C138 2009.

[51] Many countries have imperfectly made use of these provisions, raising CEACR comments, including Albania DR C138 2009, Belgium DR C138 2009, Benin DR C138 2008, Burundi DR C138 200, Cambodia DR C138 2009, Central African Republic DR C138 2009, Congo DR C138 2009, Cyprus DR C138 2009, Democratic Republic of the Congo DR C138 2009, Denmark DR C138 2009, Dominican Republic DR C138 2009, Greece DR C138 2009, Guinea DR C138 2009, Guyana DR C138 2009, Latvia DR C138 2009, Lebanon DR C138 2008, Malaysia DR C138 2008, Mali DR C138 2008, Mauritania DR C138 2008, Namibia DR C138 2008, Nepal DR C138 2008, Niger DR C138 2008, Panama DR C138 2008, Papua New Guinea DR C138 2009, Paraguay DR C138 2008, Peru DR C138 2009, Rwanda DR C138 2008, Seychelles DR C138 2009, Singapore DR C138 2008, South Africa DR C138 2008, Sudan DR C138 2009, Switzerland DR C138 2008, Syrian Arab Republic DR C138 2008, Togo DR C138 2008, Ukraine DR C138 2008, Uruguay DR C138 2008, Trinidad and Tobago O C138 2009, Venezuela O C138 2008, Honduras O C138 2009, Malaysia O C138 2009, Mauritius O C138 2008, Senegal O C138 2009.

[52] Costa Rica O C138 2008, Dominica O C138 2008, Azerbaijan O C138 2009, Malaysia O C138 2009, Papua New Guinea DR C138 2009, Yemen DR C138 2008.

[53] Honduras O C138 2009, Senegal O C138 2009.

[54] Albania DR C138 2009, Kenya O C138 2008, Senegal O C138 2009, Argentina O C138 2009, Azerbaijan O C138 2009, Indonesia O C138 2009, Nicaragua O C138 2009, Benin DR C138 2009, Central African Republic DR C138 2008, Lebanon DR C138 2008, Madagascar DR C138 2008, Malawi DR C138 2009, Sudan DR C138 2008, Swaziland DR C138 2008, Viet Nam DR C138 2008, South Africa DR C138 2008, Angola DR C138 2009, Belarus DR C138 2009, Bolivia DR C138 2009, Democratic Republic of the Congo DR C138 2009, Djibouti DR C138 2009, Ethiopia DR C138 2009, Iraq DR C138 2009, Iceland DR C138 2009, Qatar DR C138 2009, Morocco O C138 2008.

Conditions for using young persons to do light work
In some situations, states have set a minimum age for doing light work but have not complied with Convention No. 138 in setting the types of work to be considered light (for which persons younger than the normal minimum are permitted to work), hours for doing light work, or the conditions under which light work is permitted.[57] These compliance elements are qualitative; a CSR-respecting enterprise will not be able to find a private actor standard without such a standard being set by the state. Here again, the risk-averse enterprise will avoid any temptation to serve the community, for example, by allowing children to do what it thinks is light work after school or during holiday periods; the enterprise will steer completely away from any thought of using young people to do work it considers light. Enterprises attempting to meet CSR requirements would want the state to fill gaps in detailing the conditions of light work, to permit them to employ children according to those conditions.

Compulsory schooling
Convention No. 138 tells states to select a minimum age that is not less than that for the completion of compulsory schooling, where it exists. A young

---

[55] Honduras O C138 2009, Kenya O C138 2008, Central African Republic DR C138 2008, Sudan DR C138 2008, Swaziland DR C138 2008, Angola DR C138 2009, Bahamas DR C138 2009.

[56] Albania DR C138 2009, Algeria O C138 2009, Angola DR C138 2009, Antigua and Barbuda O C138 2009, Bahamas DR C138 2009, Belize DR C138 2009, Bolivia DR C138 2009, Bosnia and Herzegovina DR C138 2009, Burkina Faso DR C138 2009, Cambodia DR C138 2009, Central African Republic DR C138 2009, Comoros DR C138 2009, Cuba DR C138 2009, Dominica O C138 2009, Fiji DR C138 2009, Grenada DR C138 2009, Guatemala DR C138 2009, Jamaica DR C138 2009, Kenya O C138 2009, Malawi DR C138 2009, Malaysia O C138 2009, Mozambique DR C138 2009, Netherlands, Aruba O C138 2009, Nigeria DR C138 2009, Seychelles DR C138 2009, Zambia O C138 2009.

[57] Convention No. 138, Art. 7, para. 3. *Types*: Albania DR C138 2009, Dominica O C138 2008, Kenya O C138 2008, Azerbaijan O C138 2009, Malaysia O C138 2009, Switzerland DR C138 2008, Lebanon DR C138 2008, Peru DR C138 2008, Paraguay DR C138 2008, Singapore DR C138 2008, Tunisia DR C138 2008, Yemen DR C138 2008, South Africa DR C138 2008, Angola DR C138 2009, Grenada DR C138 2009, Iraq DR C138 2009, Trinidad and Tobago DR C138 2009, Uganda DR C138 2009; *Hours*: Albania DR C138 2009, Kenya O C138 2008, Malaysia O C138 2009, Paraguay DR C138 2008, Tunisia DR C138 2008, Yemen DR C138 2008, South Africa DR C138 2008, Angola DR C138 2009, Democratic Republic of the Congo DR C138 2009, Grenada DR C138 2009, Iraq DR C138 2009, Trinidad and Tobago DR C138 2009, Uganda DR C138 2009; *Conditions*: Albania DR C138 2009, Dominica O C138 2008, Kenya O C138 2008, Malaysia O C138 2009, Paraguay DR C138 2008, Tunisia DR C138 2008, Yemen DR C138 2008, South Africa DR C138 2008, Angola DR C138 2009, Democratic Republic of the Congo DR C138 2009, Grenada DR C138 2009, Iraq DR C138 2009, Trinidad and Tobago DR C138 2009, Uganda DR C138 2009.

person should not be tempted to engage legally in normal work before he or she has completed compulsory schooling. In practice, states err in setting minimum ages that are both lower than[58] and higher than[59] that for completion of compulsory schooling. For a private actor operating where the first case applies, setting the youth to work would be lawful in terms of the minimum age but contrary to the workers' compulsory schooling obligation. In the second case, the employer can safely rely on the prohibition of work when turning the young job seeker away to face the period of enforced idleness between the end of compulsory schooling and the beginning of lawful presence in the job market. In either situation, clarification by the state would benefit respect for a CSR initiative.

Convention No. 182 is about prioritising the worst forms of child labour (WFCL) for urgent elimination; its focus is clearly on the state. The Convention *does* define the WFCL, which can easily be understood by private actors to be an absolute prohibition directly applicable to them. So private actors should know not to employ a child – anyone under eighteen – in any of the WFCL, even in the absence of national prohibitions. For example, the CSR-respecting employer should not use, procure or offer a child for prostitution, for the production of pornography or for pornographic performances even though national law does not include such a prohibition.[60] Nor would it use, procure or offer a child for illicit activities, in particular for the production and trafficking of drugs as defined in the relevant international treaties, even in the absence of national prohibitions.[61] Likewise, an enterprise would avoid slavery or practices similar to slavery, such as the sale and trafficking of children, debt bondage and serfdom and forced or compulsory labour, including forced or compulsory recruitment of children for use in armed conflict, even though there is no national prohibition.

More interesting in respect of this relatively well-defined principle by CSR-respecting private actors are actions on elimination of the WFCL that are not directly attributable to the enterprise but rather within their 'sphere of influence'. There are examples of CSR-respecting enterprises connected

[58] Mongolia DR C138 2008.
[59] Comoros DR C138 2009, Grenada DR C138 2009, Iceland DR C138 2009, Iraq DR C138 2009, Qatar DR C138 2009, Trinidad and Tobago DR C138 2009, Uganda DR C138 2009, Kenya O C138 2009, Lebanon DR C138 2008, Philippines DR C138 2008, United Arab Emirates DR C138 2008.
[60] Azerbaijan DR C182 2009.
[61] Belize DR C182 2009, Congo DR C182 2008.

210

with the tourist industry[62] and the Internet[63] that have introduced important measures in respect of sexual exploitation and trafficking. CSR-respecting enterprises can also eschew tainted goods or raw materials and thereby respect the principle against the WFCL.[64]

The elimination of discrimination in respect of employment and occupation

The core labour standards principles on equality are the subject of the Discrimination (Employment and Occupation) Convention 1958 (No. 111) and the Equal Remuneration Convention 1951 (No. 100). But, can there be talk of 'allegations [against a company] of serious breaches of equal opportunities, *as defined by the ILO core labour standards (ILO Conventions 100 and 111 – prohibiting discrimination at work)*' (OECD 2008a: 11, emphasis added) when these Conventions define the obligations of *state actors*, and only imply – vaguely in some areas – what a breach by a private actor would mean?

Discrimination

A widely accepted principle can, indeed, be pretty well distilled for Convention No. 111: a private actor should not make any distinction, exclusion, or preference on the basis of race, colour, sex, religion, political opinion, national extraction or social origin, where that action would have the effect of nullifying or impairing equality of opportunity or treatment in employment or occupation, understood in the broadest possible terms. Under Convention No. 111, the state is obliged to act in this way in respect of matters it controls, and to promote this behaviour in the private sector. The idea, nevertheless, is sufficiently clear and adaptable to a private actor.

Equal pay for work of equal value (EPWEV)

Distilling a well-accepted principle for private actors concerning equal pay for *work of equal value* (EPWEV), the subject of Convention No. 100, is more

---

[62] In Bulgaria the responsible government agency, NGOs, and representatives of the country's tourist industry signed a Code of Ethics for the prevention of trafficking and sexual exploitation of children in the field of tourism. Bulgaria O C182 2009. Similar actions can be observed in Honduras (O C182 2008), Costa Rica and Thailand.

[63] Japan DR C182 2009.

[64] Blood diamonds and child soldiers, for example.

challenging. EPWEV means appraising the value of work done in different occupations. In a recent publication explaining the fundamental labour principles of the UN Global Compact to business, even the ILO has not said that accepting equality principle six – which itself does not mention remuneration – means doing the sex-neutral job evaluations needed to assure EPWEV; indeed, there is no mention at all of the EPWEV concept in the publication (International Labour Office 2008a). The Convention and the CEACR say states should *promote* EPWEV in the private sector.[65] Should private actors understand that acceptance of the fundamental principle in a code element on equality means proper job evaluations *must* be undertaken along the supply chain as part of a commitment against discrimination, or merely promoted? It certainly *could*, but does it?

There are potentially two reasons why this idea does not distil easily into a principle which can be applied by the private actor. The first is that the Convention's strong positive obligation for the state to promote EPWEV in the private sector 'by means appropriate to the methods in operation for determining rates of remuneration' does not convert to an equivalent private obligation. By contrast, the strong negative aspect of Convention No. 111's obligation for the state '. . . to promote . . . equality . . . with *a view to eliminating* any discrimination . . .' finds an easy private equivalent: don't discriminate. The second is the extent to which the idea of EPWEV is not understood and, as a result, not applied. As the CEACR recently pointed out to all state ratifiers, '. . . while equal remuneration for men and women for work of equal value is a *principle* that is widely accepted, the scope of the concept and its application in practice can be more difficult to grasp and apply' and as a result '. . . countries still retain legal provisions that are narrower than the principal as laid in the Convention . . .'. In this context, a clear undertaking in law and policy by the state would surely help clarify what the principle intends for the local private actor. Unfortunately, it is hard to come by.[66]

---

[65] Papua New Guinea DR C100 2009, Rwanda DR C100 2009, Swaziland DR C100 2009, Seychelles DR C100 2009, Trinidad and Tobago DR C100 2009, Saint Vincent and the Grenadines DR C100 2009, Zimbabwe DR C100 2009, China (Macau Special Administrative Region) DR C100 2009, Poland DR C100 2009.

[66] The ILO Helpdesk's Factsheet No. 5 is entitled 'Eliminating Discrimination in the Workplace'. It explains that the '[t]he principle of non-discrimination in respect of employment and occupation includes the principle of equal remuneration for men and women *who produce* work of equal value. The principle of equal pay for work of equal value means that rates and types of remuneration should be based not on an employee's sex but on

A code of conduct could, of course, include the EPWEV standard where it is not enshrined in national law.[67] Indeed, it has been suggested that CSR by definition means corporate conduct that goes beyond what is required by – or absent in – the law. Ishida describes precisely this sort of situation, in respect of gender discrimination in occupational promotion and remuneration, and Convention No. 100 in the case of Nomura Securities (Ishida 2009). There, the company settled an appeals court case to the benefit of the complainants, despite the trial court having found in 2002 that although there had been discrimination during the entire term (decades) of the complainants' employment, the remedy would be limited only to the period after the relevant law had come into force in 1999. Ishida explains that the settlement arose out of the firm's sense of social responsibility, heightened by being blacklisted by a Swedish investment service specialising in socially responsible investment. In connection with the case, the CEACR had the occasion – as it has done with so many other countries on this point – to 'recall that neither the [Japanese] Labour Standards Act nor the Equal Employment Opportunity Act fully reflects the principle of equal remuneration for women and men for work of equal value, as contained in the Convention', asking the government 'to indicate whether it is considering amending the relevant provisions of these Acts to include the Convention's principle'.[68] Closure of the governance gap more clearly conforming to the international standard would have made reliance on a CSR remedy unnecessary.

an objective evaluation of the work performed.' It goes on to suggest, among other things, that '[s]pecial training programmes could be organized to inform staff, particularly supervisors and managers, of the need to pay employees on the basis of *the value of the work* and not of who is performing the work'. Hopefully these expressions will not be understood to mean the value of the product, i.e., goods or services, produced by the job incumbent. The ILO has produced an excellent 100-page text, *Promoting Equity: Gender-neutral Job Evaluation: A Step-by-Step guide* (2008) which properly and concretely sets out the method for establishing EPWEV.

[67] To name a few, the Fair Labour Association Compliance Benchmarks (November 2006) specifically call for equal pay for work of equal value as between men and women; the Adidas Standards of Engagement (SOEs) (November 2005) names Convention No. 111, other international human rights instruments and the EPWEV concept, but the SOEs are laid out in well accepted 'no discrimination' terms consistent with the principles as reflected in Convention No. 111; the BSCI Code of Conduct (2006) names Convention No. 111 but does not mention EPWEV; the Social Accountability 8000 code (2008) does not mention EPWEV.

[68] Japan O C100 2003. In 2007 the International Labour Conference Committee on the Application of Standards took up the case of Japan and Convention No. 100, attempting to get clarity on the government's position in respect of EPWEV and the need for legislative reform.

Convention No. 111 requires ratifying states 'to declare and pursue a national policy designed to promote, by methods appropriate to national conditions and practice, equality of opportunity and treatment in respect of employment and occupation, with a view to eliminating any discrimination in respect thereof . . . by methods appropriate to national conditions and practice'.[69] While certainly doing all it can to promote the adoption of legislative frameworks, the CEACR has acknowledged that 'the inclusion of non-discrimination and equality provisions into the labour or other relevant legislation *may* be required to ensure that all men and women, in the private and public sectors, are effectively protected from discrimination in employment and occupation on all the grounds covered by the Convention'.[70] The absence of legislation or regulation in some particular areas can cause uncertainty for private initiatives; for example, Sri Lanka, an important exporter, does not have legislation prohibiting discrimination in employment and occupation.[71]

---

[69] Articles 2 and 3. The Convention indicates possible methods, including '(a) to seek the co-operation of employers' and workers' organisations and other appropriate bodies in promoting the acceptance and observance of this policy; (b) to enact such legislation and to promote such educational programmes as may be calculated to secure the acceptance and observance of the policy; (c) to repeal any statutory provisions and modify any administrative instructions or practices which are inconsistent with the policy; (d) to pursue the policy in respect of employment under the direct control of a national authority; (e) to ensure observance of the policy in the activities of vocational guidance, vocational training and placement services under the direction of a national authority; (f) to indicate in its annual reports on the application of the Convention the action taken in pursuance of the policy and the results secured by such action'.

[70] Nepal O C111 2009.

[71] Even before it ratified the Convention in 1998, it had noted that 'the absence of specific legislation prohibiting discrimination in employment and occupation' posed an obstacle to ratification, 1988 General Survey of the CEACR on Equality in Employment and Occupation, para. 13. Twenty years and a ratification later, the CEACR continues to promote the taking of legislative action in Sri Lanka. 'The Committee therefore considers that, in addition to these constitutional guarantees, the inclusion of non-discrimination and equality provisions into the labour or other relevant legislation may be required to ensure that all men and women, citizens and non-citizens, are effectively protected from discrimination in employment and occupation on all the grounds covered by the Convention, including race, colour, sex, religion, political opinion, national extraction or social origin. The Committee also recalls that the adoption of comprehensive legislation has proven to be one of the most effective means to address discrimination in employment and occupation. The Committee urges the Government to make every effort to introduce in the national legislation provisions ensuring that all men and women, citizens and non-citizens, are effectively protected from discrimination in all aspects of employment and occupation on all the grounds covered by the Convention.' Sri Lanka C111 O 2009.

Sexual harassment

The CEACR observed in 1996 that some countries were adopting legislation prohibiting sexual harassment and making it the subject of civil and/or criminal penalties.[72] In 2003, it said to ratifiers of the Convention that sexual harassment was a form of sex discrimination and should be addressed within the requirements of the Convention. Thus, it asked, 'in accordance with the Convention's requirements to prohibit sex discrimination and adopt a policy to promote equality of opportunity and treatment, [that] measures . . . be taken to address sexual harassment'.[73] Some countries have not, however, followed the CEACR's request,[74] or have limited[75] or ineffective[76] protections. Others do clearly recognise sexual harassment as discrimination.[77] A modern, CSR-concerned enterprise certainly sees sexual harassment as a form of discrimination. This is an example where meeting the international standards as understood by the CEACR may only go beyond what is required by national law and regulation, and not be in conflict with it.

The way forward

Much of this chapter deals with a process similar to that of specifying duties of private actors under international human rights instruments described by Knox (2008) – with the critical difference that 'duties' under CSR schemes are voluntary and non-binding. Knox points out that private duties under international human rights law are most often specified through international institutions with authority to interpret such law. He acknowledges that where treaty bodies are 'not authorized to make binding decisions, their non-legally binding views can have a persuasive effect, setting out interpretive positions around which state practice may coalesce. These bodies have addressed private duties but they often state only in

---

[72] 1996 General Survey, para. 40.

[73] C111 General O 2003.

[74] Bangladesh C111 O 2009, Iran C111 O 2009, Nepal C111 O 2009, Rwanda C111 O 2009, Saudi Arabia C111 O 2009, Chad C111 O 2009.

[75] Ecuador C111 O 2009, Sri Lanka C111 O 2009, Mexico C111 O 2009, Ukraine C111 O 2009, United Arab Emirates C111 O 2009.

[76] Dominican Republic C111 O 2009.

[77] Azerbaijan C111 O 2009, Belgium C111 O 2009, Greece C111 Ob2009, Norway C111 O 2009, Albania C111 O 2009, Argentina C111 2009.

general terms that parties have obligations under the treaties with respect to private behaviour without describing those obligations in detail' (ibid.: 24–25). The situation is similar for the CEACR, but, as many of the examples given in this chapter show, the core labour standards Conventions do not specify private duties in a sufficiently positive way and therefore the CEACR gives helpful clarifications by judging states once *they* have acted to impose private duties.

As the OECD has noted, at the end of the day it is one of the main responsibilities of the state to ensure that markets work for people and business can flourish within a *clear rules-based framework* (OECD 2008b). Unfortunately, many governments have a way to go to meet their responsibility in ways that conform fully to international standards. As a result, CSR-respecting companies can founder in the absence of clear rules. In these situations they may be open to reputational risks that are even greater than those they faced prior to undertaking voluntary standards of corporate responsibility.[78] Ruggie has argued that it is governments' role to protect and companies' role to respect. But what is to be done where the governance gap is such that it tends to undermine private actors' efforts to fill them?

Interpretation at the international level

Could the ILO help private actors know what duties the fundamental principles require of them, implicitly in the context of the governance gaps described above?

Although Knox notes rightly that the 'insertion of international human rights law [*read*: labour standards conforming to international Conventions] into domestic laws governing private duties will often be controversial and difficult' (Knox 2008: 27), his belief that international mechanisms can be relied on to specify duties may not be so certain in the context of the ILO and its tripartite framework. Knox says (ibid.):

> The process of specification that the human rights regime has developed, while slow, has real advantages. When states are able to agree on more

---

[78] It may be preferable to keep silent about corporate labour practices rather than assert their compliance with international standards and particularly so where the standards at the national and shop-floor level are unclear or inconsistent with international standards. Consider Piety 2009.

specific private duties, as in the labor field, they can do so immediately. When they cannot, human rights law gives an important role to international tribunals and quasi tribunals with particular expertise in human rights, which may then set out such duties incrementally, drawing on previously accepted interpretations of the law and the subsequent practice of states. Through this process, states that may be reluctant to accept duties to regulate private actors (and private actors that may be reluctant to accept them indirectly) have time to become accustomed to the idea, as the specification progresses from a nonbinding interpretation, to gradual acceptance, to binding agreement or decision.

The CEACR and the Committee on Freedom of Association (CFA)[79] have generally not been willing to directly specify duties of private actors in the course of their supervision of state obligations. However, recently there have been three interesting developments.

In March 2007, the ILO Governing Body approved the establishment of the ILO Helpdesk charged to informally answer questions posed by enterprises trying to better understand international labour standards in the world of work.[80] The Helpdesk opened around November 2008, working under an agreed and detailed operational plan.[81] According to the service's promotional brochure, the Helpdesk's 'primary audience are the people who deal with day-to-day company operations and supply chain management, and who develop private policies shaping those operations, particularly concerning respect for workers' rights'. It 'deals with questions relating to international labour standards and draws on guidance provided by the ILO Declaration of Fundamental Principles and Rights at Work, the ILO MNE Declaration and a range of other declarations, conclusions, guidelines, tools and other instruments. The Helpdesk addresses how these instruments might guide company operations.'[82] The Helpdesk offers a series of Factsheets that are to be 'specifically focused on helping enterprises that want to ensure their operations are aligned with labour

---

[79] See, for example, CFA case No. 2571 involving El Salvador (2007), and alleged anti-union behaviour by a company. The CFA recommendations, which tell the government what it should do in respect of the company, do not help the company figure out what it should do: http://webfusion.ilo.org/public/db/standards/normes/libsynd/LSGetParasByCase.cfm?PARA=8491&FILE=2595&hdroff=1&DISPLAY=RECOMMENDATION#RECOMMENDATION

[80] GB.300/14, para. 11 (November 2007).

[81] GB.301/12, para. 3 (March 2008), GB.301/MNE/2 (March 2008).

[82] ILO Helpdesk promotional brochure, available at: http://www.ilo.org/public/english/employment/multi/download/helpdesk-en.pdf

standards'.[83] Although several two- to four-page Factsheets based on questions presented to the Helpdesk have been published,[84] it is too soon to conclude whether the facility will be able to make pronouncements that are sufficiently specific and decisive to be operationalised; replies are prepared by a 'multi-disciplinary team', which includes the social partners bureaux,[85] who could press for non-specific language when difficult questions arise.[86] Already in November 2009, the employers' group in the Governing Body, 'stressed that the Helpdesk had been designed as an information tool to give concise information to concrete questions and not as a tool to promote ILO standards or the MNE Declaration'.[87] Such views do not bode well for any idea that the new facility would help private actors better understand international labour standards Conventions or principles, even in support of implementing their own CSR initiatives.

The mission of the ILO Helpdesk is consistent with the second development, the adoption by the International Labour Conference of the 2008 Declaration. The Declaration authorises the Organisation to develop 'new partnerships with non-state entities and economic actors, such as multinational enterprises and trade unions operating at the global sectoral level'.[88] This first-of-its-kind mandate for the Organisation opens the door for any range of developments designed to give CSR-respecting enterprises the authoritative guidance they need.

Lastly, in November 2008 the ILO Governing Body asked its secretariat to prepare a study on the interpretation of international labour Conventions, potentially concerning how existing provisions in the ILO Constitution authorising an interpretative tribunal could for the first time be given effect.[89] A paper on the matter was promised to be put before the Governing

---

[83] ILO Helpdesk Factsheet, 'Putting Decent Work Principles into Practice: Labour-Management Cooperation for Responsible Enterprise Restructuring', available at: http://www.ilo.org/wcmsp5/groups/public/—-ed_emp/—-emp_ent/—-multi/documents/publication/wcms_116340.pdf

[84] These can be seen at: http://www.ilo.org/dyn/basi/VpiSearch.ViewDetails?p_lang=en&p_doc_id=34

[85] GB.301/MNE/2, para. 20 (March 2008).

[86] The work of the Helpdesk is complemented by the ongoing technical cooperation work of the ILO going more and more to support private initiatives. Concerning EPWEV, see fn 66; or concerning forced labour, see a seven-booklet set entitled *Combating Forced Labour: A Handbook for Employers and Business* (ILO 2008).

[87] GB.306/11, para. 7 (November 2009).

[88] 2008 Declaration, II.A.(v).

[89] GB.303/PV, para. 254. Article 37 provides that notwithstanding the jurisdiction of the International Court of Justice to decide any question or dispute relating to the interpretation

Body in March 2010 or soon thereafter;[90] in the event, its preparation and presentation remained pending as at May 2011. The employers in the Governing Body stressed that they wanted the study 'to be useful, help to enhance the clarity and reliability of ILO Conventions and improve understanding thereof . . .'.[91] Here, too, it is not yet clear whether such a tribunal would be more ready than other ILO supervisory bodies to specify the duties of private actors for CSR uses.

Social dialogue aimed at filling gaps

The three developments described above would not be needed if governments would more speedily move to conform to ILO Conventions they have ratified and principles they are obliged to promote and respect under the 1998 Declaration. Alas, some would argue that the CSR movement itself would be redundant if only governments would more aggressively specify and enforce the duties of private actors in ways conforming to international standards.

Accepting the current situation, corporate actors could promote the sustainable implementation of their own CSR schemes by pushing states to fill the governance gaps that only they can fill relative to international labour standards. The ILO has here too been active in promoting developments through technical cooperation activities. Fenwick and Kring (2007) describe a representative sampling of ILO technical cooperation activities promoting the ILO's fundamental principles and rights at work in Indonesia, Morocco, Vietnam and Brazil. They paint a picture, among other things, of the possibilities for CSR-respecting enterprises to engage with governments in the context of promoting states' implementation of ratified ILO Conventions or movement toward better realisation of fundamental principles. Put simply, they can help get governments to establish the duties of private actors in ways that conform to the international standards.

Although Ruggie has eschewed the concept of 'sphere of influence' as a concept to define the scope of due diligence required to fulfil the

---

of an ILO Convention, the 'Governing Body may make and submit to the Conference for approval rules providing for the appointment of a tribunal for the expeditious determination of any dispute or question relating to the interpretation of a Convention which may be referred thereto by the Governing Body. . .'.

[90] GB.306/LILS/4(Rev.), para. 12.

[91] GB.304/9/2, para. 10.

responsibility to respect human rights standards,[92] the idea is a good one when it is turned on its head to suggest that enterprises act to get governments to close governance gaps in respect of their existing international obligations. The ILO has been promoting this approach since its inception in the name of social dialogue. These efforts may not have been made with the idea of solving implementation challenges for private voluntary initiatives, but they nevertheless have this result.[93] In another forum, the newly drafted international guidance standard on social responsibility, ISO 26000, suggests that private actors should consider legitimate opportunities and channels to seek to influence relevant organisations and authorities to remedy conflicts between national and international rules.[94]

It is in the interest of well-meaning code owners to engage with the state with a view to filling gaps in national standards that make it difficult to implement private standards. As suggested here, it is in companies' interests to have closure in these respects; CSR will be easier to implement where this is done. In combination with changing approaches to auditing, from control and compliance to one of commitment (Locke, Amengual and Mangla 2009) and relationship building (Frenkel and Scott 2002), maybe there is hope that CSR can deliver actual changes in working conditions.

Conclusion

In a 2005 survey of 269 risk managers, the Economic Intelligence Unit (EIU) found virtual unanimity in the idea that reputational risk has risen sharply in recent years. Study respondents said that 'higher standards of governance imposed by regulators' was the third most important reason for an increased focus on reputational risk within their company[95] and that the biggest threat to reputation is failure to comply with regulatory or legal obligations. This fits well with the idea that in the case of labour principles,

---

[92] Clarifying the concepts of 'Sphere of influence' and 'Complicity', Report of the Special Representative of the Secretary-General on the Issue of Human Rights and Transnational Corporations and other Business Enterprises, A/HRC/8/16 (15 May 2008).

[93] Reliance on tripartite agreement for the change of non-compliant national law can be seen in CEACR comments. See, for example, Bolivia O C105 2009, Indonesia O C87 2009.

[94] Draft International Standard, ISO 26000, para. 4.7.

[95] Preceded only by two other motivations: (1) reputation becoming a key source of competitive advantage as products/services become less differentiated; and (2) faster dissemination of 'bad news' through global media/communication channels.

an absence of meaningful regulation can heighten reputational risk by keeping the character of applicable standards vague and thus difficult to operationalise (EIU 2005). Reputational risk likewise flows from the labour dimension of CSR despite its being a voluntary internal regulation linked to standards external to the CSR-respecting enterprise.

The success of the 1998 Declaration in prioritising the four core labour standards used to benchmark labour principles in CSR codes and initiatives and prompting the ratification by states of the corresponding ILO Conventions is challenged by implementation gaps by both the public and private actors. This chapter has argued that these governance gaps challenge the standards themselves as they are applied locally either by the state or the private actor, and that the nature of some standards requires state action to fill gaps if even private actors are to apply the standards. Private actors are in a position to help remedy the situation and particularly so if they are made aware of its nature. Action needs to be taken one way or another if CSR is to be part of sustainable development. CSR-concerned enterprises willing to engage in social dialogue with slow moving or reticent state actors are well placed to take this action and should recognise self-interest in so doing.

References

Alston, P. (2004a) 'Shrinking the International Labor Code: An Unintended Consequence of the 1998 ILO Declaration On Fundamental Principles And Rights At Work?', *New York University Journal Of International Law & Politics* 36: 221.

Alston, P. (2004b) '"Core Labour Standards" and the Transformation of the International Labour Rights Regime', *European Journal of International Law* 15: 457.

Alston, P. (2005) 'Facing up to the Complexities of the ILO's Core Labour Standards Agenda', *European Journal of International Law* 16: 267.

Atkinson, R.D. (2002) *Prison Labor: It's More than Breaking Rocks* (Progressive Policy Institute).

Bakvis, P. and McCoy, M. (2008) 'Core Labour Standards and International Organizations: What Inroads Has Labour Made?', *Briefing Papers* 6 (F.-E.-Stiftung).

Blanchard, F. (2004) 'Une page d'histoire de l'OIT: la Pologne' ['Poland: A Page From the ILO's History'], in J.-C. Javillier, B. Gernigon and G. Politakis (eds) *Les normes internationales du travail: un patrimoine pour l'avenir; mélanges en l'honneur de Nicolas Valticos* [*International Labour Standards: Heritage for the Future; Selected Essays in Honour of Nicolas Valticos*] (ILO).

Boivin, I. and Odero, A. (2006). 'The Committee of Experts on the Application of Conventions and Recommendations: Progress Achieved in National Labour Legislation', *International Labour Review* 145(3): 207.

Chigara, B. (2007) 'Latecomers to the ILO and the Authorship and Ownership of the International Labour Code', *Human Rights Quarterly* 29(3): 706.

Earth Rights International (2009) *Getting it Wrong: Flawed "Corporate Social Responsibility" and Misrepresentations Surrounding Total and Chevron's Yadana Gas Pipeline in Military-Ruled Burma (Myanmar)* (September 2009, Earth Rights International).

Economist Intellegence Unit (2005) 'Reputation: Risk of Risks', an Economist Intelligence Unit White Paper sponsored by Ace, Cisco Systems, Deutsche Bank, IBM and KPMG, December 2005.

Elliot, K.A. and Freeman, R.B. (2004) 'White Hats or Don Quixotes? Human Rights Vigilantes in the Global Economy', in *Emerging Labor Market Institutions for the Twenty-First Century* (National Bureau of Economic Research, Inc.).

Fenwick, C. and Kring, T. (2007) *Rights at Work: An Assessment of the Declaration's Technical Cooperation in Selected Countries* (ILO).

Frenkel, S.J. and Scott, D. (2002) 'Compliance, Collaboration, and Codes of Labor Practice: The Adidas Connection', *California Management Review* 45(1): 29.

Humblet, M. and Zarkas-Martres, M. (2004) 'International Labour Standards in the Service of Social Justice', in J.-C. Javillier and A. Odero (eds) *International Labour Standards: A Global Approach: 75th Anniversary of the Committee Of Experts On The Application Of Conventions And Recommendations*, 2nd revised edition (ILO).

International Labour Office (2007) *Eradication of Forced Labour* (ILO).

International Labour Office (2008a) *The Labour Principles of the United Nations Global Compact: A Guide for Business* (ILO).

International Labour Office (2008b) *Freedom of Association in Practice Lessons Learned: Global Report under the Follow-Up to the ILO Declaration on Fundamental Principles and Rights at Work 2008* (ILO).

Ishida, M. (2009) 'Corporate Social Responsibility, Socially Responsible Investment and Labour Law in Japan: The Lessons from the Nomura Securities Case', Paper presented at World Congress: International Society for Labour and Social Security Law, 1–4 September 2009 (Sydney).

Javillier, J.-C., Gernigon, B. and Politakis, G. (eds) (2004) *Les normes internationales du travail: un patrimoine pour l'avenir; mélanges en l'honneur de Nicolas Valticos* [*International Labour Standards: Heritage for the Future; Selected Essays in Honour of Nicolas Valticos*] (ILO).

Javillier, J.-C. and Odero, A. et al. (2004) *International Labour Standards: A Global Approach: 75th Anniversary of the Committee Of Experts On The Application Of Conventions And Recommendations*, 2nd revised edition (ILO).

Kellerson, H. (1998) 'The ILO Declaration of 1998 on Fundamental Principles and Rights: A Challenge for the Future', *International Labour Review* 137(2): 223.

Knox, J. (2008) 'Horizontal Human Rights Law', *The American Journal of International Law* 102(1): 1.

Langille, B. (2005) 'Core Labour Rights – The True Story (Reply to Alston)', *European Journal of International Law* 16: 409.

Locke, R., Amengual, M. and Mangla, A. (2009) 'Virtue out of Necessity? Compliance, Commitment, and the Improvement of Labor Conditions in Global Supply Chains', *Politics & Society* 37: 319.

Locke, R., Kochan, T., Romis, M. and Oin, F. (2007) 'Beyond Corporate Codes of Conduct: Work Organisation and Labour Standards at Nike's Suppliers', *International Labour Review* 146: 21.

McIntyre, R. (2006) 'Are Workers Rights Human Rights and Would It Matter If They Were?', *Human Rights & Human Welfare* 6: 1.

Maupain, F. (2005) 'Revitalization Not Retreat: The Real Potential of the 1998 ILO Declaration for the Universal Protection of Workers' Rights', *The European Journal of International Law* 16: 439.

N'Diaye, M. (2004) 'The Annual Review and the Promotion of the 1998 ILO Declaration on Fundamental Principles and Rights at Work: Developments and Initial Impact Assessment', in J.-C. Javillier, B. Gernigon and G. Politakis (eds) *Les normes internationales du travail: un patrimoine pour l'avenir; mélanges en l'honneur de Nicolas Valticos* [*International Labour Standards: Heritage for the Future; Selected Essays in Honour of Nicolas Valticos*] (ILO).

OECD (2001) 'Codes of Corporate Conduct: Expanded Review of their Content', in *Corporate Responsibility: Private Initiatives and Public Goals* (OECD).

OECD (2008a) 'Corporate Responsibility Practices in the Area of Employment and Industrial Relations', in *Employment and Industrial Relations: Promoting Responsible Business Conduct in a Globalising Economy* (OECD).

OECD (2008b) 'Overview of Selected Initiatives and Instruments Relevant to Corporate Social Responsibility', in *OECD-ILO Conference on Corporate Social Responsibility* (OECD).

Piety, T.R. (2009) 'Why the ACLU was Wrong about Nike, Inc. v. Kasky (April 6, 2009)', *Tulsa Law Review* 41: 715.

Ruggie, J. (2008) 'Protect, Respect and Remedy: A Framework for Business and Human Rights', Report of the Special Representative of the Secretary-General on the issue of human rights and transnational corporations (United Nations) A/HRC/8/5 (7 April 2008).

Servais, M. (2004) 'Globalisation and Decent Work Policy: Reflections Upon a New Legal Approach', *International Labour Review* 143: 187.

Trebilcock, A. (2004) 'The ILO Declaration on Fundamental Principles and Rights at Work and its Follow-up', in J.-C. Javillier, A. Odero et al. (eds) *International Labour Standards: A Global Approach: 75th Anniversary of the Committee Of Experts On The Application Of Conventions And Recommendations*, 2nd revised edition (ILO).

World Bank Group (2003) *Company Codes of Conduct and International Standards: An Analytical Comparison* (World Bank Group).

12

Big unions and big business

*Can international framework agreements
promote sustainable development at a local level?*

TONIA NOVITZ*

Introduction

In the twenty-first century, the phenomenon of international collective bargaining has gradually attracted more attention. This collective bargaining is taking place through the medium of international framework agreements (IFAs), concluded between global trade union federations (GUFs) and multinational companies (MNCs). Since 2000, the numbers of such agreements increased exponentially as an alternative to unilateral corporate Codes of Conduct declared by MNCs (European Foundation for the Improvement of Living and Working Conditions 2008, Papadakis 2008a, Telljohann 2009, Sciarra 2010: 230–233).

This chapter investigates how IFAs could assist in securing economic, social and environmental development objectives. The obvious difficulty

* Professor of Labour Law, University of Bristol. This is a preliminary paper which serves as a prelude to a larger project relating to international framework agreements and to the connections between sustainable development and labour standards. A rather different version of this paper was included in a Polish labour law collection in honour of Andrzej Swiatkowski, *Studia z zakresu prawa pracy I polityki spotecznej* [*Studies in Labour Law and Social Policy*] (2009) and some opinions in this paper were also presented in Novitz, T. (2010) 'Core Labour Standards Conditionalities: A Means by which to Achieve Sustainable Development?', in J. Faundez and C. Tan (eds) *International Law, Economic Globalization And Developing Countries* (Edward Elgar). Thanks go to colleagues at the University of Bristol who provided me with initial feedback on early drafts and to participants in the British Academy Conference in May 2009. All errors and omissions are my own.

224

is that we are talking here about 'big unions' and 'big business'. Can they secure change, not only at the global level where agreements are easily reached in the abstract, but also at the local level such that development-oriented reforms are actually implemented in practice? My contention, in this chapter, is that IFAs, by their very nature, have this potential. They can forge important intersections between the global and the local spheres of deliberation. In so doing, they may give opportunities to workers to identify local issues of economic, social and environmental concern and participate in decisions relating to their employer's responses to such concerns. There are obstacles that must be overcome, which are identified in this chapter, but IFAs may well have an impact on development and its sustainability.

My assertion turns on a particular understanding of 'sustainable development', namely that this concept does not only possess a substantive element reflected in, for example, the Millennium Development Goals (or MDGs), but also a participatory aspect, as explained in the introduction to this collection. We need to understand development as not entirely technocratic and expert led, but as having scope for reasonable differences of opinion on the manner in which development is to be pursued in particular local circumstances. For this reason, this chapter begins by addressing differing and contested views of sustainable development, with reference to the principles elaborated upon in the Rio Declaration of 1992 and the Johannesburg Declaration of 2002. This chapter draws on the view taken in the latter instrument that there is 'a collective responsibility to advance and strengthen interdependent and mutually reinforcing pillars' of sustainable development: economic development, social development and environmental protection.[1] Results-based and process-oriented approaches to development are compared and contrasted. It is argued that sustainable development should be understood also, if not primarily, in participatory terms.

The next part of this chapter then considers what collective bargaining at the global level has to offer in terms of promoting sustainable development at a local level. A brief history of initiatives taken to achieve the signature of IFAs is presented, noting differences between the numerous agreements now reached. The obstacles to conclusion of such agreements in the context of the current economic climate are considered, alongside

---

[1] See the Johannesburg Declaration on Sustainable Development 2002, para. 5.

other barriers to collective bargaining. In so doing, two discrete dimensions of these agreements are subjected to scrutiny: the substantive clauses included in IFAs and the procedures set up for their implementation.

A defining feature of IFAs is that they make mention of labour standards endorsed by the International Labour Organisation (ILO), including 'core labour standards' and particular ILO Conventions, including most notably those relating to freedom of association and collective bargaining. Some substantive clauses contained in the IFAs also refer specifically to 'sustainable development' as a discrete objective, but the meaning of this clause is not spelt out. The procedural clauses are perhaps the most interesting facet of the IFAs, because they offer the potential for reconciliation of tensions between social, economic and environmental aspects of development. Negotiation between big unions and big business might seem an unlikely candidate for the full realisation of local environmental and other development objectives, being so apparently distant from the concerns of those most directly concerned. Yet, it may be possible to view IFAs as a means by which to achieve more meaningful social dialogue from the ground upwards. As Nikolaus Hammer has observed, IFAs 'do not create new actors as such but rather provide platforms and entry points for labour across different spaces and scales . . .' (Hammer 2005: 527–528). Indeed, the conclusion of an IFA is often the result of extensive localised action, which GUFs coordinate and assist.

Finally, the process of social dialogue does not end with the signature of an IFA. After that date, the non-legal mechanisms provided for enforcement of an IFA become significant. They may provide control to the GUF or a European Works Council (EWC) capable of exercising influence to change domestic situations. To that extent they may seem imperfect, insofar as they leave enforcement not to those affected on the ground, but to a more privileged group of worker representatives in another country who may not be so directly affected by the social conditions or environmental pollutants experienced by the workforce on the ground. However, IFAs can go further in terms of maintaining dialogue between these different groups of workers, insofar as they provide for 'review committees' which allow national (and even local) representation. It would seem that such procedures have the potential to influence relations between an MNC and subcontractors or suppliers, enabling local trade union recognition (Sobczak 2003). In addition, of considerable potential significance are 'subsidiarity' clauses which, when inserted into an IFA, allow for complaints to be addressed at a local level, enabling the economic, social

226

and environmental concerns of a particular community to be voiced by workers who live within it.

The procedural and substantive dimensions of sustainable development

It has been observed that 'one of the most striking characteristics of the term sustainable development is that it means so many different things to different people and organizations' (Robinson 2004: 369). For example, environmentalists associate the term with 'a dualistic relationship between nature and humanity' (Hopwood, Mellor and O'Brien 2005: 38), while in an industrial setting, labour lawyers understand the term as being connected to the achievement of durable social objectives.

An attempt to reconcile these divergent understandings was made via the 'three pillars' approach adopted in the Johannesburg Declaration on Sustainable Development 2002, which emphasises the interaction of economic development, social development and environmental protection. Additionally, by stressing the significance of collective participation in the enterprise of promotion of development, the Johannesburg Declaration continued a tradition, drawing on both the UN Declaration on the Right to Development of 1986 and the Rio Declaration on Environment and Development 1992. Article 1(1) of the UN Declaration not only stressed that development is a human right, but that it is one 'by virtue of which every human person and all peoples are entitled to participate in, contribute to, and enjoy economic, social, cultural and political development, in which all human rights and fundamental freedoms can be fully realized'. This is because, as Article 2(1) of the UN Declaration established, 'the human person is the central subject of development and should be the active participant and beneficiary of the right to development'. Principle 10 of the Rio Declaration likewise observed that 'environmental issues are best handled with participation of all concerned citizens, at the relevant level'. This perspective was reiterated again in paragraph 26 of the Johannesburg Declaration on Sustainable Development 2002, which recognised 'that sustainable development requires a long-term perspective and broad-based participation in policy formulation, decision-making and implementation at all levels'.

Yet, despite this rhetorical recognition of an entitlement to participatory involvement in the *process* of development, development has historically been assessed in practice in terms of *outcomes*. Previously, so-called 'developing countries' were placed under pressure to adopt 'Western-style' modes of public governance and economic management, which experts deemed appropriate (Trubek and Santos 2006). During the 1980s and 1990s, targets for progress were set, the achievement of which would be empirically ascertainable, be they economic or other statistical indicators. For example, the Washington Consensus, which came to govern the operations of the International Monetary Fund (IMF) and World Bank Group (and the conditions under which funding was offered), may be regarded as having taken this form. As Stiglitz (1998: 5) has observed:

> The success of the Washington consensus as an intellectual doctrine rests on its simplicity: its policy recommendations could be administered by economists using little more than simple accounting frameworks. A few economic indicators – inflation, money supply growth, interest rates, budget and trade deficits – could serve as the basis for a set of policy recommendations. Indeed, in some cases economists would fly into a country, look at and attempt to verify these data, and make macroeconomic recommendations for policy reforms all in the space of a couple of weeks.

Arguably, the quest for achievement of the Millennium Development Goals (MDG) raises similar issues, in that targets are set from on high, regardless of local priorities (Satterthwaite 2003, Black and White 2006, Saith 2006). Even one of the original architects of this ambitious project, Vandemoortele (2009), has voiced concern that there has been a capture of the MDG process, such that money-metric and donor-centric views of development are prominent. He sees there being a need for social partnership if the MDG are to be met (Vandemoortele 2008).

Within a results-based framework for development, social and labour standards tend to be seen as subsidiary social goods which promote and sustain economic growth or other humanitarian objectives. If the objective is to facilitate competitiveness of exports on international markets, then it follows that labour markets should be deregulated, abolishing labour laws which would otherwise impose labour standards on employers and in so doing enhance the cost of labour. In such a context, collective organisation and participatory representation aimed at raising wages and constraining managerial discretion have been viewed as rigidities that were best avoided (Morgan-Foster 2003, Kaufmann 2007: 102).

By way of contrast, the notion that development is a *process* which has to be understood in procedural terms can be allied to the view that commentators such as Sen and Nussbaum take of 'development as freedom', according to which the role of development is to enhance human capabilities of present and future generations (Sen 1999 and Nussbaum 2000). Such a perspective would suggest that labour standards are not merely a by-product of other development objectives, nor are they merely a means to achieve economic or other goals. Rather, such labour rights as freedom of association, collective bargaining and collective action can be regarded as constitutive of a participatory process which gives credibility to stated development objectives, thereby encouraging their implementation and thereby their longer term sustainability (Novitz 2003: chapter 1, Bogg 2009).

Sen's human rights-based approach has been adopted and utilised in the field of labour standards by the ILO. In his early writing for the ILO in the 1970s, Sen proposed that the Organisation seek to take a broad and generous approach to the idea of 'working rights', which he considers is now instantiated in the 'Decent Work' philosophy adopted by ILO Director-General, Juan Somavia.[2] The notion of 'Decent Work' encompasses the protection of fundamental rights, employment protection, social protection and social dialogue. In this way, Somavia has linked the emphasis on 'core labour standards' or 'rights at work' identified in the ILO Declaration of 1998, which draw on the 'fundamental' or 'core' ILO Conventions,[3] with social dialogue as a procedure to ensure that such rights receive the respect they deserve in practice. In particular, Somavia has made a claim that the primary procedural mechanism within the ILO 'tripartism' can 'play a central role in defining the convergence of public policies and market mechanisms that is needed to achieve the balances that are essential for sustainable development'.[4]

For these reasons, when analysing the substantive terms contained in IFAs, my interest lies not only in express statements made relating to sustainable development but also in indirect references to the ILO Conventions and other standards which could be linked in various ways

[2] International Labour Conference 87th Session 1–17 June 1999. Address by Mr Amartya Sen, available at: http://www.ilo.org/public/english/standards/relm/ilc/ilc87/a-sen.htm
[3] These are ILO Conventions Nos 87 and 98 on Freedom of Association and Collective Bargaining (1948 and 1949); Conventions Nos 29 and 105 on the Elimination of All Forms of Forced and Compulsory Labour (1930 and 1957); ILO Convention No. 138 on the Minimum Age for Admission to Employment (1973) and Convention No. 182 on the Worst Forms of Child Labour (1999); and ILO Conventions Nos 100 and 111 on the Elimination of Discrimination in Respect of Employment and Occupation (1957 and 1958).
[4] *Decent Work for Sustainable Development*, Director-General's Introduction to the International Labour Conference 2007 (ILC 96-2007/Report I(A): 3–4.

229

to aspects of sustainable development. Moreover, I want to see whether the procedural provision made for further social dialogue under IFAs has scope for enhancing the participation of those who might be understood as beneficiaries of development.

The negotiation of 'international framework agreements'

IFAs are the result of negotiations between 'big business' as we understand multinational companies to be, and the 'big unions' or GUFs. The following organisations are commonly termed GUFs: the Building and Woodworkers International (BWI), Education International (EI), the International Federation of Chemical, Energy, Mine and General Workers' Unions (ICEM), the International Federation of Journalists (IFJ), the International Metalworkers' Federation (IMF), the International Transport Workers' Federation (ITF), the International Textile, Garment and Leather Workers' Federation (ITGLWF), the International Union of Food, Agricultural, Hotel, Restaurant, Catering, Tobacco and Allied Workers' Associations (IUF), Public Service International (PSI), the Global Union for Skills and Services (UNI), and the International Arts and Entertainment Alliance (IAEA).[5] Of these, eight have signed IFAs with 70 MNCs (Stevis 2010: 3–4).

IFAs originated in the late 1980s, but have taken some time to evolve in terms of content and coverage. The first agreements concluded in 1989 between Danone and the International Union of Food Workers (IUF) took the form of 'a Plan for Economic and Social Information in Companies of the [then] BSN Group' and an 'Action Programme for the Promotion of Equality of Men and Women at the Workplace'. There followed an 'Agreement on Skills Training' in 1992 and finally an IFA proper in 1994: 'IUF/BSN Joint Declaration on Trade Union Rights' (Hammer 2005: 515, Gallin 2008). There followed an eventual 'flurry of agreements' between MNCs and GUFs, particularly between 2002–2006 (Stevis 2010: 2). By 2008, 72 IFAs had been concluded which covered approximately 5 million workers.[6]

There is no complete consensus as to the definition of an IFA, but some of the defining features of such an agreement have been identified as being that:

[5] See http://www.global-unions.org/spip.php?rubrique25
[6] See http://www.eurofound/europa/eu. See also Torres 2008 and Papadakis 2008a: 103.

- it is a global agreement, covering the entire enterprise;
- a global union federation is a signatory;
- ILO Conventions are a source of reference;
- freedom of association and the right to collective bargaining are protected under the terms of the agreement;
- the agreement includes a requirement that the MNC exercises influence over suppliers, subsidiaries and joint ventures;
- there is provision for effective dissemination of information so as to facilitate implementation;
- there is provision for trade union involvement in implementation; and
- there is a right to bring complaints.

(Miller 2004: 216, Hammer 2005: 518, Riisgaard
2005: 709, Herrnstadt 2007–2008: 192)

The negotiation of IFAs is arguably a departure from the standard role of the GUFs, prior to 2000. These organisations have traditionally been drawn into forms of political representation within institutional structures, such as the tripartite ILO within the UN framework, and the official 'social dialogue' processes of the European Union (EU). By way of contrast, IFAs arise by virtue of 'transnational industrial relations organizing and cam-paigning' outside the formal context of such international and regional organisations (Hammer 2005: 514).

Moreover, while these agreements are ultimately concluded by GUFs, the 'big unions', they are also usually the result of extensive and sustained campaigning at the local, national and regional level. As Miller (2004: 231) observes, 'mapping or profiling the supply chain or owned operations of a particular multinational and the experiences of workers within such structures require a multilevel research effort'. Subsequently, coordinated multilevel campaigns will be necessary 'to bring the employer to the bargaining table' (ibid.: 232).

It should be noted that the whole point of IFAs is that they are not merely corporate 'codes of conduct' or unilateral statements of intent, but are jointly negotiated texts. 'In this regard they move the issue of corporate social responsibility from unilateral managerial control . . . into the domain of collective bargaining' (ibid.: 216). These are, however, akin to UK collec-tive agreements, in that they are seldom legally enforceable.[7] As Dan Gallin

---

[7] See International Metalworkers' Federation, *Background to International Framework Agreements in the IMF* (2006) at 12: 'no legal enforcement mechanisms exist at the global level'. See also Hammer 2005: 518.

(2008: 10–11) has observed: 'there is no international legal framework . . . to provide a guaranteed legal status to any labour/management agreement reached at international level'. As we shall see, this has implications for the implementation of such agreements.

There has been an attempt to prevent the negotiation of IFAs being the sole prerogative of 'big unions' and thereby distant from the interests that they represent. Rather than just being concluded by representatives of the GUF, there is a trend towards also obtaining the signature of the MNCs' World Works Council (WWC) and sometimes by the relevant European Works Council (EWC). This has been a growing trend in sectors represented by the IMF and ICEM (Hammer 2005: 523). There can however be difficulties in the EWCs negotiating the text of an IFA, since some EWC agreements rule out any negotiating role (Gallin 2008: 19–20). Despite this diversification, however, it may be fair to say that still much depends on the 'good institutional representation' of the national union within the global union, WWC and/or EWC, that is, whether it connects to local unions, their agendas and concerns (Hammer 2005: 524).

Predominantly, the conclusion of IFAs has been limited to MNCs which have their base in Europe. As at 2005, no IFAs had been negotiated with North-American MNCs (ibid.: 525). Herrnstadt (2007–2008: 191) has offered four different, if related, reasons for this outcome. The first is that the culture of 'dialogue' has been developed through legal mechanisms in Europe; the second is that there is no legal basis in the US for social dialogue; indeed, third, in the United States many employers are openly hostile to unions. Certainly, IFAs are unlikely to be agreed by an MNC in the absence of a 'corporate culture committed to social responsibility and dialogue' (Stevis 2010: 12). Fourth, Herrnstadt has observed that 'US workers and their unions do not share many of the protections enjoyed by many of their European counterparts', so that for US workers issues such as health care, retirement security, job security and benefits tend to take priority over IFAs in discussions with employers.

However, one might question the validity of this observation as at 2010. One obvious exception to this rule has been the agreement concluded between the US firm, Chiquita, and the IUF and the Latin-American Coordination of Banana Workers' Unions (COLSIBA) (Riisgaard 2005: 717). Nor does this perspective on the exclusion of US companies make sense in respect of truly global companies, such as Group 4 Securicor (G4S), which operates in 110 companies across the world. Notably, a hard-fought campaign led to the conclusion of an IFA between UNI and G4S in

December 2008.[8] Indeed, UNI seems to be overcoming traditional bound-aries, having signed an IFA with a Canadian company in 2007, IFAs with Brazilian companies in 2008 and 2009, as well as with a Japanese company in 2008 (Stevis 2010: 3–4).

The Chiquita agreement in particular demonstrates that regional union organisations which represent workers in the key MNC sites of production can also instigate and then be signatories to an IFA. Indeed, what may be most significant in respect of that agreement is that it was 'the first IFA negotiated and signed with a coordinating body of unions from developing countries' (Riisgaard 2005: 722). This is important in that such alliances present an opportunity to bridge geographical differences between unions representing 'rich' workers in the North and the unions representing workers in the South. 'Dialogue can ensure that campaigns are built around the interests of those doing the work and in this way, the voices of workers in the free trade zones of the world can be heard alongside those of concerned western consumers' (Wills 2002: 678). As Herrnstadt (2007–2008: 190) has observed, a 'common purpose of IFAs is to prevent corporations from pitting workers in one country against workers in other countries'.

Substantive provisions in IFAs

Reference to ILO Conventions

It is evident that, in terms of the substantive standards laid down in IFAs, reference can and has been made to a variety of ILO Conventions and Recommendations, such that not only 'core labour standards' are included.[9] However, it is the core ILO Conventions which undoubtedly

---

[8] See http://www.global-unions.org/spip.php?rubrique68, and http://www.uniglobal union.org/Apps/iportal.nsf/pages/20090202_vlnuEn

[9] These have been listed by Hammer 2005: 518 as Convention No. 1 on Hours of Work 1919, Convention No. 29 on Forced Labour, Convention No. 47 on the Forty-Hour Week 1935, ILO Convention No. 87 on Freedom of Association and Protection of the Right to Organise 1948, Convention No. 94 on Labour Clauses (Public Contracts) 1949, Convention No. 95 on Protection of Wages 1949, Convention No. 98 on the Right to Organise and Collective Bargaining 1948, Convention No. 100 on Equal Remuneration 1951, Convention No. 105 on Abolition of Forced Labour 1957, Convention No. 111 on Discrimination (Employment and Occupation) 1958, Convention No. 131 on Minimum Wage Fixing 1970, Convention No. 135 on Workers' Representatives 1971, Convention No. 138 on Minimum Age 1973, Convention No. 155 on Occupational Safety and Health 1981, Convention No. 156 on Workers with Family

receive the most (and almost invariable) attention. They are usually listed as a cohesive block of obligations. Occasionally, more vague wording is used. Examples include: 'compliance with international labour standards, and in particular the ILO conventions on trade union freedom and the right to organize and international standards on the respect of human rights'[10] and 'the social rights and principles described in this declaration take the Conventions of the ILO into consideration'.[11]

Freedom of association and the right to collective bargaining receive the most attention, perhaps because these are instruments negotiated by and for the benefit of trade unions. However, the range of workers' rights anticipated is interesting and suggests that the impact of core labour standards has not been as much to marginalise other labour standards as was at first feared (cf. Alston 2004).

Reference to 'national legal and industry standards'

There would seem to be an increasing tendency, where traditional bargaining issues such as pay, hours, holidays, sick pay, health and safety, training or redundancies arise, for there to be reference to 'national legal and industry standards'. This is similar to the OECD Guidelines for Multinational Enterprises, which try to relate standards back to national labour laws (Murray 2001).

This form of cross-referencing is however potentially problematic. 'It makes little sense from a labor group's perspective to negotiate an agreement with a company that sets forth standards that it is already required to honor through national law' (Herrnstadt 2007–2008: 197). Moreover, such a clause belies the significance of reference to international labour standards. 'Global social dialogue and industrial relations cannot be based on national standards' (Stevis 2010: 8).

Also, often developing countries have difficulty attracting foreign direct investment, and thereby seek to attract multinational employers by either

Responsibilities 1981, Convention No. 162 on Abestos 1986, Convention No. 167 on Safety and Health in Construction 1988, Convention No. 182 on the Worst Forms of Child Labour 1999; also Recommendation No. 116 on Reduction of Hours of Work 1962 and Recommendation No. 143 on Workers Representatives 1971.

[10] IFA between Endesa and ICEM, April 2002, as recorded by Hammer 2005: 516–517.

[11] IFA between Volkswagen and IMF, Group Global Works Council, June 2002, as recorded by Hammer, 2005: 516–517.

lowering the standards previously set in national legislation, or offering one-off incentives, such as, for example, through the mechanism of an Exclusive Economic Zone (EEZ), in which the application of national labour laws are commonly excluded (Blackett 2001). For developing countries, such a statement may effectively render these terms in an IFA nugatory.

Direct reference to sustainable development

It is not always clear from the text of IFAs to which paradigm of development the parties intend to refer. The most bold and far-reaching IFAs link sustainable development with corporate social responsibility and core labour standards. For example, one agreement between the IMF and GEA states:

> will support to the best of its ability the combating of underdevelopment in third world countries and stands by its social responsibility. In this context it . . . supports all the internal and external initiatives of a corporate social responsibility (CSR). It agrees to observe, secure, or further extend the generally accepted ILO core working standards and human rights.[12]

Another agreement between Impreglio S.p.A and IFBWW/FENEAL-UIL/FILCA-CISL/FILLEA/CGIL concluded in 2004 states that:

> The parties commit themselves to work in this direction to achieve social justice and sustainable development in the activities and undertakings of Impreglio and its contractors, subcontractors and suppliers.

This agreement goes on to make reference to a variety of labour standards, including the core ILO Conventions. It also adds:

> Impreglio S.p.A. considers the respect for workers rights to be a crucial element in sustainable development and will therefore engage only those contractors, subcontractors and suppliers which recognize and respect the criteria listed above.

What remains unclear is how sustainable development as a concept adds to or enhances the protection of workers' rights and whether it has any independent meaning in these agreements. It is also unclear what would happen where objectives of sustainable development, such as protection

---

[12] IFA between GEA and IMF, EMF, EWC, June 2003, as recorded by Hammer 2005: 516–517 and cited at 520.

of a domestic industry for reasons of economic development, clashed with workers' determination to gain higher wages and thereby a greater share in the profits of their labour. There might also be tension between local workers affected by industrial pollutants and workers in other parts of the enterprise who were prepared to tolerate local environmental damage in order to preserve profitability and jobs. Such matters would seem to require further attention and clarification by the parties. One may wonder whether the absence of such clarification is due to the fact that workers with a direct interest in local social, economic and environmental development issues are not necessarily engaged in drafting the texts of the IFAs.

Environmental concerns

The International Organisation of Employers (IOE) has also identified 'Common Trends in IFAs', pointing to the fact that almost half make provision for environmental concerns. They observe that some IFAs make specific reference to the Rio Declaration of Environment and Development, while others merely recognise more generally the importance of 'protection of the environment'.[13] The means for enforcement of these clauses are however subject to the same (often limited) complaints mechanisms as the labour standards set out in the IFA. Indeed, the negotiation between competing development objectives, worker interests and employers' concerns all turn ultimately on the procedures for the implementation of IFAs.

Procedures for the implementation of IFA provisions concerned with sustainable development

Gallin (2008: 10–11) has noted that, in the absence of concrete legal mechanisms for their enforcement, the implementation of IFAs depends 'even more on the balance of power between the contracting parties at the time they are concluded' and one might think also on the balance of power subsequently when unions call for their implementation. The dynamics of domestic industrial relations may also play a role. Stevis (2010: 7) suggests

---

[13] International Organisation of Employers, 'Common Trends Across IFAs' available at: http://www.ioe-emp.org/fileadmin/user_upload/documents_pdf/ifas/Common_trends_ifas.pdf

that what matters is the relative influence of labour unions in various countries, which may for example differ between the US and Brazil.

As Hammer (2005: 518) observes, as far as IFAs are concerned, 'labour is one of the main actors in the implementation as well as a regular monitoring process'. However, there is more to be said than this, for different kinds of labour representation occur in the negotiation of the IFA to that which engage in implementation and further monitoring. 'While trade union specific efforts to create global social policy instruments cannot succeed without a critical element of centrally coordinated research and networking, such activity in turn has to link into locally generated organizing initiatives, which in turn can only be sustained when and where workers are both able and willing to collectively address injustice at their place of work' (Miller 2004: 232). Also, in the words of Ron Oswald of the IUF, once space for local trade unionism has been secured through an IFA, his GUF relies on 'active and energetic and militant local organizing to fill that space. If they don't we've done it for nothing' (cited in Wills 2002: 685).

It must also be observed that the scope for such collective action may be determined by the wording of the IFA in question. There are notable differences between different IFAs in that, while some are devoted to the recognition of core and other labour standards, others 'come much closer to bargaining agreements, in that they contain detailed provisions about regular meetings, deal with a range of issues beyond core labour rights and are meant to be discussed, renegotiated or prolonged after certain intervals' (Hammer 2005: 519). The level of detail may well matter insofar as it makes the agreement more efficacious and thereby responsive to those affected on the ground by MNC activities and their concerns relating to development issues.

Many agreements contemplate regular procedural review by the MNC and GUF jointly at regular intervals. These can make some provision for inclusive participation, such as one union member for each country, thereby ensuring some geographical spread in representation.[14] The establishment of 'review committees' can give unions access to the senior management of the company, thereby providing an opportunity 'to override union-hostile local management' (Riisgaard 2005: 727). This was a tactic that was utilised in the IFA with Accor, so that when strike leaders were sacked in Indonesia, the IUF could intervene directly by contacting

---

[14] See IFA between Endesa and ICEM, January 2002, cited by Hammer 2005: 516–517 and 525.

the MNC human resources department based in Paris (Miller 2004: 696). Similarly, Stevis (2010: 4) reports that the Daimler IFA has assisted in the resolution of disputes in Brazil and Turkey. For European-based MNCs, the EWC may play a role, not so much in negotiating an agreement (as we have seen above), but rather in its implementation, especially where the IFA provides for formal review at every annual meeting of the EWC (such as under the Accor agreement). '[T]his allows non-European concerns to find their way onto the agenda of the EWC' (Wills 2002: 686–687). Also, where problems have arisen in relation to contractors or subcontractors in the US, European senior management have been called upon to intervene (Bourque 2008: 39).

In terms of more local engagement, most IFAs do provide for dissemination of information relating to the IFA. The difficulty is that very few IFAs address this issue in the kind of detail which would ensure effective education or distribution of information relating to the IFA (Herrnstadt 2007–2008: 201). All too often, in older agreements, the onus was placed on the GUF to act, usually by holding workshops to enhance access to information (Wills 2002: 688). The danger in such circumstances is that unions themselves disseminate 'information almost solely to union members, thereby limiting the potential of the agreement to be used as a lever for non-organized workers to join unions' (Riisgaard 2005: 723–724). However, GUFs have become more ambitious over time in their negotiation of IFAs, and now are more likely to demand specific training programmes for employees on site which relate to implementation of the IFA (Hammer 2005: 516–517 and 522). Much however will still depend on the availability of resources on site in developing countries. For example, Miller (2004: 231) observes that 'attempts to network electronically can fail due to the absence of on-line computers with a constant supply of electricity in some countries'.

Local engagement can be further promoted by what Hammer (2005: 524) has described as a 'subsidiarity principle', in other words a clause included in an IFA stating 'a preference to discuss and solve matters at local level' before referring them to headquarter management and the relevant global union federation. This may seem in some ways problematic, as workers at the local level may have less bargaining power, and less in the way of expertise than the more powerful 'big union' with all its experience. However, such a clause does allow the shop floor to have a say over the issues that they see arising, and ensures that there can be some responsiveness to development issues that arise at the local level. For example, where issues arise relating to industrial pollutants affecting a particular community, there is potential to engage a local response more effectively so as to ensure that industrial development is sustainable.

This brings us to the other significant procedural aspect of these agreements, which arises in respect of supply chain regulation. Some IFAs allow an independent NGO (albeit of the MNC's choice) to make inspections of suppliers and state that the MNC agrees to terminate their business relationship with a supplier that does not take appropriate corrective measures within an agreed time limit or where there are repeated violations.[15] However, not all make provision for such drastic action. Indeed, the 2001 IFA between Chiquita, the IUF and COLSIBA has been identified as being problematic because, while 'Chiquita agreed to require its suppliers' respect for core workers' rights . . .' the provision was 'dependent on Chiquita's relative degree of influence over its suppliers and the availability of appropriate and commercially viable supply alternatives' (Riisgaard 2005: 726). It may be difficult also for the union to insist on a more stringent set of standards and penalties, since withdrawal of a contract from a supplier may lead to a loss of jobs and members.

Nevertheless, even a flawed IFA can bring about substantial change and improvements in terms of worker participation. The side effects of the Chiquita agreement were the recognition of a union on a new site in Honduras, ongoing dialogue between unions and Chiquita at a national level in Costa Rica, the additional signing of collective agreements in Chile, and the preservation of unionisation on the sale of Chiquita's Colombian operations to another banana producer. Riisgaard's conclusion following her study of the operation of the Chiquita IFA (ibid.: 729–731) was that these are 'examples of union consultation and social dialogue' which illustrate 'the value of the IFA . . . IFAs thereby constitute a sophisticated multilevel response to the challenges of MNCs' geographically dispersed production systems and outsourcing strategies, creating space for union organizing and social dialogue' (ibid.).

Conclusion

This chapter has argued that if economic, social and environmental development is to be sustainable, development has to be understood in

---

[15] IFA between H&M and UNI, January 2004, cited in Hammer 2005: 516–517 and at 526.

procedural as well as substantive terms. Otherwise, we risk subscription to a model of development that is too static and circumscribed by larger vested interests. If we consider that 'development as freedom' (or at least as empowerment) is central to the achievement of sustainable development, then procedures (and their participants) do matter. Ironically, even though they are concluded by big unions and big business initially at the macro level, this is what the implementation of IFAs at a local level has to offer. IFAs provide access to smaller interest groups, so that they can shape development through the medium of trade union representation, thereby ensuring engagement with local community interests.

It should be noted that IFAs often differ in terms of their substantive and procedural terms. GUFs now seek to ensure that a 'new generation' of IFAs have 'stronger implementation and dispute resolution procedures' (Stevis 2010: 2), which has made union officials reluctant to sign new agreements with MNCs which do not measure up to these more stringent standards. While this determination on the part of GUFs has led to a slowing in the conclusion of IFAs, this may be the only sensible strategy to ensure that there is scope for genuine local participation, and thereby sustainable outcomes.

References

Alston, P. (2004) '"Core Labour Standards" and the Transformation of the International Labour Rights Regime', *European Journal of International Law* 15: 457.

Bakvis, P. and McCoy, M. (2008) *Core Labour Standards and International Organizations: What Inroads Has Labour Made?*, Friedrich-Ebert-Stiftung Briefing Papers No. 6 (Friedrich-Ebert-Stiftung).

Black, R. and White, H. (eds) (2006) *Targeting Development: Critical Perspectives on the Millennium Development Goals* (Routledge).

Blackett, A. (2001) 'Global Governance, Legal Pluralism and the Decentered State: A Labor Law Critique of Codes of Corporate Conduct', *Indiana Journal of Global Legal Studies* 8: 401.

Bogg, A. (2009) *The Democratic Aspects of Trade Union Recognition* (Hart Publishing).

Bourque, R. (2008) 'International Framework Agreements and the Future of Collective Bargaining in Multinational Companies', *Just Labour: A Canadian Journal of Work and Society* 12: 30.

European Foundation for the Improvement of Living and Working Conditions (2008), *Codes of Conduct and International Framework Agreements: New Forms of Governance at Company Level* (OOPEC).

Gallin, D. (2008) 'Transnational Companies: International Framework Agreements: A Reassessment', in a policy paper released on www.globallabour.info/

Grossman, G. and Sykes, A. (2007) 'A Preference for Development: The Law and Economics of GSP', in G. Bermann and P. Mavroidis (eds) *WTO Law and Developing Countries* (Cambridge University Press).

Hammer, N. (2005) 'International Framework Agreements: Global Industrial Relations Between Rights and Bargaining', *Transfer* 11(4): 511.

Hepple, B. (2006) *Labour Laws and Global Trade* (Hart Publishing).

Hepple, B. (1997) 'New Approaches to International Labour Regulation', *Industrial Law Journal* 26: 353–366.

Herrnstadt, O. (2007–2008) 'Are International Framework Agreements a Path to Corporate Social Responsibility?', *University of Pennsylvania Journal of Business and Employment Law* 10: 187.

Hopwood, B., Mellor, M. and O'Brien, G. (2005) 'Sustainable Development: Mapping Different Approaches', *Sustainable Development* 13: 38–52.

Howse, R. and Langille, B. (2006) 'The World Trade Organization and Labour Rights: Man Bites Dog', in V. Leary and D. Warner (eds) *Social Issues, Globalisation and International Institutions: Labour Rights and the EU, ILO, OECD and WTO* (Martinus Nijhoff).

Kaufmann, C. (2007) *Globalisation and Labour Rights: The Conflict Between Core Labour Rights and International Economic Law* (Hart Publishing).

Miller, D. (2004) 'Preparing for the Long Haul: Negotiating International Framework Agreements in the Global Textile, Garment and Footwear Sector', *Global Social Policy* 4(2): 215.

Morgan-Foster, J. (2003) 'The Relationship of IMF Structural Adjustment Programs to Economic, Social and Cultural Rights: The Argentine Case Revisited', *Michigan Journal of International Law* 24: 577.

Murray, J. (2001) 'A New Phase in the Regulation of Multinational Enterprises: The Role of the OECD', *Industrial Law Journal* 30: 255.

Novitz, T. (2003) *International and European Protection of the Right to Strike* (Oxford University Press).

Novitz, T. (2009) 'In Search of a Coherent Social Policy: EU Import and Export of ILO Labour Standards', in J. Orbie and L. Tortell (eds) *The European Union and the Social Dimension of Globalization: How the EU Influences the World* (Routledge).

Novitz, T. (2010) 'Core Labour Standards Conditionalities: A Means by which to Achieve Sustainable Development?', in J. Faundez and C. Tan (eds) *International Law, Economic Globalization And Developing Countries* (Edward Elgar).

Nussbaum, M. (2000) *Women and Human Development: The Capabilities Approach* (Cambridge University Press).

Papadakis, K. (2008a) 'Research on Transnational Social Dialogue and International Framework Agreements (IFAs)', *International Labour Review* 147(1): 100.

Papadakis, K. (ed.) (2008b) *Cross-Border Social Dialogue and Agreements: An Emerging Industrial Relations Framework* (ILO-IILS).

Riisgaard, L. (2005) 'International Framework Agreements: A New Model for Securing Workers Rights?', *Industrial Relations* 44(4): 707.

Robinson, J. (2004) 'Squaring the Circle? Some Thoughts on the Idea of Sustainable Development', *Ecological Economics* 48: 369.

Saith, A. (2006) 'From Universal Values to Millennium Development Goals: Lost in Translation', *Development and Change* 37(6): 1167.

Satterthwaite, D. (2003) 'The Millennium Development Goals and Urban Poverty Reduction: Great Expectations and Nonsense Statistics', *Environment and Urbanization* 15(2): 179.

Sciarra, S. (2010) 'Notions of Solidarity in Times of Economic Uncertainty', *Industrial Law Journal* 39(3): 223.

Sen, A. (1999) *Development as Freedom* (Oxford University Press).

Sobczak, A. (2003) 'Codes of Conduct in Subcontracting Networks: A Labour Law Perspective', *Journal of Business Ethics* 87: 225.

Stevis, D. (2010) *International Framework Agreements and Global Social Dialogue* (Employment Sector Working Paper No. 47, ILO).

Stiglitz, J. (1998) 'More Instruments and Broader Goals: Moving Toward the Post-Washington Consensus', the 1998 WIDER Annual Lecture (Helsinki, Finland, 7 January 1998), available at: http://time.dufe.edu.cn/wencong/washington consensus/instrumentsbroadergoals.pdf

Telljohann, V., Da Costra, I., Müller, T., Rehfeldt, U. and Zimmer, R. (2009) 'European and International Framework Agreements: New Tools of Transnational Industrial Relations', *Transfer: European Review of Labour and Research* 15(3–4): 505.

Torres, R. (2008) 'Preface', in K. Papadakis (ed.) *Cross-Border Social Dialogue and Agreements: An Emerging Global Industrial Relations Framework* (International Institute for Labour Studies).

Trubek, D. and Santos, A. (2006) 'The Third Moment in Law and Development Theory and the Emergence of a New Critical Practice', in D. Trubek and A. Santos (eds) *The New Law and Economic Development* (Cambridge University Press).

Vandemoortele, J. (2008) 'Making Sense of the MDGs', *Development* 51(2): 220.

Vandemoortele, J. (2009) 'The MDG Conundrum: Meeting the Targets Without Missing the Point', *Development Policy Review* 27(4): 355.

Wills, J. (2002) 'Bargaining for the Space to Organize in the Global Economy: A Review of the Accor-IUF Trade Union Rights Agreement', *Review of International Political Economy* 9(4): 675.

An afterword

Impressions and suggestions
for a way forward

ROLPH VAN DER HOEVEN*

This contribution provides a somewhat personal review of various contributions made to this volume and interventions offered at the conference held at the British Academy in May 2009.

A general comment is that we have been talking more about the role of labour standards in development than specifically about 'sustainable development'. However, I do not see this as a shortcoming as the discussion on labour standards and development poses already so many challenges that it is only when we have a clear picture that the link to sustainability will be easy to make.

One also needs to realise that there still exists in certain circles quite some opposition to linking labour standards to development and its sustainability. Even some progressive Third World activists, for example, see linking labour standards to development as a ploy by rich countries to pose additional conditionality on poorer countries with a view to erecting trade barriers in rich countries to protect their labour markets. This was, for example, clear in the negotiations of the text of the Johannesburg Conference on Sustainable Development in 2002, where only after great difficulties a text suggested by the International Labour Organisation (ILO) mentioning the importance of employment and workers' rights could be accepted in the final communiqué.[1]

---

* Professor of Employment and Development Economics at the Institute of Social Studies (ISS) in The Hague.

[1] World Summit on Sustainable Development, September 2002, Johannesburg Declaration on Sustainable Development, para. 28: 'We also agree to provide assistance to increase income-generating employment opportunities, taking into account the Declaration on Fundamental Principles and Rights at Work of the International Labour Organisation.'

In the first part of this volume, Bob Hepple QC has reminded us of the different nature of various labour standards; they may be static, dynamic, risk spreading and empowering. By delineating standards along these lines, one could make the point that not all labour standards have the same effect on the pattern of development. Hepple points out that it is important to situate the discussion on labour standards in the context of the current financial crisis, which has rapidly become a social crisis, with a risk of leading to greater informalisation and use of precarious labour.

One positive point which the crisis has brought about is a change in appreciation of the need for better regulation of financial markets; in a similar vein one could thus argue also for a review of the regulation of labour markets. In that context it might be interesting to note that some progressive bankers call for a positive appreciation of the so-called Nordic model, which combines free markets with a high degree of income redistribution, a highly developed system of labour standards, labour market flexibility combined with adequate social security and a high level of government expenditure on public goods. This is a model which, as Beate Sjåfjell observes, Norwegian social actors are attempting to utilise in the implementation of EU law regarding environmental management. The question of course is how relevant the Nordic experience could be for developing countries and their economic and social, as well as environmental, development.

Many of the contributions in this volume use as their reference not the Nordic model but what the ILO had labelled 'decent work': striving simultaneously for improved labour standards, employment, social security and social dialogue.[2] The challenge of course is to prevent 'decent work' from becoming a cheap slogan, as happened to other useful concepts, and to ensure that it continues to be a basis for genuine research and dialogue, where one considers carefully the possible trade-offs between achievement of the various elements of decent work.

Brian Langille has hinted at something like this, insofar as he reports that thinking is progressing among the international financial institutions, where a review of the so-called Washington Consensus on economic policies is taking place. He calls, however, for a rethinking of the model of labour policies and standards, which he has labelled the Geneva Consensus. According to him, 'business as usual' cannot continue in the

---

[2] *ILO Declaration on Social Justice for a Fair Globalization*, 2008 (ILO).

field of labour policies and labour standards. He argues that these should be less prescriptive, with greater consideration of overarching government policies and less focus on the progress of individual labour standards. The system of international labour standards should become part of policy coherence and cooperation at the international level. A similar point was also made in the report of the World Commission on the Social Dimension of Globalisation.[3] One could even argue that coherence at an international level is a necessary element of globalisation, as under the current system of globalisation no international agency can achieve its own policy objective with only its own instruments. (For example, the ILO can not obtain employment creation without changes in international financial markets and the Internationl Monetary Fund (IMF) can not strive for low inflation without sound industrial relations and agreed wage-setting mechanisms.) However, accepting the need for greater international coherence, and the fact that no single organisation can achieve its own objectives, implies increased international democratic control to avoid the bureaucrats of international agencies presuming to make important policy decisions. *Improved international coherence implies improved democratic control of international organisations.*

It is also clear from the contributions on anti-discrimination, poverty and exclusion that anti-discriminatory laws on their own can not change policy. A change in attitudes and mindsets is equally important. As Judy Fudge and Jacqui True articulate, there is a need for systemic changes in society. However, Mark Bell demonstrates how legal mechanisms can generate public debate, which placed pressure on governments to change their policies and advance the position of the Roma.

A problem when looking at indicators of discrimination and child poverty is knowing who to hold responsible for deficient indicators regarding child rights and child welfare. Should we hold responsible the families of women and working children, governments of countries where women and children work, the international community, or citizens in the North for allowing a sharp world divide? It is thus necessary that to a discussion on indicators we add investigation of the kind of indicators which can lead to accountability by different groups of people and institutions. However, even if the lines of accountability are clear, it is

---

[3] World Commission on the Social Dimension of Globalization, *A Fair Globalization: Creating Opportunities for All*, 2004 (ILO).

not always easy to delineate what proper action is needed to combat discrimination and child labour, and especially the worst forms of it.

Sonia Bhalotra argues, rightly, that to solve the issue of child labour and policies ideally calls for a general equilibrium approach, as there are so many variables and policies which depend on each other. As a general rule stemming from a general equilibrium approach, policy measures need to remove binding constraints. These depend, however, on the socio-economic situation in each particular country. The major challenge, then, is for legal measures to be instrumental in removing binding constraints rather than dealing with issues which do not lead to removing binding constraints. This means that the issue of child labour should be analysed in an economy-wide setting and that legal instruments which simply forbid child labour may not always have the expected results, which brings us to the capacity of corporate social responsibility to address this aspect of development and whether this can be achieved in a sustainable way.

In this context, both the laws relating to regional markets (such as those in the European Union) and global markets (generated by the World Trade Organisation) become relevant. There is a social and economic dimension to environmental protection, as outlined by Beate Sjåfjell, which is embedded in the EU treaties. Also, Adelle Blackett has proposed a better framework for trade, aid and labour laws, which has important applications for migrant workers.

The question of aid remains as relevant as it was back in the 1960s, when Western governments were introducing Official Development Assistance. They justified doing so on two premises: firstly, that development aid would accelerate development and so reign in migration as income differences between poor and rich countries became smaller; and, secondly, that by supporting industrialisation goods would move from poorer to richer countries. However, as the experience over the last 40 years has shown, development aid in most cases could not really kick-start the economy, and conversion of incomes between poorer and richer countries did not always take place; hence the need to review the current conceptualisation of trade, aid, migration and the labour markets.

A point for debate at the British Academy conference was whether bilateral trade agreements, which reflect the powerful position of the richer nations vis-à-vis the developing countries, should be used as an instrument to force developing countries to accept improvement of labour standards. Many in the audience felt that this debate was passé, as the issue of the social clause in bilateral trade agreements had been off the table for some time in ILO committees on policies for the Social Dimensions of Globalisation, and there was the issue of whether restricting exports from developing countries might retard their development. It was noted from the audience that restricting trade through social clauses, especially in times of crisis, would provide a double blow to workers in developing countries.

Charlotte Villiers, David Tajgman and Tonia Novitz review various experiences with corporate social responsibility and social dialogue, as does Surya Deva. All agree that the new development of 'Corporate Social Responsibility' (CSR) was significant, but should be followed critically as CSR was not a panacea. There are even instances where employers favour Corporate Social Responsibility as an alternative to the national legislation of labour and social issues. Some of the participants at the conference argued that in that respect CSR could even be regressive. Moreover, the question was raised of whether one should prefer a system in which companies maximised profits but paid proper taxes and adhered strictly to labour standards (and did not object to a gradual development of labour standards through social dialogue), or prefer a system where companies through self-regulation developed systems of CSR while weakening labour standards. Also, since firms organise themselves in international bodies to cooperate on CSR one could well argue, as Tonia Novitz did, that more attention should be given to international framework agreements between companies and trade unions across the globe.

Many issues relevant to the role of labour standards and sustainable development were made during the British Academy conference; the question now is how to take these discussions forward especially in the light of the current financial, economic and social crisis.

First, it would be good to reiterate that the current crisis was caused by huge problems in the capital and financial markets, and much less by problems in markets for international trade, and certainly not by problems in the labour market. A major conceptual mistake during the last decade was that many economists and politicians regarded capital market liberalisation as a logical follow-up to trade liberalisation. They expected the positive and negative consequences of internal and external capital market liberalisation to be similar to those of trade liberalisation. The social outfall of globalisation (as, for example, documented by the report of the World Commission on the Social Dimension of Globalisation) and the depth of the financial crisis has proven this to be wrong. The crisis was caused by unregulated internal and external capital markets. External capital market liberalisation has also caused greater economic volatility which has led to increasing inequality within countries. Moreover, poorer countries have greater difficulties dealing with greater volatility as they often lack proper financial instruments and the social infrastructure to deal with greater volatility.

The current globalisation and the fallout of the crisis force us therefore to be cognisant of growing inequality between and within countries, and to devise policies to counter this. One notices that both politicians and people in the street speak more about inequality than a couple of years ago. This opportunity should be seized, and issues of inequality need to be put upfront in many policy debates. There are those who argue that growing inequality is a consequence of the current economic system, and that if one is aiming at economic growth, inequality is an automatic by-product of that. However, history can provide examples where fast growth and low inequality were simultaneously possible.[4] One example is that which is now labelled the golden age of economic development, in which many countries in Europe after the Second World War grew quickly within a context of relative equality. (In the Netherlands, for example, reduced inequality, together with economic growth, price stability, full employment and a balanced external account, formed the five principal objectives of government policy.) A second example is the equitable growth pattern of the so-called Asian tigers in the 1960s and 1970s, caused by earlier policies of land redistribution and investment in education. Although there are many differences between these two situations, one can notice a common element: both employ system controlled capital. In the European countries this took place through social pacts between trade unions and employers. In Asia, capital was controlled by government bureaucrats.

So it is important in crisis responses to design policies which re-establish the role of labour in development. Hence, stimulus measures currently undertaken should focus on the creation of employment, education and training. Wage deflation should be avoided as falling wages exert a negative effect on final demand. Also lengthening access to employment benefits can contribute to maintaining final demand.

These issues all relate directly to different labour standards, which have perforce to play an important role in any decent response to the crisis, and should be part of every social dialogue agenda. Arguing for a social clause

---

[4] Van der Hoeven, R. (2008), 'Income Inequality Revisited: Can One Bring Sense Back into Economic Policy?', inaugural address, ISS Public Lectures Series 2008, No. 2, The Hague.

reduces final demand on a global scale and thus hurts many workers in the current crisis, but a better realisation of the current labour standards can play an important role in diminishing the social consequences of the crisis and in building a sustainable socio-economic system to avoid – or face – future crises.

Index